Victor J. Valcarcel
Intelligent Banking

Victor J. Valcarcel

Intelligent Banking

Python Programming for Banking and Finance

DE GRUYTER

Author's Note: No generative AI vendors or General Purpose Artificial Intelligence (GPAI) tools were used in any aspect of the crafting of this book–including but not limited to: ideation, writing, editing, graphing, coding, and summarization.

ISBN 978-3-11-119278-9
e-ISBN (PDF) 978-3-11-119312-0
e-ISBN (EPUB) 978-3-11-119336-6

Library of Congress Control Number: 2025937602

Bibliographic information published by the Deutsche Nationalbibliothek
The Deutsche Nationalbibliothek lists this publication in the Deutsche Nationalbibliografie; detailed bibliographic data are available on the Internet at http://dnb.dnb.de.

© 2025 Walter de Gruyter GmbH, Berlin/Boston, Genthiner Straße 13, 10785 Berlin
Cover image: [M] Barbara Gizzi [F] Nikada / E+ / Getty Images; [M] Barbara Gizzi [F] matejmo / iStock / Getty Images Plus
Typesetting: VTeX UAB, Lithuania

www.degruyter.com
Questions about General Product Safety Regulation:
productsafety@degruyterbrill.com

A mi madre, por todo

Acknowledgments

I want to thank Stefan Giesen and Steven Hardman at De Gruyter for taking the initiative on the "original handshake," and particularly to Steven for gracefully stewarding me through the early days. I am deeply indebted to my content editor Jaya Dalal, also at De Gruyter, who was a constant source of masterful and responsive editorial support. Her many great ideas helped shape the project in a meaningful way.

I could not be more thankful for Taowen Hu and Mindy Valcarcel for their painstaking and thorough editing of the final manuscript. Their attention to detail played a crucial role and their constant support was paramount to my finishing, relatively on time… ahem.

I am indebted to Enrique Martinez-Garcia for his great support and ideas in the early days.

I want to thank Maria Teresa Morla, Ivan and Secundino, Mark Wohar, John Keating, Lee Smith, Kevin Siqueira, Dann Arce and Jennifer Holmes, for their encouragement and valuable input at all stages of the project.

I am grateful to William Barnett, Yuanchen Bing, Robin Chen, Fernando Colunga, Yundi Lu, and Yuan Ma and to my family (mama, Esther, Esther y Julio, Carmen y Luis, Suso, Pedro, Merche, papa, y todos los demas) for their patience and understanding when this work sometimes kept me away from being as responsive as I would have liked.

I am grateful to Shu Wu for teaching me that kindness does belong in the study of financial economics. Rest easy my friend.

This book is the culmination of a multiyear project collecting my own class notes for my M.S. course in International Banking and Monetary Systems at the University of Texas at Dallas. I am thankful for all the student feedback I have received on the course over the years, particularly those in the inaugural class: Dareem Antoine, Taylor Fisher, Nada Iqbal, Prattasha Islam, Colin Mckenzie, Ashutosh Patel, Artimes Rashidi Torghi, and Mumuksha Singla.

And, once again, a final word of thanks to Tom Clark, Stefan Giesen, Albrecht Doehnert, Gerhard Boomgaarden, Steven Hardman, Jaya Dalal, Natalie Wachsmann, Vilma Vaičeliūnienė, and other folks at De Gruyter who helped make this project a labor of love.

https://doi.org/10.1515/9783111193120-207

Contents

Part I: Money and the Government

Part IV: Machine Learning

List of Figures

https://doi.org/10.1515/9783111193120-204

List of Tables

https://doi.org/10.1515/9783111193120-205

Introduction

Contents

Traditional money and banking textbooks establish the central tenets of the science of macroeconomics and financial markets. Their main audience is undergraduate economics students. As such, they tend to offer comprehensive treatments with large breadth and scope. Material is presented in an academic fashion. Given their voluminous treatments, traditional money and banking textbooks may also serve as occasional reference beyond graduation.

There is another track where books on capital markets operate, which falls largely on what is commonly referred to as "trade books." These books tend to be more advanced, since their intended audiences are professionals or continuing education clientele. These books are often technical and data-driven, but they are generally void of fundamental exposition of economic theory or the institutional aspects of various financial markets.

Since the ultimate purpose and intended audiences for these two types of book are quite different, a gap opens between the traditional textbook and the trade book. *This book bridges that gap.* It is neither a traditional textbook nor is it a trade book—though it combines aspects of both.

In the U.S., if you are an undergraduate student in economics, you are rarely trained in programming—particularly programming that is targeted to applications in economics and finance. Instead, if you are an economics or finance major, you would typically be exposed to the fundamentals of money and banking from traditional textbooks. This often leaves economics and finance majors untrained in programming for financial applications. Picking up programming skills from trade books would then be simply left until after graduation.

On the other hand, if you are an engineering and computer science major, you would finish your studies at university well trained in programming, but with a sparse understanding of the fundamentals of financial markets. The main objective of this book is to pull double duty and immerse you in economic concepts of financial markets and banking with an emphasis on programming. Thus, the main audience of this book is *undergraduate students in economics, finance, and other quantitative fields.* If you are in these fields, *this book was written for you.*

Traditional money and banking textbooks are written in a strictly academic fashion. Thus, they tend to be broad in scope with a large number of chapters often numbering

https://doi.org/10.1515/9783111193120-202

20, 25, and beyond! Two full semesters of intense training may still not do justice to all the material offered in these books. Instructors are left covering treatments at back-breaking speed. Another byproduct of these large treatments is that substantial portions of the prototypical money and banking textbook are left unattended by the instructor. So, parts of the book are left fallow.

This is not your typical money and banking textbook. Far from being encyclopedic, this is a lean book that leans heavily on Python programming. It was written so that it can be covered in its entirety over a single semester at a leisurely pace. Therefore, I have sacrificed breadth in the vast array of economic notions typically afforded by the standard textbook in favor of the depth in some of the fundamental concepts by reinforcing them with programming.

It is increasingly common that students in other (less technical) areas outside economics, finance, computer science, and engineering turn to studying finance, banking, and financial markets for master's degrees. While it is difficult to avoid equations on a book on this subject, I have curated the material for a less mathematical and more accessible reading. I leave the more technical details or expanded treatments for other excellent books such as *Python for Finance* by Yves Hilpisch or *The Economics of Money, Banking and Financial Markets* by Frederic Mishkin. My choice of topics covered stems from my own university teaching experience with undergraduate and graduate courses in banking and financial markets. Therefore, if you are pursuing an *MBA or MS in finance, this book may be useful to you.*

In this book, we will cover the fundamentals of various monetary markets and several main treatments covered by more typical money and banking textbooks. And we will forgo some of the breadth usually found in the traditional textbooks in favor of a deeper treatment of technical topics and programming, more typically found in trade books. Specifically, we will lean heavily on Python programming to contextualize the fundamental concepts of money and banking. Our goal is to gain general Python skills (e. g., importing Python libraries, setting up Python environments to work, reading in data) as well as specific skills for Python programming for banking (e. g., modeling yield curves, forecasting stock prices, regressing market yields).

The book contains snippets of Python code interspersed throughout. A companion website https://www.degruyterbrill.com/document/isbn/9783111193120/html is provided with all the Python snippets and additional expanded codes.

0.1 Structure and Treatments

The book is divided into four parts: Part I—*Money and the Government*, Part II—*Time, Probability, and Risk*, Part III—*Financial Markets*, and Part IV—*Machine Learning*.

The first chapter of *Money and the Government* describes the role of government in the management and determination of the money supply. It describes money as a vehicle for incurring government debt. Fiscal policy broadly involves taxing, spending, and borrowing. This chapter focuses on the latter. Governments generally borrow by issuing "*I-owe-you's*," which we call bonds and we discuss in later chapters. These bonds are often issued by national and local governments. This chapter describes some historical trends in debt of various parts of the economy.

Another aspect of money in the government refers to its management. This falls under the umbrella of monetary policy. The second chapter of *Money and the Government* describes the role the U. S. central bank—the Federal Reserve system—has in the determination of the money supply and its connection with interest rates. This chapter defines the money supply and discusses two different ways to aggregate money balances: simple-sum (equal weighing) aggregation versus Divisia (liquidity-weighing) aggregation. The chapter also describes interest rates obtained in the market, such as the federal funds rate, and differentiates them from managed rates, like the discount window rate or interest on reserve balances (IORB). Finally, it makes some connections between the Federal Reserve's own balance sheet, the monetary base, and bank reserves.

The second part of the book is titled *Time, Probability, and Risk*. This part contains three chapters. The first chapter of this part of the book introduces the concept of interest rates by connecting them with the concepts of monetary assets discussed in previous sections. Interest rates place value on monetary assets at different times by bringing them backward or forward in time to a time when they can be compared. This first chapter covers the foundations of the analysis of time value of money with important concepts of future value and present value.

The second chapter of *Time, Probability, and Risk* covers the main axioms of probability theory and establishes the concepts of expectations, the central limit theorem, and long-term averaging. All these concepts are crucial to modeling the levels and trends of interest rates and many other financial variables. The third chapter of *Time, Probability, and Risk* covers the fundamentals of risk by differentiating between expected values and volatilities of various financial instruments. It explains the trade-offs between financial risk and financial returns. And it covers the basics of risk management.

The third part of the book is titled *Financial Markets*. This part is subdivided into three chapters—the first of which presents the bond market. It covers discount and coupon bonds issues by treasuries as well as corporations. It discusses yields, returns, and risk in the bond market. The next chapter covers theories of interest rates. It discusses interest rate spreads, risk spreads, and the term structure of interest rates. The final chapter in this section covers the stock market. It discusses valuation of single stocks as well as overall index measures. It covers methods for assessing risk and returns of stock. It explains the concept of Monte Carlo simulations and gives a primer on forecasting equity prices.

The final part of the book is titled *Machine Learning*. Beginning from the concept of a perceptron, it covers its connection with neural networks and linear regression. It also discusses basic tasks of machine learning, such as classification, prediction, and inference.

0.2 Why Python?

Banks and financial companies are increasingly demanding these skills from recent college graduates. Yet, traditional money and banking textbooks rarely offer these skills. If you are a typical economics major, you would likely need to supplement what you get from the traditional approach to money and banking, with coursework in computer science to add to your general knowledge of programming. Importantly, these skills would not be directed to applications in finance or economics—leaving you to make those connections on your own, possibly after college graduation.

Banking and finance have always required high degrees of human intelligence, which is now beginning to be artificially enhanced. Programming languages are the nexus of interaction between human and artificial intelligence. And banks and financial institutions have already begun to make the transition by requiring programming training of many of their analysts.

Important financial companies such as JPMorgan Chase and Citi require their asset management trainees to learn how to code (typically in Python). This fosters better communication between the business teams and the technology teams. These two major banks, as well as other financial institutions, now run summer Python coding camps for their recent hires. This clearly reflects the lack of Python programming training available to business and economics students outside engineering schools. This book was written in part to remedy this.

A report by PricewaterhouseCoopers LLP, found that almost one-third of financial services jobs could be displaced by automation—related to machine learning and AI— by the mid-2030s. In the opinion of this author, the advent of AI analytics will not simply remove jobs in banking and finance. Instead, it is more likely AI will expand the definition of the roles financial analysts and bankers are known for. It is also likely it will create new types of jobs, some ancillary and some central to the expertise one expects from financial analysts, wealth managers, and bankers.

Job seekers with fluency in machine learning, artificial intelligence, and data sciences will likely be in even higher demand than ever before. This motivates a revamping of the curriculum of financial markets and economics to emphasize these skills at earlier stages of the educational track. This book argues for some introduction of these programming skills at the beginning stages of college-level economics and financial degrees rather than at the last stages. And often these skills are not gained at college at all! Instead, these skills have been typically acquired beyond graduation—for example with coding camps offered by the banking industry for their newly minted employees. This book was written for students who might want to get a head start on acquiring these tools.

A distinct advantage of this book is that it is an introduction to first-principle concepts of finance and financial markets while providing a first introduction to Python programming. It is not meant for advanced practitioners or Ph. D. students who may have taken multiple courses in each. If you are taking your first steps in the world of finance or economics, and you want to learn some programming along the way, this book is for you.

0.3 Integrated Development Environments (IDEs)

An integrated development environment (IDE) is a software application that provides a comprehensive suite of components with similar user interfaces acting as a single program in which all development can be done.

While IDEs may vary widely, they tend to include: a source code editor where programming is done, a compiler/interpreter that runs the code, and some graphical user interface (GUI) that can offer some added features, like graphing, editing, code completion, syntax highlighting, debugging, etc.

The fact that IDEs are integrated environments allows for creating, running, and debugging code all in one. Some programmers prefer to work exclusively in code editors where code can be written, edited, and saved. But then it must be subsequently run elsewhere. Code editors are generally simpler than IDEs, as they do not include many other IDE components.

If we Google *Best IDEs for Python programming*, we get many different ones: PyCharm, IDLE, Spyder, Atom, Sublime, Vim, and Jupyter Notebook are particularly popular. See Figure 0.1. All of these can be downloaded and installed in our computer as free shareware—though some IDEs may have a premium paid version, they are generally

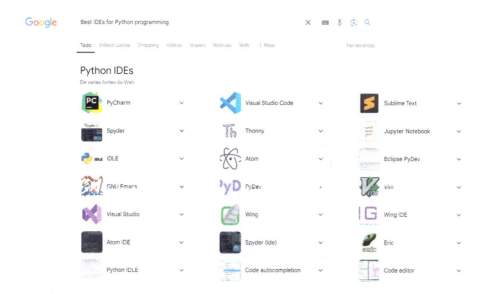

Figure 0.1: Searching for IDEs to work with Python.

just cosmetic upgrades. All the analysis in this book can be accomplished free of charge with these shareware IDEs. Throughout the book we will be using *JupyterLab*.

Again, these can be installed locally on our machine free of charge. An alternative to installing IDEs on our machine is to work on cloud-based IDEs. Cloud IDEs rely on powerful servers hosted in remote data centers. When we open a cloud IDE in your browser, it spins up a virtual environment—essentially a remote container or virtual machine—that acts as our development workspace. This workspace includes all the tools and dependencies we need for a specific version of Python we might need. The advantages of cloud-based IDEs include the ability to collaborate with partners and friends in real time as well as the ability to leverage computational power of remote servers that may often exceed the memory and processing capabilities of our own machine. A disadvantage is that they require a stable internet connection and/or WIFI signal, and processing speed can be less reliable over WIFI than locally in our computer.

0.4 Setting up a Python Environment

The ancient Romans had a popular refrain: *"Omnes viae Romam ducunt"* roughly translating to *"All roads lead to Rome."* At the height of the Roman Empire, more than 350 major roads resembling the spokes on a large wheel spanned roughly 50,000 miles, ranging as far away as Hispania (modern day Spain, my country of origin), or from the "Hadrian's Wall" in Scotland, or from the Euphrates River in Mesopotamia (modern day Iraq), or from Northern Germany, or from the Sahara desert in North Africa—all leading to Rome as the final destination, the center of the wheel.

We could say Rome was at the center of a highly integrated network. One could start from far-ranging origins, but it did not matter whether one started their journey from Northern Europe, Southern Europe, Northern Africa, or the Middle East, one could invariably arrive in Rome.

Similarly, we could say that Python is the center of a highly integrated network of software applications and programming. Python is a rich ecosystem with wide applicability across multiple fields. Just as it did not matter whether you were a German, a Scot, or a Spaniard... you could arrive in Rome—it does not matter whether you are a software engineer, a physicist, or an economist... you can arrive at Python!

Moreover, the rich Python ecosystem allows for multiple ways to accomplish similar tasks. For example, there are myriad ways to set up a Python environment. Just as the road from Northern Europe, Southern Europe, or North Africa would lead to Rome, setting up a working environment locally from an MS-DOS prompt or from a graphical unit interface (GUI) or setting up an environment in the cloud, all lead to a working Python setup.

There is a wealth of information on the internet on how to set up a Python environment: in the Windows operating system, in the Mac OS system, or in Linux OS. Just as many roads lead to Rome, many roads lead to a working Python setup. Just as Rome was a rich network of roads and cities, Python is also a rich ecosystem of dozens of IDEs and hundreds of libraries. There are multiple ways to set up a Python environment locally in your computer or in the cloud. You may already have a Python setup yourself, or you may find a setup that works for you. There is no right or wrong setup, there is just what works for you. And you may find along the way that a setup can be quite idiosyncratic and mostly driven by personal preference. But at the end of the day, it does not really matter for your day-to-day work. One can be just as productive working with different setups.

I will now discuss a step-by-step setup to getting Python working on your PC so you can run the codes and follow along throughout the various chapters of this book. While all of this can also be done for Mac OS or Linux operating systems, the discussion below focuses on the Microsoft Windows operating system.

0.4.1 Laying the Groundwork: Installing Anaconda

There are many ways to install Python on our computer. One of the most popular ones is through the distributor/repository called *Anaconda*. Anaconda (or simply Conda) is an open source distribution platform for Python and other languages created by Anaconda, Inc.—an American company founded in 2012. As of 2025, Anaconda claims it has about 50 million users worldwide. The reason for its popularity is that it serves as a package manager and it is free (though it also has a subscription-based premium version). Python is an object-oriented programming language. What makes it powerful is its rich and deep ecosystem of libraries, packages, and applications. Often, different packages and libraries are developed independently and may not necessarily play nice (compatibility-wise) with each other. These packages act as a patchwork in the fabric that is Python. Anaconda's main service is to fit these patches together into "the Python quilt" and create environments where the libraries and native Python work well together.

We can download and install Anaconda from their website free of charge. Anaconda provides download and installing documentation for the three major operating systems on their their webpage. Anaconda also provides a GUI called Anaconda Navigator, which offers a simple and intuitive toolkit for installing and managing packages as shown in in Figure 0.2.

A different way to download and install Anaconda without the Navigator GUI is to do so through a command line interface (or CLI), which is a program on our computer that processes text commands to do various tasks. Conda is a CLI program, which means it can only be used via the command line. On Windows computers, Anaconda recommends that we use the Anaconda Prompt CLI to work with Conda. This CLI is called *Conda Powershell* and it is included in the installation for free. On MacOS and Linux, users can use their built-in command line applications.

Anaconda contains a large suite of packages. There is a streamlined version called Miniconda, which is a smaller version of Anaconda that includes only Conda, Python, the

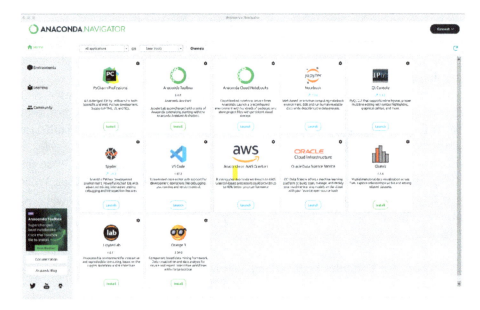

Figure 0.2: Anaconda Navigator's graphical user interface.

packages they depend on, and a small number of other packages. The smaller Miniconda allows for a streamlined installation, which we can then grow organically by installing packages as we need them. We discuss this practice below.

0.4.2 Getting Started: Step-by-step

Let's get started by downloading and installing Miniconda.
–   Turn our computer on and ensure we are connected to the internet.
–   Open a web browser and navigate to the Miniconda installation webpage, or the Miniconda repository of all legacy versions.

Figure 0.3 shows what the installation website looks like in 2025. In the future, the layout of the Anaconda webpage website may look slightly different but the features and functionality should remain the same.

And scrolling down the same page, we can find the Miniconda installation button, which I highlighted in yellow. Click on it to install it on our computer. See Figure 0.4.

Figure 0.5 shows that I downloaded Miniconda to my Windows 11 machine via Google Chrome. You can find it on your browser's Downloads icon (highlighted in green). We can install it in our computer by clicking on the self-extracting link (highlighted in yellow).

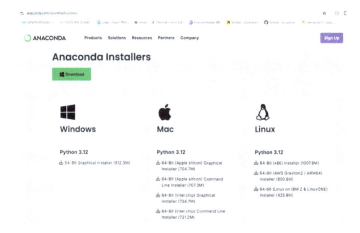

Figure 0.3: Anaconda install page.

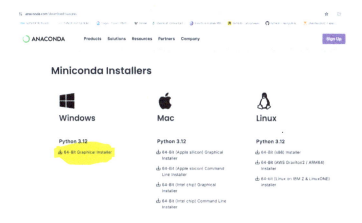

Figure 0.4: Miniconda install page.

Figure 0.5: Miniconda downloaded locally to a Windows 11 PC.

Then we can follow the self installer, which will ask for a directory to save our Conda and Python environments to.

SILENT INSTALL

Another way to install Conda is through what is known as a "silent installation." On a Windows 11 PC:

- Select the Start menu (the Windows icon) on the taskbar or press the Windows key.
- Type 'cmd.'
- Select the Command Prompt from the list.

The command prompt will open to wherever the default path is located, which may look something like what is shown in Figure 0.6.

Figure 0.6: A standard command prompt.

Then type the following three commands:

```
curl https://repo.anaconda.com/miniconda/Miniconda3-latest-Windows-x86_64.exe
-o .\miniconda.exe
start /wait ''`'' .\miniconda.exe /S
del .\miniconda.exe
```

These three lines instruct the computer to download the latest 64-bit Windows installer. We might want to rename it to a shorter file name or leave the three lines untouched. This performs a silent install, and then deletes the installer. It is called silent because it runs quietly in native MS-DOS, it does not open any screens, and all we can see as proof that it downloaded and installed is the following in the command prompt. See Figure 0.7.

Command Prompt

```
Microsoft Windows [Version 10.0.26100.3194]
(c) Microsoft Corporation. All rights reserved.

C:\Users\vicva>curl https://repo.anaconda.com/miniconda/Miniconda3-latest-Windows-x86_64.exe --output .\Downloads\Minico
nda3-latest-Windows-x86_64.exe
  % Total    % Received % Xferd  Average Speed   Time    Time     Time  Current
                                 Dload  Upload   Total   Spent    Left  Speed
100 88.9M  100 88.9M    0     0  10.8M      0  0:00:08  0:00:08 --:--:-- 10.3M
```

Figure 0.7: Silent installation of Miniconda on a Windows 11 machine.

The command prompt now shows that 100% of the 88.9M Miniconda package was successfully installed on my Windows 11 machine.

There are additional ways to install Miniconda, such as from the Windows Powershell or directly from the Anaconda Navigator GUI. Instructions on these, as well as on how to install for Mac IOS and Linux are all available on the Anaconda website.

0.4.3 Working from the Miniconda Powershell

As we mentioned earlier, Python is a rich ecosystem of libraries and packages. These libraries are often developed independently, so they constitute a patchwork, and Conda is the quilt that gathers and patches up the various libraries. We will be doing analysis in an IDE. But before we can start working, we must set up an environment to do so. Miniconda is what we will use to set up the environment to work. Once we have installed Miniconda on our Windows 11 machine, we can simply go to the search box next to the Windows icon and type "miniconda". See Figure 0.8.

Figure 0.8: Finding the Miniconda Powershell in the computer.

Clicking on the Miniconda Powershell is our first step into the world of Python. Clicking on it will open a window in our machine that will look reminiscent of an MS-DOS prompt. It will typically look like a black screen very similar to the Command Prompt screen shown in Figure 0.6. Or it may look different if we have reformatted the look of the Conda Powershell in advance.

Since I have played with the look of my own Powershell in the past, my Conda Powershell does not look black. Regardless of how it looks, the prompt will automatically open wherever the Miniconda installation placed the base install on our computer. See Figure 0.9.

Figure 0.9: Conda base prompt.

At the Conda prompt, typing *"conda - -version"* will return the version of Conda installed in our computer. Our Miniconda installation would have already installed a few libraries along with the base installation. Typing *"conda list"* at the prompt will show the list of libraries originally installed with Miniconda. See Figure 0.10.

```
(base) PS C:\Users\vicva> conda list
# packages in environment at C:\Users\vicva\miniconda3:
#
# Name                      Version              Build  Channel
appdirs                     1.4.4            pyhd3eb1b0_0
arch                        4.15          py38he774522_0    bashtage
blas                        1.0                    mkl
bottleneck                  1.3.5         py38h080aedc_0
brotlipy                    0.7.0        py38h2bbff1b_1003
ca-certificates             2023.01.10         haa95532_0
certifi                     2022.12.7     py38haa95532_0
cffi                        1.15.1        py38h2bbff1b_3
charset-normalizer          2.0.4            pyhd3eb1b0_0
colorama                    0.4.6         py38haa95532_0
conda                       23.1.0        py38haa95532_0
conda-package-handling      2.0.2         py38haa95532_0
conda-package-streaming     0.7.0         py38haa95532_0
console_shortcut            0.1.1                      4
cryptography                39.0.1        py38h21b164f_0
cython                      0.29.33       py38hd77b12b_0
icc_rt                      2022.1.0           h6049295_2
idna                        3.4           py38haa95532_0
```

Figure 0.10: A list of libraries installed in the (base) Conda installation.

We can always install more libraries onto our (base) installation as needed. However, I recommend keeping our base installation as light as possible. Why?

Let's remember that Python libraries are often developed and updated independently by different parties—Who knows? You might create your own libraries yourself in the future? As a package manager, Conda patches up all these independent libraries and often creates dependencies that get these various libraries to play nice with each other. Since these Python libraries are independent, some libraries tend to be updated more regularly than others. This means that sometimes some libraries or packages get updated and no longer work nicely with the other libraries until other updates take place. So, it is a common occurrence that a project works one day and the next day, if a library gets updated, it stops working.

Here is where the utility of Conda really shines! Conda is not only a package manager, but also an environment manager. This means that we can set up an environment in Conda that is project specific. We can set up the libraries and packages we want under a given environment. And this environment acts as a *freezer*. If we do not update the libraries within that environment, the code is nearly guaranteed to continue to work even if versions subsequently change and libraries get updated.

Therefore, we can create different environments for different projects. We can create as many environments as we want and use them for different projects or for multipurpose. We can keep the libraries in an environment *frozen* or update them. We can share environments with friends. We can clone environments and we can delete environments when we no longer need them. *Environments are our friends!*

0.4.4 Python Environments with Conda

First, we want to find out whether we have Conda environments set up in our computer. At the Conda prompt, typing *"conda env list"* returns whatever environments we may have. If we just installed Conda, we likely have a single environment created with the base installation. We call this the (base) environment. See Figure 0.11.

Figure 0.11: Conda (base) environment.

But again, a best practice is to leave (base) light and unencumbered with *library/pckg bloat* and, instead, to work in other environments. To do this, let us create the first environment. At the Conda prompt, type *"conda create"* followed by a space and a double hyphen and the word "name". Whatever we write after the command "name" will be the name we are giving to the new environment. The name must be alphanumeric and it may not contain spaces. Let's call our environment 'Banking Intelligence 1'. This name will not work because of the spaces. An easy workaround is to connect words with underscores, hyphens, or periods.

To sum up, type "*conda create - -name Banking_Intelligence_1*. See Figure 0.12.

```
(base) PS C:\Users\vicva> conda create --name Banking_Intelligence_1
Collecting package metadata (current_repodata.json): done
Solving environment: done

==> WARNING: A newer version of conda exists. <==
  current version: 23.1.0
  latest version: 25.1.1

Please update conda by running

    $ conda update -n base -c defaults conda

Or to minimize the number of packages updated during conda update use

    conda install conda=25.1.1

## Package Plan ##

  environment location: C:\Users\vicva\miniconda3\envs\Banking_Intelligence_1

Proceed ([y]/n)?
```

Figure 0.12: Create a new environment called Banking Intelligence 1.

This command gathers the necessary files and asks whether we want to proceed. Notice a warning that a newer version of Conda exists. (This will likely not appear on your end if you installed Conda recently.) But in any event, this will create the new environment without incident. Typing "*y*" for "*yes*" creates the package and returns us to the (base) prompt. See Figure 0.13.

To verify that we did create our new environment, type again "*conda env list*" at the prompt and we can see two environments now. See Figure 0.14.

Notice there is an asterisk next to (base), the asterisk denotes the environment that is currently active. Let us now activate our new environment. At the prompt, type "*conda activate Banking_Intelligence_1*" and then type again "*conda env list*" and we can see that our newly installed environment is now activated as we can see its name in the parenthesis at the prompt and we can see the asterisk next to the name in the environment list. See Figure 0.15.

For practice, take some time now and create another environment called Banking Intelligence 2 and activate it. You should arrive at a new environment list that looks like Figure 0.16.

Now let us say that in a few months we no longer need this newest environment and decide to delete it from your environments folder. This can be easily accomplished with

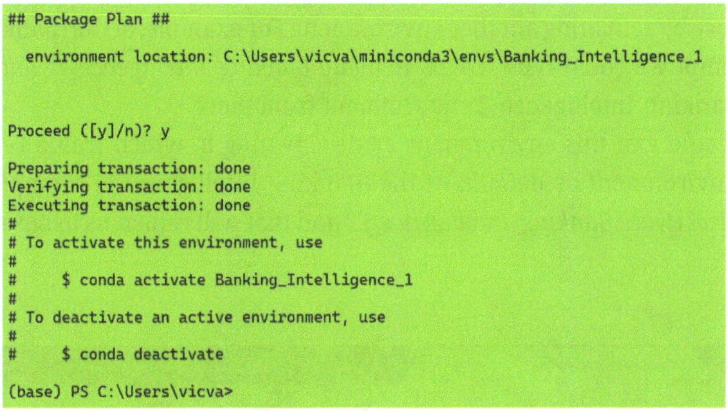

```
## Package Plan ##

  environment location: C:\Users\vicva\miniconda3\envs\Banking_Intelligence_1


Proceed ([y]/n)? y

Preparing transaction: done
Verifying transaction: done
Executing transaction: done
#
# To activate this environment, use
#
#     $ conda activate Banking_Intelligence_1
#
# To deactivate an active environment, use
#
#     $ conda deactivate

(base) PS C:\Users\vicva>
```

Figure 0.13: A new environment called Banking Intelligence 1 is installed.

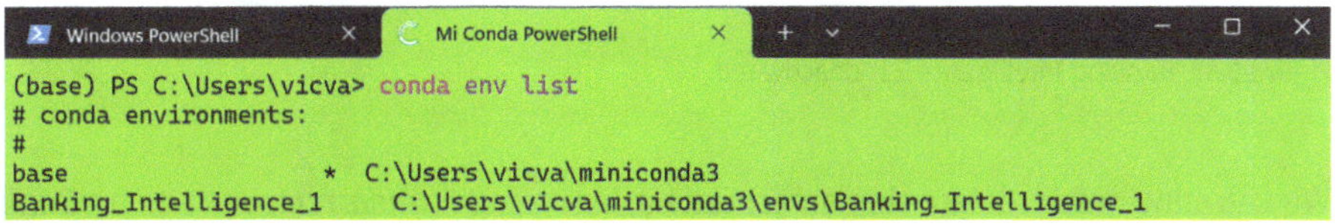

```
Windows PowerShell    ×     Mi Conda PowerShell    ×    +  ∨                      —  □  ×
(base) PS C:\Users\vicva> conda env list
# conda environments:
#
base                    *  C:\Users\vicva\miniconda3
Banking_Intelligence_1     C:\Users\vicva\miniconda3\envs\Banking_Intelligence_1
```

Figure 0.14: Banking Intelligence 1 is a new environment.

```
Windows PowerShell    ×     Mi Conda PowerShell    ×    +  ∨                      —  □  ×
(base) PS C:\Users\vicva> conda activate Banking_Intelligence_1
(Banking_Intelligence_1) PS C:\Users\vicva> conda env list
# conda environments:
#
base                       C:\Users\vicva\miniconda3
Banking_Intelligence_1  *  C:\Users\vicva\miniconda3\envs\Banking_Intelligence_1
```

Figure 0.15: Banking Intelligence 1 is activated.

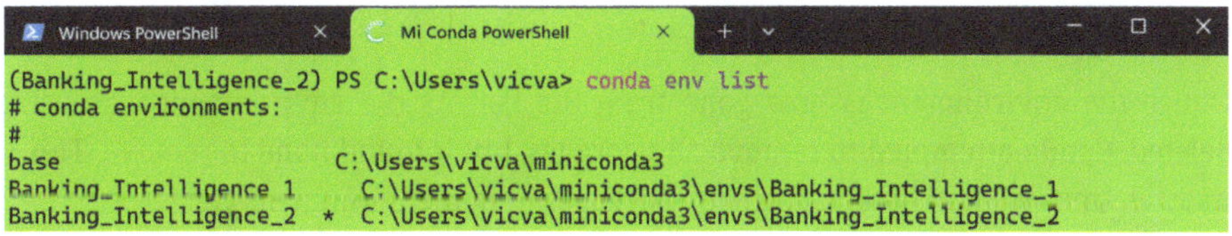

```
Windows PowerShell    ×     Mi Conda PowerShell    ×    +  ∨                      —  □  ×
(Banking_Intelligence_2) PS C:\Users\vicva> conda env list
# conda environments:
#
base                       C:\Users\vicva\miniconda3
Banking_Intelligence_1     C:\Users\vicva\miniconda3\envs\Banking_Intelligence_1
Banking_Intelligence_2  *  C:\Users\vicva\miniconda3\envs\Banking_Intelligence_2
```

Figure 0.16: Banking Intelligence 2 is activated.

the Conda command *"remove."* However, we cannot delete the environment while the environment is active. We need to exit the environment first before removing it from the computer.

We can do it as before by activating another environment. For example, at the (Banking_Intelligence_2) prompt we could type *"conda activate Banking_Intelligence_1"* and we could then delete Banking_Intelligence_2 environment from there.

Alternatively, we could exit this environment by deactivating it, which would return us to the (base) environment by default. At the (Banking_Intelligence_2) prompt, we could type *"conda deactivate Banking_Intelligence_2"* and that will return us to base. See Figure 0.17.

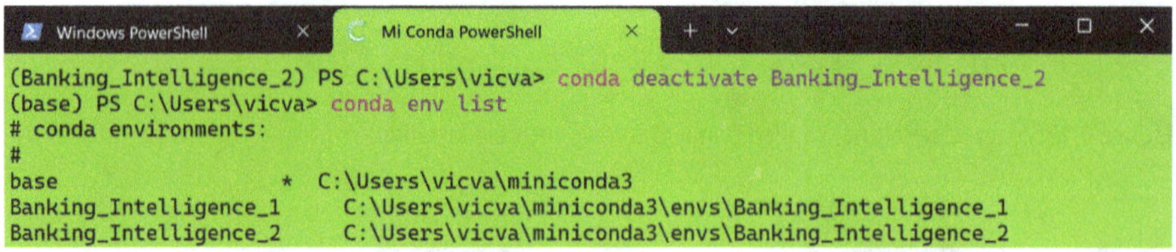

```
Windows PowerShell      ×        Mi Conda PowerShell      ×     +  ⌄                          —   □   ×
(Banking_Intelligence_2) PS C:\Users\vicva> conda deactivate Banking_Intelligence_2
(base) PS C:\Users\vicva> conda env list
# conda environments:
#
base                        *  C:\Users\vicva\miniconda3
Banking_Intelligence_1         C:\Users\vicva\miniconda3\envs\Banking_Intelligence_1
Banking_Intelligence_2         C:\Users\vicva\miniconda3\envs\Banking_Intelligence_2
```

Figure 0.17: Banking Intelligence 2 is deactivated.

We can now safely delete this environment by typing *"conda remove - -name Banking_Intelligence_2 - - all"*. See Figure 0.18.

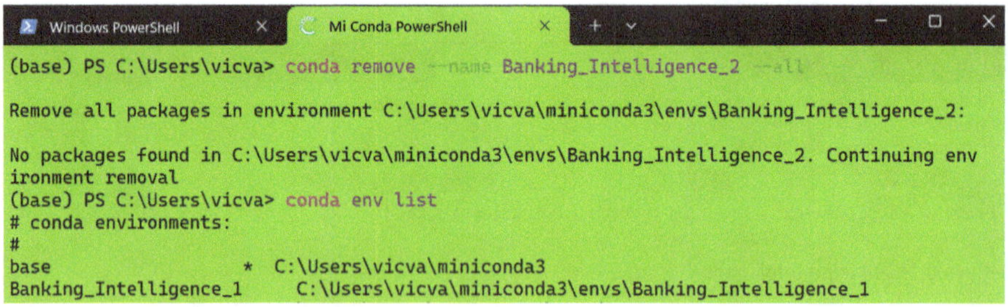

```
Windows PowerShell      ×        Mi Conda PowerShell      ×     +  ⌄                          —   □   ×
(base) PS C:\Users\vicva> conda remove --name Banking_Intelligence_2 --all

Remove all packages in environment C:\Users\vicva\miniconda3\envs\Banking_Intelligence_2:

No packages found in C:\Users\vicva\miniconda3\envs\Banking_Intelligence_2. Continuing env
ironment removal
(base) PS C:\Users\vicva> conda env list
# conda environments:
#
base                        *  C:\Users\vicva\miniconda3
Banking_Intelligence_1         C:\Users\vicva\miniconda3\envs\Banking_Intelligence_1
```

Figure 0.18: Banking Intelligence 2 has been deleted from the environment list.

Notice the environment is now gone from the list. As the environment was being deleted, Conda attempted to remove all packages, but it found none to remove. This is natural, since we had not installed any packages in that environment yet.

0.4.5 Python Libraries in Conda

Returning to our *'Banking Intelligence 1'* environment, if we type *"conda list"* it returns an empty set since we have not yet installed any libraries in this new environment. See Figure 0.19.

Figure 0.19: Banking Intelligence 1 environment is empty.

Let's now install the IDE we will use in this book. We will install the Jupyter suite locally in our computer through the Conda Power shell. The Jupyter suite is a powerful IDE that enables interactive computing across many programming languages (the name is an amalgamation of the *Ju*lia, *Py*thon and *R* programming languages) in a web browser environment. Jupyter is an open-source, free software written in the open-standards paradigm, which means it is completely free of licensing and allows for free use, to be repurposed and freely distributed. This allows both the software and the code in this book to be available free of charge without any limitations or guarantees.

Jupyter suite provides a range of packages and libraries organized around two main IDEs: *Jupyter Notebook* and *JupyterLab*. Jupyter Notebook is the first IDE; therefore, it is older and possibly more popular. In recent years, JupyterLab is increasingly gaining popularity. All the codes in this book were written in JupyterLab. Those Python programmers (who often call themselves Pythonistas) who have been coding in Jupyter Notebook find transitioning to JupyterLab virtually seamless. If we are starting out fresh today, we need not begin from 'Notebook'; we can begin to work and learn directly from 'Lab'. One can do virtually the same things in both. The differences are mostly cosmetic, apart from the look of the 'shell' and a few additional toolbars and capabilities of the web browser one uses to work with the IDE.

One can install a package or a library in the Conda Powershell with the command *conda install* followed by the name of the library. Often Conda will install the desired package as well as all the required sub-packages, libraries, sub-libraries, and dependencies required for the package to run. At the (Banking_Intelligence_1) prompt of the Conda Power shell, typing *"conda install jupyter"* will gather all requisite components and ask to *proceed([y],n)?* See Figures 0.20 and 0.21.

Typing 'y' will gather the packages and dependencies and install the Jupyter suite in the active environment. Once the suite and all its dependencies are installed, we can simply scroll down the shell to look for the libraries that were installed (the list is always organized alphabetically). See Figure 0.22.

Alternatively, if we want to check whether a particular library or package is currently installed in the active environment, we can simply type the name of the package or library followed by two dashes and the word "version." For example, at the prompt typing *"jupyter - -version"* returns the version of the libraries in the Jupyter suite. See Figure 0.23.

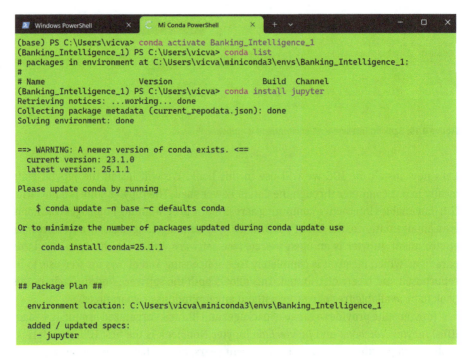

Figure 0.20: Installing the Jupyter Suite.

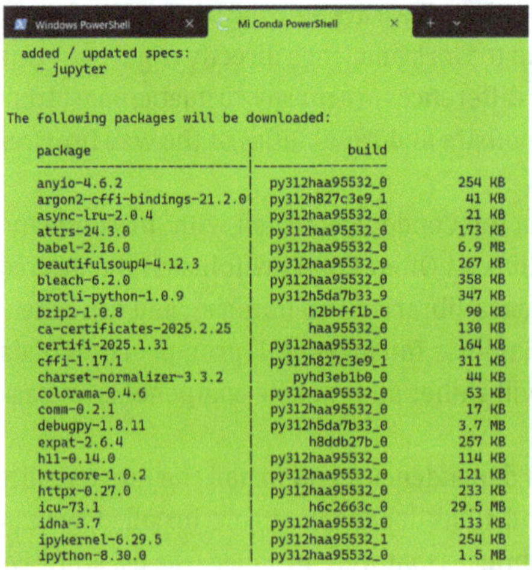

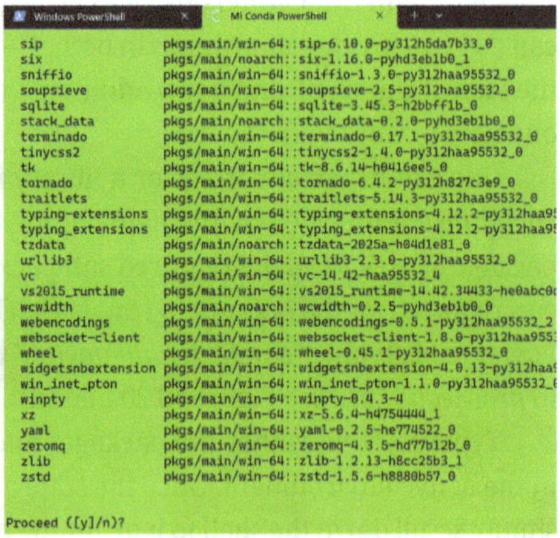

Figure 0.21: Installing the Jupyter Suite (ctd).

We can easily see JupyterLab was also installed. Had it not been installed, we would need to type "*conda install jupyterlab.*" This would verify that the dependencies and libraries are all ready—if some libraries required some updating, Conda would prompt

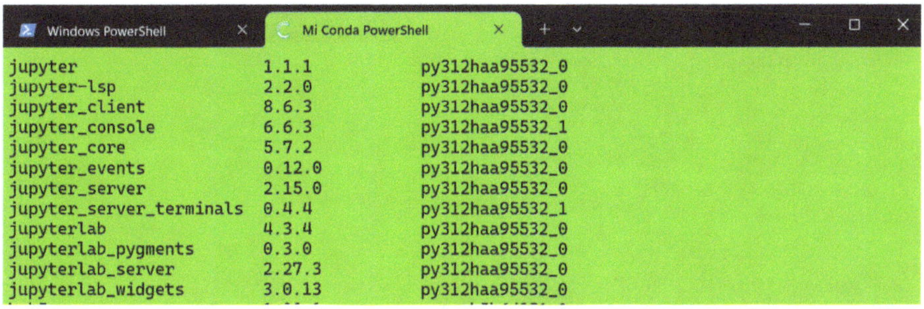

Figure 0.22: Scrolling down the Conda Powershell to find the Jupyter installation.

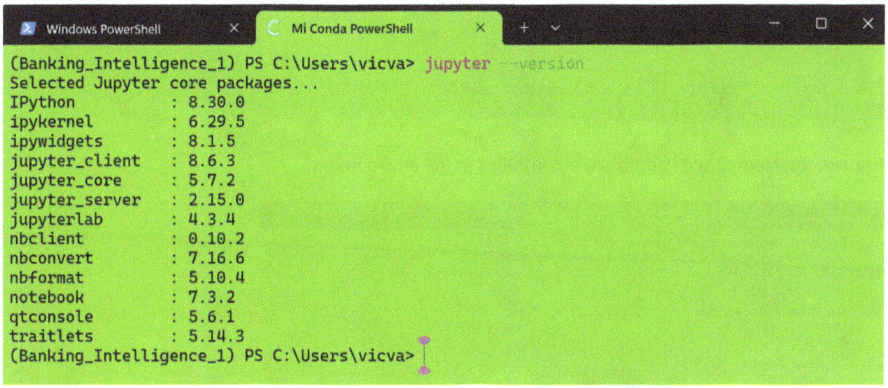

Figure 0.23: Versions of the various Jupyter libraries.

us whether we want to update them at this time or not—and subsequently it would install JupyterLab. Remember that this installation of the Jupyter suite has *only* been downloaded and installed in the currently active environment and not in (base) or in any other environment we might have created.

Two other libraries we will use often throughout the book are Numpy and Pandas. If we type "*numpy - -version*" or "*pandas - -version*," we get an error if the library is not installed in the (Banking_Intelligence_1) environment. See Figure 0.24.

At the prompt, we can easily install Numpy by typing "*conda install numpy*." See Figure 0.25.

Similarly, we can easily install Pandas by typing "*conda install pandas*." Once we have completed this, we can verify these libraries are installed in the current environment by typing: "*conda list numpy*" and "*conda list pandas*." See Figure 0.26.

We will use Numpy and Pandas frequently throughout the book. We will also need other libraries and packages in this book and, later on, other projects you might undertake. Any additional library can be downloaded and installed in the same way as we described so far for Jupyter, Numpy and Pandas.

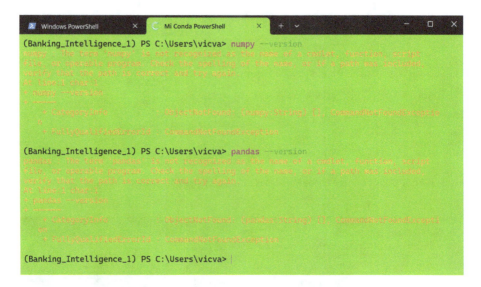

Figure 0.24: Numpy and Pandas are not installed in the environment.

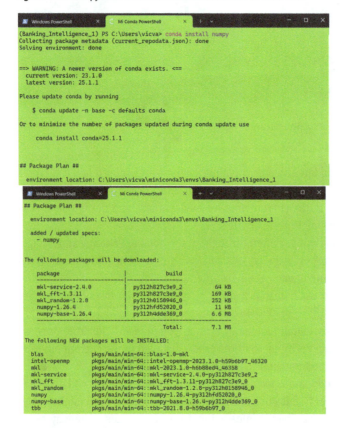

Figure 0.25: Installing Numpy.

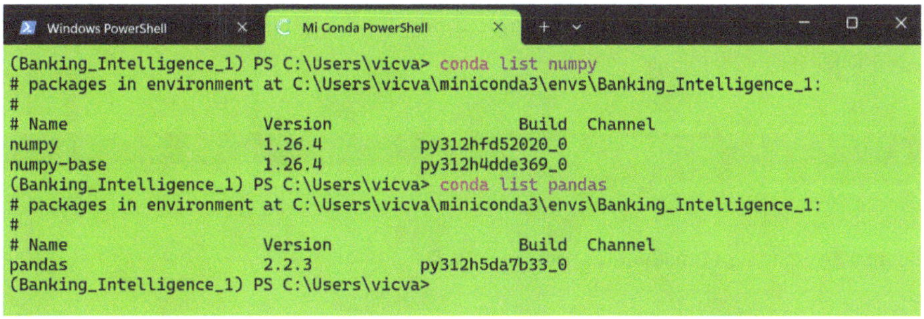

Figure 0.26: The Numpy and Pandas libraries are now installed.

Sometimes, we may need a relatively large suite of libraries and packages, and (re-)installing them one-by-one may be time consuming. Let's say that we have all the packages we need in our 'Banking_Intelligence_1' environment and we have been working in that environment for a while. Now, say, we want to create another environment—in our computer or in a different computer—that shares all the same libraries. Reinstalling each library and package one-by-one is always an option, but it can be time consuming. Also, the packages we might download today could be newly updated versions and, instead, we may want to keep the same versions of the libraries we had used before.

There are two ways to reinstall all the same versions of the libraries and packages onto a new environment, depending on whether we want the environment in the same machine or whether we want to create it in a different computer.

To easily replicate all the libraries we have in our environment onto a new environment in the same computer, we can simply clone the environment. Let's say we want to create a new environment called *Banking_Intelligence_5* and we want it to be identical to our *Banking_Intelligence_1*. This can be easily done at the Conda Powershell prompt by typing: "*conda create - - Banking_Intelligence_5 - - clone Banking_Intelligence_1*."

0.4.6 (Re-)creating a Conda Environment via YAML

There is a somewhat more involved process to replicate an existing environment onto another computer. When working with Conda, a YAML file can be used to list all the necessary packages for our project. This makes it easy to share our environment across different computers or with friends, which ensures all the necessary packages and correct versions are available in a new environment to run our code.

Starting from the environment we want to copy—say, 'Banking_Intelligence_1'— we can export the current environment (with all libraries and packages in their current versions) by exporting it as *.yml* file in our computer. At the Conda Powershell, typing "*conda env export > 'name your new environment'.yml*" will save a YAML file with the name we gave it locally in our computer—in the same directory where your environment is located. See Figure 0.27.

Figure 0.27: Exporting a Conda environment to a YAML file.

This example creates a file I called *"MyIB_env."* Typing *"notepad myIB_env.yml"* at the Conda prompt opens the YAML file, which contains a listing of all the libraries and packages installed in the *"'Banking_Intelligence_1'"* environment. The *"myIB_env.yml"* YAML file is saved in the default folder. We can simply find it using the search box next to the start button on a Windows 11 machine. For example, the full path to my YAML file on my own computer was saved in *"C:\Users \vicva \MyIB _env.yml."*

We can now create a new environment with all the libraries/packages reflected in the YAML file. Typically, we could do this by typing at the Conda Powershell prompt: *"conda env create -f MyIB_env.yml."* However, notice that opening the *"myIB_env.yml"* YAML file in a notepad reveals the name of the original environment *'Banking_Intelligence_1'*. See Figure 0.28.

Figure 0.28: Exporting a Conda environment to a YAML file.

This means that—while the name of the YAML file is *"myIB_env.yml"*—the name of the environment the YAML file calls is the original name *"Banking_Intelligence_1."* So, if we attempt to create the environment from the YAML file, Conda will throw an

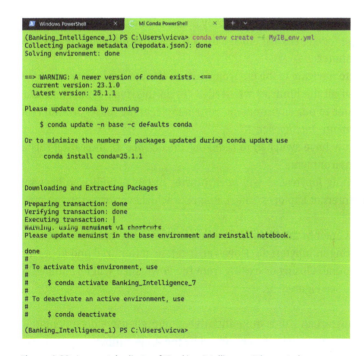

```
    MyIB_env.yml                    ×    +

File    Edit    View

name: Banking_Intelligence_7
channels:
  - defaults
dependencies:
  - anyio=4.6.2=py312haa95532_0
  - argon2-cffi=21.3.0=pyhd3eb1b0_0
  - argon2-cffi-bindings=21.2.0=py312h827c3e9_1
  - asttokens=2.0.5=pyhd3eb1b0_0
  - async-lru=2.0.4=py312haa95532_0
  - attrs=24.3.0=py312haa95532_0
  - babel=2.16.0=py312haa95532_0
  - beautifulsoup4=4.12.3=py312haa95532_0
  - blas=1.0=mkl
  - bleach=6.2.0=py312haa95532 0
```

Figure 0.29: Changing the name in the YAML file to *'Banking_Intelligence_7'*.

error because the name of that environment (*Banking_Intelligence_1*) is already taken. But we can simply open the notepad, and right after the name field, type whatever new name we would like to give to the new environment and save the notepad. For example, let's change the name in the name field from *Banking_Intelligence_1* to *Banking_Intelligence_7*. See Figure 0.29.

```
 Windows PowerShell        ×      Mi Conda PowerShell        ×    +  ˅

(Banking_Intelligence_1) PS C:\Users\vicva> conda env create -f MyIB_env.yml
Collecting package metadata (repodata.json): done
Solving environment: done

==> WARNING: A newer version of conda exists. <==
  current version: 23.1.0
  latest version: 25.1.1

Please update conda by running

    $ conda update -n base -c defaults conda

Or to minimize the number of packages updated during conda update use

    conda install conda=25.1.1


Downloading and Extracting Packages

Preparing transaction: done
Verifying transaction: done
Executing transaction: |
Warning: using menuinst v1 shortcuts
Please update menuinst in the base environment and reinstall notebook.

done
#
# To activate this environment, use
#
#     $ conda activate Banking_Intelligence_7
#
# To deactivate an active environment, use
#
#     $ conda deactivate

(Banking_Intelligence_1) PS C:\Users\vicva>
```

Figure 0.30: An exact duplicate of *'Banking_Intelligence_1'* is created.

We are now ready to create a new environment. At the Conda Powershell prompt type: "*conda env create -f MyIB_env.yml.*" See Figure 0.30.

And voila! We can verify by typing "*conda env list*" that the new environment *Banking_Intelligence_7*, which is an exact replica of *Banking_Intelligence_1*, is now in our list of environments. See Figure 0.31.

Figure 0.31: An exact duplicate of '*Banking_Intelligence_1*' is now in the environment list.

A YAML file with all the libraries required to run the codes for this book is available on the companion website https://www.degruyterbrill.com/document/isbn/9783111193120/html.

0.5 Working our *Intelligent Banking* Book with JupyterLab

Once we have installed all the requisite libraries in our environment and we are ready to start, do the following:
– Open a Conda Powershell, which automatically opens in the (base) environment.
– At the prompt, type "*conda env list*" to see the various environments we have installed in your computer.
– We will now want to navigate to the environment we want to use—where we have previously installed all the libraries we needed. To do this, type "*conda activate*" followed by the name of our environment. For example, at the (base) prompt type "*conda activate Banking_Intelligence_1.*"
– The prompt will now have switched to *(Banking_Intelligence_1)*, indicating this is now the current environment.
– At this prompt, typing *JupyterLab* will open Jupyter in our default web browser (such as Chrome, Internet Explorer, Safari, Bing… or whichever browser you most frequently use).
– Once JupyterLab is open in the browser, the Conda Powershell must be kept open while we are working in JupyterLab. However, it can be minimized and kept running in the background. Closing or exiting from the Powershell will terminate the JupyterLab session. See Figure 0.32.

The interface of the JupyterLab IDE is quite intuitive. Comprehensive documentation for getting started coding in JupyterLab is provided by the Project Jupyter open source project. The various worksheets provided for each chapter of the book will typically begin by importing the requisite libraries from the environment where the libraries were installed.

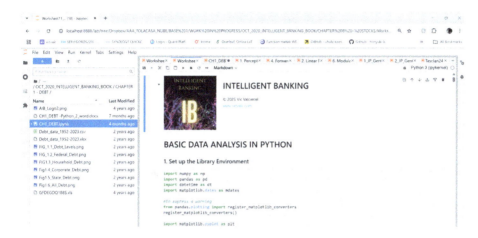

Figure 0.32: JupyterLab on a Chrome browser.

We will want to make sure the libraries (e. g., Numpy, Pandas, etc.) are installed in the current environment. JupyterLab will show an error if we attempt to import a library that is not installed in the environment. If we ever get an error after we import a library, we must return to the Conda Powershell and install it (see previous sections). Alternatively, some libraries can be installed/updated directly in JupyterLab. Please consult the great wealth of free documentation for JupyterLab at https://jupyterlab.readthedocs.io/en/latest/.

A bank of JupyterLab scripts to run the codes for this book is available at the companion website https://www.degruyterbrill.com/document/isbn/9783111193120/html. Let's get to the fun and the business of finance and banking!

Part I: **Money and the Government**

1 Debt and the U. S. Treasury

Contents

Debt obligations play a vital role in macroeconomic systems. Debt issuance, instrumentation and fluctuations affect households, non-financial firms such as most corporations, financial firms such as banks, and governments. This chapter provides a broad overview on some trends and patterns of debt in the United States.

1.1 Debt Measurement

Macroeconomic debt can be measured in absolute and relative terms, with the latter providing more informative content. Figure 1.1 shows various levels of macroeconomic debt in the United States between 1952 and 2023.

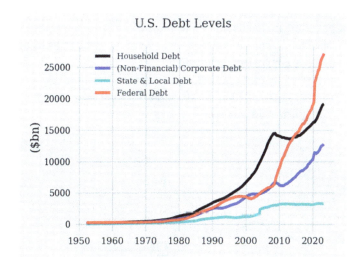

Figure 1.1: Historical levels of debt in the United States.

Figure 1.1 highlights that, while all measures of debt have experienced growth since the middle of the 20th century, household debt has represented the largest component of debt most of that period. However, the Great Financial Crisis (GFC) that led to the Great

https://doi.org/10.1515/9783111193120-002

Recession of 2008, represented a major shift in debt dynamics. After 2008, the federal debt began growing much more rapidly, outstripping all other debt growth, so that by the mid 2010s, federal debt overtook household debt as the largest component of debt. Since the COVID-19 period of 2020, the distance between the U.S. federal debt and all other debt has only been made larger.

1.2 The United States Federal Government Debt

On any given year, the federal government makes decisions on spending programs that add up to a federal budget. The government also collects various taxes throughout the year, which represent the government's revenues for the year.

When the government spends less than it collects in taxes, it runs a budget surplus. This means the government has some measure of revenues leftover after it has made its expenditures. This leads to the question of what to do with the surplus. This is not a question that gets asked often, as the United States has rarely enjoyed budget surpluses. The question was asked at the end of the 1990s when the end of the Clinton presidency left the government with a surplus. What to do with that surplus became a point of debate in the 2000 United States presidential election, where suggestions to use it to pay down the national debt or to add them to the Social Security funds were bandied about.

A balanced budget implies that the government roughly spends the same amount of U.S. dollars as it collects in taxes. Balanced budgets have also been relatively rare in the United States, at least since the 1970s.

Any year the federal government spends above and beyond its own revenue, which stems mainly from tax collection, it runs a budget deficit. Since the deficit has to be financed by taking on new debt, any budget deficit automatically adds to the national debt. The national debt is affected by many factors, including government taxing and spending decisions, government's participation in capital markets, business cycle fluctuations, natural disasters, militarization, and wars.

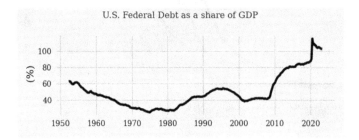

Figure 1.2: Historical levels of federal debt in the United States.

Figure 1.2 shows the United States federal debt as a share of gross domestic product (GDP). In the postwar period through about 1980, the absolute level of U.S. government debt grew at a slower rate than GDP, leading to a secular downward trend of U. S. relative debt relative to GDP.

After 1980, federal debt began to grow faster than GDP. The debt-to-GDP ratio steadily increased until the middle of the 1990s, when the United States economy experienced a sustained economic expansion (or boom) due to the information technology (IT) revolution and the mass adoption of the internet. From the middle of the 1990s, the federal debt-to-GDP ratio began to decline until about 2000 (commonly associated with the end of the dot com bubble of the 1990s) and then the ratio stabilized around 40%. In the aftermath of the GFC and the Great Recession of 2008, this ratio increased massively from 40% to over 80% by the end of 2019. Then the ratio experienced another massive hike in 2020 when, in response to the COVID-19 global pandemic, the federal debt was allowed to exceed 100% of GDP—a ratio that was only reached once before during World War II.

1.3 The United States Treasury Department

While policy decisions on federal spending and taxation are made by the legislative and executive branches of the United States government, policy actions are implemented by the United States Treasury Department. The Treasury is the arm of the federal government responsible for implementing fiscal policy: this involves federal government spending, taxation (through its largest bureau, the Internal Revenue Service, or IRS) and debt management.

From the Treasury's own website, the basic functions of the Department of the Treasury include:
1. Managing federal finances.
2. Collecting taxes, duties, and monies paid to and due to the U. S. and paying all bills of the U. S.
3. Currency and coinage.
4. Managing government accounts and the public debt.
5. Supervising national banks and thrift institutions.
6. Advising on domestic and international financial, monetary, economic, trade, and tax policy.
7. Enforcing federal finance and tax laws.
8. Investigating and prosecuting tax evaders, counterfeiters, and forgers.

1.4 Residential (Household) Debt

The largest share of debt incurred by United States households goes to housing services in the form of mortgage debt. Mortgage debt as a share of GDP has increased steadily since 1945.

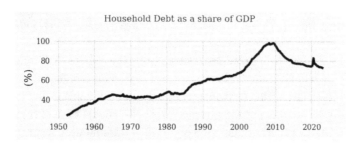

Figure 1.3: Historical levels for household debt in the United States.

Figure 1.3 shows the 1990s and early 2000s saw a dramatic increase in mortgage debt. Many factors accounted for this run-up in mortgage debt, including a policy during the President George W. Bush administration to drive up home ownership for families. Bubble behavior, which was typically reserved for financial markets, was now for the first time showing up in real estate. Many purchased houses on the expectation that their price would continue to increase. When prices begin to rise faster than the fundamental value of the house, this "decoupling" between value and price led to prices simply increasing because they were expected to increase.

This dynamic—that current prices tend to increase simply on the expectation that they will continue to do so—may lead to a self-fulfilling prophecy that may hold for a while... until the bubble pops!

It is possible this "irrational exuberance" (as Alan Greenspan, a former Federal Reserve chairperson, called it)—which led many households to speculate that housing demand and home prices would continue to increase ad infinitum— would have been less destructive had it had been financed by homeowners' income, savings, and wealth.

However, very low financing costs and high competition in commercial banking made it possible for homeowners to finance overvalued home purchases through mortgages. High competition in residential lending meant commercial banks derived low margins from issuing these loans. In order to compete, financial institutions relaxed lending standards. The term NINJA loans (no income—no job—no assets... no problem) became popular.

It could be argued that banks aided and abetted this runaway speculation. But this overabundance of mortgages exposed both homeowners and banking institutions to higher risk. When the bubble burst in 2007, housing prices declined sharply. Many homeowners were left with mortgage debt that was higher than the value of the home. This led to high delinquency, large losses for lenders, and bank bankruptcies and failures. The term Depression 2.0 became a rallying word for the massive monetary and fiscal response that would follow in 2008 and beyond. We will discuss more of this later in the book.

1.5 Other Debt

Non-financial firms also incur debt. Firms often finance investment in property, plant, and equipment by taking out loans.

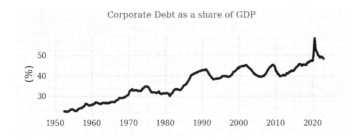

Figure 1.4: Historical levels for corporate debt in the United States.

Figure 1.4 shows that, fueled by the IT boom of the 1990s and more general productivity gains, corporate debt began increasing in the 1990s. This expansion continued until the GFC and the Great Recession of 2008. Low interest rates after 2007 contributed to low financing costs, which fueled a renewal in corporate borrowing through the 2010s. The global pandemic of 2020 saw a substantial spike in corporate debt, likely driven by low interest rates and the low cost of debt financing at the time. However, the spike was relatively short lived and corporate debt realigned rather quickly, returning to pre-COVID-19 levels by 2021. In addition to the federal government, other government entities in the United States, namely state and local governments, also take out loans to finance government works, education, infrastructure spending, etc.

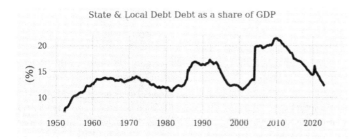

Figure 1.5: Historical levels for state and local debt in the United States.

Figure 1.5 shows that the debt incurred by state and local governments has represented the lowest levels of macroeconomic debt. It has ranged between 10% and 15% of GDP for most of the postwar period, except for the period following the Great Recession of 2008, when it spiked to about 20% of GDP before returning to its historical values.

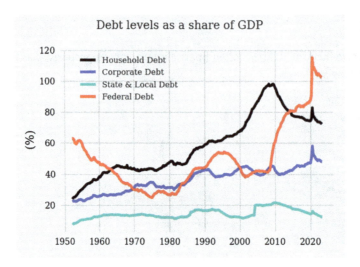

Figure 1.6: Various levels of debt in the United States.

Figure 1.6 shows that as a share of GDP, both household and corporate debt has steadily increased in the United States. However, in the aftermath of the GFC, household debt moderated somewhat. State and local debt has remained fairly level as a share of GDP. The federal debt has skyrocketed since GFC and through the global pandemic period, exceeding 100% of GDP. This leaves an open question as to whether this high level of debt is sustainable in the long run.

Thinking About It...

The national debt is the accumulation of various levels of government borrowing along with associated interest owed to the investors who purchased these securities. As the federal government experiences reoccurring deficits, which is common, the national debt grows. *See link to the U. S. Treasury*

Simply put, the national debt is similar to a person using a credit card for purchases and not paying off the full balance each month. The cost of purchases exceeding the amount paid off represents a deficit, while accumulated deficits over time represent a person's overall debt.

Debt dynamics have fundamentally shifted since the mid-20th century, with particularly dramatic changes occurring after the 2008 Global Financial Crisis and the 2020 COVID-19 pandemic. Historically, household debt, primarily in the form of mortgages, dominated the debt landscape in the United States for many decades. However, a significant transformation occurred after the 2008 financial crisis, when federal debt began growing at an unprecedented rate. This trend accelerated further during the COVID-19 pandemic, leading federal debt to surpass household debt as the largest component of the national debt.

Household debt patterns reveal interesting trends, especially in mortgage debt. The 1990s and early 2000s saw a dramatic increase in mortgage debt, driven by various factors, including government policies promoting home ownership and speculative behavior in real estate markets. This culminated in the 2008 housing crisis, characterized by relaxed lending standards (including notorious "NINJA loans") and ultimately leading to widespread foreclosures and bank failures. Tracking debt is crucial for understanding the broader economic landscape of the United States, as these debt patterns reflect and influence major economic events, policy decisions, and societal changes over the past several decades.

1.6 Glossary

Balanced Budget A situation where government spending equals government revenue in a given fiscal year. Like budget surpluses, balanced budgets have been relatively rare in the U. S. since the 1970s.

Budget Deficit The situation that occurs when the federal government's spending exceeds its revenue (primarily from tax collection) in a given fiscal year. Any budget deficit must be financed by taking on new debt, which adds to the national debt. Budget deficits can be influenced by various factors, including economic conditions, policy decisions, and unexpected events like natural disasters.

Budget Surplus The opposite of a budget deficit—when the government collects more in taxes and other revenue than it spends in a given year. Budget surpluses have been relatively rare in recent U. S. history, with a notable period occurring during the late 1990s at the end of the Clinton presidency.

Corporate Debt Debt incurred by non-financial companies, typically used to finance investments in property, plant, equipment, and other business operations. This form of debt often fluctuates with economic cycles and interest rates, as seen in the IT boom of the 1990s and the post-2008 low interest rate environment.

Debt-to-GDP Ratio A key metric for measuring relative debt levels, calculated by dividing total debt by the Gross Domestic Product (GDP). This ratio provides more informative content than absolute debt values, as it shows debt in relation to the economy's size and capacity to generate income.

Deficit Spending When the government spends above and beyond the revenues it collects from taxation, it runs a deficit. Deficit spending automatically contributes to growing the national debt.

Federal Debt (National Debt) The total amount owed by the U. S. federal government, which accumulates over time as a result of budget deficits. The federal debt has grown dramatically since the 2008 financial crisis and exceeded 100% of GDP following the COVID-19 pandemic.

Fiscal Policy Government actions regarding taxation and spending, implemented by the U. S. Treasury Department. Fiscal policy decisions affect the federal budget, debt levels, and overall economic activity.

Fundamental Value The actual worth of an asset based on its underlying characteristics and income-generating potential, as opposed to speculative market prices. The disconnect between fundamental values and market prices can indicate bubble conditions.

Global Financial Crisis (GFC) The severe financial crisis of 2008 that led to the Great Recession, marked by the collapse of the housing market, widespread bank failures, and a significant increase in federal debt. This event represented a major shift in debt dynamics across all sectors.

Gross Domestic Product (GDP) The market value of all final goods and direct services sold in a country over a calendar year. It can be reflected in currency units or as an index.

Household Debt Debt incurred by individuals and families, with mortgage debt typically representing the largest component. Household debt was historically the largest component of total U. S. debt until being surpassed by federal debt in the mid-2010s.

Internal Revenue Service (IRS) The largest bureau of the Treasury Department, responsible for collecting taxes and enforcing tax laws. The IRS plays a crucial role in government revenue collection, which affects budget deficits and debt levels.

Irrational Exuberance A term popularized by former Federal Reserve Chairperson Alan Greenspan, referring to unsustainable investor enthusiasm that drives asset prices well above their fundamental values.

Lending Standards The criteria used by financial institutions to evaluate potential borrowers and decide whether to extend loans. The relaxation of these standards contributed to the housing bubble and subsequent financial crisis.

Monetary Response Actions taken by the Federal Reserve and other monetary authorities to address economic crises, often including interest rate adjustments and other measures that affect borrowing costs and debt levels.

Mortgage Debt The primary component of household debt, representing loans used to purchase homes. Mortgage debt played a central role in the 2008 financial crisis due to relaxed lending standards and speculative behavior in the housing market.

NINJA Loans An acronym for "No Income, No Job, No Assets" loans that became notorious during the housing bubble of the early 2000s. These loans exemplified the dangerously relaxed lending standards that contributed to the 2008 financial crisis.

Real Estate Bubble A period when housing prices rise far above their fundamental values, driven by speculative behavior and expectations of continued price increases. The bursting of the real estate bubble in 2007 triggered the Global Financial Crisis.

State and Local Government Debt Debt incurred by state and local governments to finance public works, education, and infrastructure. This has historically been the smallest component of total U. S. debt, typically ranging between 10 and 15% of GDP.

Sustainable Debt A level of debt that can be maintained over the long term without causing economic instability or requiring dramatic policy changes. The sustainability of current U. S. federal debt levels (over 100% of GDP) remains an open question.

Treasury Department The executive agency responsible for managing federal finances, including debt management, tax collection, and fiscal policy implementation. The Treasury issues government debt securities to finance budget deficits.

2 Money and the Federal Reserve

Contents

In this chapter, we discuss the central bank of the United States—referred to as the Federal Reserve, or simply the Fed. The Fed is charged by the U. S. Congress with conducting monetary policy. To do that, it must measure the supply of money, manage credit to the banking system, oversee banking practices, help regulate interbank transactions, and inform Congress of the state of the economy.

2.1 The Federal Reserve System

Most countries have a central bank. A central bank is unlike the bank you and I may have a bank account with a neighborhood branch close by. Banks like Bank of America, Wells Fargo, Truist, Banco de Santander, Deutsche Bank, Bank of Yokohama, etc. are financial institutions who have at least two stakeholders: customers (like you or I) and shareholders (owners and managers of the bank). The objective of these financial institutions is to maximize profits and shareholder value and to compete for (and serve) customers.

A central bank has different objectives and stakeholders from commercial banks. First, the central bank's stakeholders are the public and residents/citizens of the country. For example, if I am a citizen of the U. S., technically I am automatically served by the central bank of the U. S., whereas if I want to be served by Wells Fargo in the U. S., then I need to enter into a contractual agreement with the bank for service (i. e., open an account with the bank). Second, a central bank is a nonprofit seeking institution. The objectives of central banks may vary from country to country, but they work to maximize the welfare of the country and, by extension, the welfare of its citizens.

As a result of various central bank panics plaguing the U. S. economy at the end of the 19th and beginning of the 20th centuries, the U. S. Congress, with the approval of President Woodrow Wilson, passed into law the Federal Reserve Act of 1913 (see Figure 2.1 below). This act of Congress established the Federal Reserve as the central bank of the U. S.

Section 2A of the Federal Reserve Act outlines the objectives of the Fed as follows:

https://doi.org/10.1515/9783111193120-003

Figure 2.1: President Wilson signs the Federal Reserve Act of 1913.

> The Board of Governors of the Federal Reserve System and the Federal Open Market Committee shall maintain long run growth of the monetary and credit aggregates commensurate with the economy's long run potential to increase production, so as to promote effectively the goals of maximum employment, stable prices, and moderate long-term interest rates.

Note that the objectives are maximum employment, price stability, and moderate long-term interest rates. Importantly, monetary and credit aggregates are listed as implicit "levers" though which it was understood the objectives could be reached.

So, the understanding was that the Fed could maintain (i. e., manage) long-run growth of the money supply to accomplish price stability and maximum employment. However, as we discuss below, it is not clear that the Federal Reserve has complete control of the money supply. Similarly, it is not clear that the Federal Reserve has complete control over the market rate that banks charge each other for very short-term loans (which is called the effective Federal Funds rate).

The Federal Reserve Act establishes the Fed as a special kind of bank—one that is not allowed to maximize its own profits. Instead, it is charged with the dual mandate of price stability and maximum employment. Even as a nonprofit institution, this act of Congress allows the Fed to hold a balance sheet made up of assets and liabilities. This enables the Fed to hold monetary instruments, typically U. S. government securities such as bills and bonds, as well as currency and other assets. Therefore, while it is not clear how much control the Fed has over the money supply or interbank rates, we can be more definitive about the Federal Reserve's ability to control its own balance sheet.

This means that any given trading day, the Fed can buy and sell U. S. government securities in the open market and manage the size of its balance sheet. When the Fed sells securities in the open market, the portfolio of securities it holds goes down (shrinking the size of its balance sheet). When the Fed buys securities in the open market, the portfolio of securities it holds increases (enlarging the size of its balance sheet). So, the Fed enjoys very good control over the treasuries it holds in its balance sheet. And this gives it a lot of control over bank reserves, which we define below. After all, we do not call it the Federal Money System, we call it the Federal Reserve System. The Fed controls bank reserves. But you and I care about money, not bank reserves. In the next sections, we discuss how the Fed can influence (but not control) the money supply and monetary aggregates through its control of bank reserves.

2.2 Monetary Aggregates and the Money Supply

There are myriad monetary assets that people hold in a national economy. For example, an individual might hold paper currency (cash) in her pocket. She might also deposit some of her cash or part of her income directly in a bank and hold it in the form of bank deposits. She might also hold cryptocurrencies (outside the banking system) and corporate bonds (debt issued by firms). A firm might also hold bank deposits, shares of stock, and Treasury bonds. Governments might hold gold reserves and other nations' currencies, as well as their own currencies.

Why hold these various monetary assets? For two main reasons:

1. they render some value in exchange (i. e., they can be used to trade for other monetary assets, various goods, or various services).
2. they render some intrinsic value (i. e., they render some monetary service, such as investment returns, access to capital markets, inflation protection, or storage of value, to name a few).

Different monetary assets may have different properties from one another. This means these monetary assets can be similar to each other in some respects and quite different from each other in other respects. The difficulty lies in keeping an accurate measure of the total amount, or the total value, of these various monetary assets in an economy. This falls under the typical purview of a central bank.

Simply summing all these various monetary assets into a single measure sounds simple enough. But it is deceptively simple. The reason is that each monetary asset that we might think of falls along a spectrum between value in exchange and intrinsic value—the two categories mentioned above.

The easier it is to use a monetary asset for exchange, the more liquid it is. Cash (e. g., the U. S. dollar in the U. S.) is the most liquid of assets because it can be directly exchanged for goods and services. A checking account of U. S. dollars in the U. S. is generally perfectly substitutable for cash (absent capital rationing by the government or banks), so that it is also very liquid. Foreign cash (e. g., the Euro) is a little bit less liquid in the U. S. because it generally is not accepted as a means of payment. It requires the extra step of exchanging it for the dollar before we can access goods/services. A U. S. Treasury bond cannot typically be used to buy groceries at the corner store. It is less liquid than cash because it takes a few more steps to convert the bond into cash before it can be used to access goods/services. Liquidity is a relative term that denotes how quickly and easily a monetary asset can be converted into cash.

For example, a checking account is relatively liquid because, generally, it is easily convertible into cash. On the other hand, a certificate of deposit (CD) is less liquid because the buyer of a CD generally needs to wait a pre-specified period before the CD can be converted back into cash. So the CD provides less liquidity to the buyer but it provides other monetary services, such as an interest payment. Generally, we can think of the interest rate a particular asset offers as the monetary service it provides to the holder in exchange for parting with liquidity.

Therefore, monetary assets lie along a spectrum between liquidity and monetary services—as Figure 2.2 highlights.

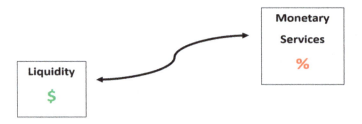

Figure 2.2: The two main purposes of holding monetary assets.

Now, the difficulty arises for central banks when they add up all these monetary assets into a measure of the money supply. The money supply is an aggregate of various monetary assets that range in degrees of liquidity.

Therefore, the money supply (M) is necessarily an arbitrary measure that depends on what gets included or not as part of the aggregate. Central banks differ on their preferred measure of the money supply, or which monetary assets are reflected in the money supply. Most central banks, however, agree that whatever is reflected in their M measure must be an asset to the public and a liability to banks and/or the central bank.

The Federal Reserve uses two measures of the money supply for the U.S.: M1 and M2. M1 is the primary measure of the money supply. From the Federal Reserve inception in 1913 to 2020, M1 was the measure of the medium of exchange. Since March 2020, this has become less clear. Historically, M1 consisted of currency in circulation, checkable deposits available to customers on demand (also known as demand deposits or checking accounts), and nonbank traveler's checks. M2 added savings deposits to M1. Saving deposits constituted roughly 60% of M2, making them the largest component of M2.

2.3 Divisia Monetary Aggregates and Simple-Sum Monetary Aggregates

Savings deposits are different from checking account deposits. Checking deposits typically pay no interest and, therefore, must be made available when the depositor demands them back. This means they are highly liquid. On the other hand, savings deposits provide a trade. Savings holders are paid an interest rate in exchange for a promise not to demand the funds back on short notice, or all at once. This means it takes a little more time to convert savings deposits into cash (known as liquidating). The interest rate savings provide are the reward to depositors for parting with liquidity.

Since checking and savings deposits have different liquidity profiles, they really are different types of deposits. It made sense for the Fed to separate them into the different aggregates (as it used to since 1913), where M1 was a narrower and more liquid measure of the money supply—since it excluded savings—and M2 was the broader and less liquid measure—since it included the vast balances of U. S. savings.

All of this changed in May 2020, when—bucking over 100 years of tradition—the Federal Reserve made an unprecedented change to these monetary aggregates. The Fed took savings out of M2 and began to include them in M1 instead. At first glance, this might seem like a harmless change. But it has portentous implications, and it may lead to big problems in the way money is measured.

First, in one fell swoop, M1 is now a much broader measure of the money supply than it ever was. As we discuss later, there may be advantages from keeping track of a narrow measure of the money supply. Second, M1 now conglomerates highly liquid checking accounts and less liquid savings accounts. Adding together assets with different liquidity profiles is highly misguided and leads to large measurement errors. Professor William A. Barnett showed this in an influential paper in 1980.

Professor Barnett argued the way Federal Reserve adds up deposits into their (M1 or M2) monetary aggregates is highly misguided. The reason is that all deposits are simply summed up into the aggregate without regard for their liquidity. For example, imagine that in last month's economy we had $2 of currency (C = $2) and $3 of checking deposits (D = $3) and no savings (S = $0). The Federal Reserve would simply add up all of these into their M2 measure.

$$M2_{[Last\ Month]} = (C = \$2) + (D = \$3) + (S = \$0) = \$5.$$

Now, say that this month (today) currency was reduced by $1, all checking deposits moved to savings and an extra $1 of savings was added. The Federal Reserve would again sum up all these deposits today to conclude the money supply remains unchanged:

$$M2_{[This\ Month]} = (C = \$1) + (D = \$0) + (S = \$4) = \$5.$$

According to this simple-sum calculation, last month the money supply was $5 and this month it remains at $5. But these are not necessarily comparable. Last month's M2 measure was much more liquid, and this month's measure seems to add up to the same quantity, but it is generating interest (since S is interest-yielding). Essentially, simply summing up all deposits implicitly assigns them equal importance.

If we have three deposits C, D, and S to add up, then giving them the same importance can be done by assigning each an equal value of [1/3]. This is called a weight. Equal weights shows:

$$M2_{[\text{Last Month}]} = 3 * \left[\left(\frac{1}{3}\right)(C = \$2) + \left(\frac{1}{3}\right)(D = \$3) + \left(\frac{1}{3}\right)(S = \$0) = \$5 \right]$$

and

$$M2_{[\text{Last Month}]} = 3 * \left[\left(\frac{1}{3}\right)(C = \$1) + \left(\frac{1}{3}\right)(D = \$0) + \left(\frac{1}{3}\right)(S = \$4) = \$5 \right].$$

Adding up this way suggests that this simple-sum aggregate is essentially the same as aggregating with equal weights. Equal importance assumes D and S are perfect substitutes. But they are not!

Professor Barnett first raised this problematic way of simply summing up assets into a monetary aggregate, which became known as the *Barnett Critique*. He invented what became known as the Divisia Monetary Aggregate. A Divisia aggregate is a weighted sum (instead of a simple-sum) monetary index that assigns different weights according to the liquidity and monetary services each component provides.

In our example above, imagine that liquidity gets assigned more importance, so that liquid deposits receive a weight of (2/5) and the less liquid deposits receive a weight of (1/5). The Divisia measures would be calculated as follows:

$$M2_{[\text{Last Month}]} = 3 * \left[\left(\frac{2}{5}\right)(C = \$2) + \left(\frac{2}{5}\right)(D = \$3) + \left(\frac{1}{5}\right)(S = \$0) = \$6 \right]$$

and

$$M2_{[\text{This Month}]} = 3 * \left[\left(\frac{2}{5}\right)(C = \$1) + \left(\frac{2}{5}\right)(D = \$0) + \left(\frac{1}{5}\right)(S = \$4) = \$3.6 \right].$$

This would suggest the money supply has decreased from last month to this month, which better reflects the loss in liquidity that took place between the two months as a consequence of deposit substitution.

Beginning in the 1980s, research studies of the effects of monetary policy mostly abandoned analysis of monetary aggregates in favor of interest rates, because economists stopped finding monetary aggregate data useful for modeling. However, the vast majority of economists focused on simple-sum measures the Federal Reserve produces, which is problematic, as we discussed. On the other hand, growing research literature is finding that correctly measured monetary aggregates like the Divisia measure of the money supply are very useful for modeling.

2.4 The Determinants of the Money Supply

The Federal Reserve is responsible for controlling the money supply and regulating the banking system. However, while the Fed can influence the money supply, it cannot completely control it, since there are other actors in the money supply determination. For example, the banking system creates the deposit accounts that are a major component of the money supply. In addition, the nonbank public (all households and firms) decides the form in which they wish to hold money (e. g., currency vs. deposits).

Beginning with some definitions: Currency in circulation (C) is paper money and coins held by the nonbank public. Vault cash is currency held by banks. Currency in M1 is currency held by the nonbank public, which is what is left after subtracting vault cash from currency in circulation.

Bank reserves (R) are deposit accounts that commercial banks keep in their accounts with the Fed plus vault cash. Reserve deposits are assets for banks and liabilities for the Fed. Why? Because banks can request that the Fed repay the deposits on demand with Federal Reserve Notes.

The process starts with the monetary base. Monetary base (or high-powered money) is the sum of bank reserves and currency in circulation.

$$MB = C + R.$$

The monetary base is an important determinant of the money supply, because it acts as a base effect. There is also a multiplier effect, so that the monetary base can generate more money M1 or M2 in the economy (the money multiplier). The money multiplier links the monetary base to the money supply. There is a close connection between the monetary base and the Fed's balance sheet. See Figure 2.3.

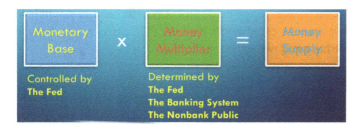

Figure 2.3: The model of money supply determination.

When the money multiplier is stable, the Fed can hold a strong influence over the money supply by controlling the monetary base. The Fed's management of the monetary base is, by and large, accomplished through the market for reserves.

The Fed supplies reserves to the banking sector. We discuss how this is done below. On the other side of the coin, commercial banks demand reserves. There are two main reasons why commercial banks demand reserves. One, reserves provide core funding to the bank. So, the more reserves the bank holds, the better it can withstand an unexpected deposit outflow or a bank run. Two, reserves furnish the bank with financial capital, which in turn can be used to generate loans. The more reserves a bank has, the more ability it has to generate loans, which is the most important source of profit for the bank.

So, reserves play double duty for commercial banks, and they create a trade-off. Reserves act as insurance against unexpected deposit outflows, and they can be turned into profitable loans. The more reserves the commercial bank hoards, the more capitalized it is at the cost of fewer opportunities for loan issuance. On the other hand, the more the bank converts its reserves holdings into loans, the more profits it can generate, at the cost of its ability to weather a major deposit outflow—when customers run to the bank to withdraw their deposits.

So, more reserves provide more insurance and lower profits. Fewer reserves translate to less insurance and higher profits. So how does the bank find the optimal trade-off? In other words, what are the optimal levels of reserves holdings? Banks spend a lot of time and resources on this question.

Profits are beneficial for the specific bank that collects them through loan issuance. On the other hand, the insurance provided by holding more reserves makes for a better capitalized bank. Since banks are highly interconnected, more reserves are beneficial not only to the specific bank, but to the whole banking system.

Since one of the tasks of the Federal Reserve is to safeguard the banking system, it has always fallen under its purview to find ways to induce banks to remain well capitalized. In the past, the Fed would set a required reserve ratio. This required reserve ratio (rr) is the percentage of checkable deposits that the Fed specifies that banks must hold as reserves.

So, the Fed would require banks to hold a portion of their total reserves (R). These were called required reserves (RR). So, banks would hold required reserves to comply with the Fed's rule. Sometimes, they would hold extra. Any reserves they would hold above the Fed's requirement were called excess reserves (ER). Banks would demand reserves according to the following two equations:

$$RR = rr * (\text{New Deposits}),$$
$$R = RR + ER.$$

These equations suggest that if the Fed wanted banks to slow down loan creation, it could simply raise the reserve ratio, thereby requiring banks to keep more reserves "in the vault" and issue fewer loans. Conversely, if the Fed wanted banks to issue more loans, it would lower required reserves by reducing the reserve ratio. Therefore, the required reserve ratio was one of the tools the Federal Reserve would use to conduct monetary policy.

This all changed in March 2020, when the Federal Reserve effectively ended its reserve requirement. On the Fed's website—you can read the details in Figure 2.4 below—

the Fed also explains the elimination of required reserves prompted the consolidation of other statistical releases of various money measures; which suggests this to be a momentous change in policy.

Figure 2.4: A notable change in Federal Reserve policy.

One way to think about this is that if there is no longer a requirement for banks to hold reserves, then required reserves are zero and all reserves are now excess reserves (in excess of zero) and the equations above now look like:

$$RR = (0\%) * \text{New Deposits},$$
$$R = \cancel{RR} + ER.$$

Depository institutions are no longer required to keep reserves. So, what keeps them well capitalized? In 2008, the Federal Reserve began offering a new interest rate for whatever level of reserves banks voluntarily keep in the vault. This is called interest on reserves (IOR). This rate is managed exclusively by the Fed. Since the Fed retains exclusive control over the setting of this rate, IOR effectively establishes a floor against other rates that banks could sell their reserves at. This gives the Fed some loose degree of influence over banks' demand for reserves.

While the Fed began to pay interest on reserves in 2008, IOR did not have traction because it was effectively set at zero for a long time after and, presumably, the reserve ratio still mattered from 2008 to 2020. But after 2020, the Federal Reserve switched instruments of monetary policy. Before 2020, it had used the proverbial "stick." Banks would be penalized if they held reserves below the requirement. After 2020, it switched to IOR as the proverbial "carrot," rewarding banks for keeping reserves, as Figure 2.5 suggests.

The Fed's approach to managing reserve demand

(rr) is the stick   (IOR) is the carrot

Figure 2.5: The Federal Reserve switches one of their tools of monetary policy abandoning the reserve ratio and adopting IOR in 2020.

Therefore, in 2020, the Federal Reserve effectively traded one of their tools of monetary policy for another by abandoning the reserve ratio and adopting IOR.

IOR is a relatively new tool of monetary policy the Federal Reserve can use to have an impact on the determination of the money supply. IOR's impact will manifest mainly through the money multiplier in our model, shown in (the middle box of) Figure 2.3. We discuss this in more detail below. But first, the left box in Figure 2.3 suggests that determination of the money supply can also be accomplished by management of the monetary base.

2.5 The Monetary Base

The Federal Reserve changes the monetary base by altering the levels of assets it holds in its balance sheet—one way to do this is through management of the Fed's System Open Market Account (SOMA) portfolio. The Fed's buys and sells securities in the open market, usually U. S. Treasury securities, but also mortgage-backed securities (MBSs) since 2008.

When the Fed purchases these securities, its SOMA portfolio balances increase, and when the Fed sells securities, its SOMA portfolio balances decreases.

These transactions are carried out electronically with primary dealers by the Fed's trading desk. As of May 2024, there were 24 primary dealers (commercial banks, investment banks, and securities dealers).[1]

These primary dealers are approved to hold reserve accounts with the Federal Reserve. This means they are part of the banking system in the U. S. For instance, if the Federal Reserve were to inject $100 of reserves into one of these banks, say Bank of America (BoA), then $100 would be credited to the reserve account of BoA. Technically, since BoA is part of the banking system, reserves in the banking system would increase by $100.

---

1 ASL Capital Markets Inc.; Bank of Montreal; Chicago Branch; Bank of Nova Scotia, New York Agency; BNP Paribas Securities Corp.; Barclays Capital Inc.; BofA Securities Inc.; Cantor Fitzgerald & Co.; Citigroup Global Markets Inc.; Daiwa Capital Markets America Inc.; Deutsche Bank Securities Inc.; Goldman Sachs & Co. LLC; HSBC Securities (USA) Inc.; Jefferies LLC; J. P. Morgan Securities LLC; Mizuho Securities USA LLC; Morgan Stanley & Co. LLC; NatWest Markets Securities Inc.; Nomura Securities International Inc.; RBC Capital Markets LLC; Santander U. S. Capital Markets LLC; Societe Generale, New York Branch; TD Securities (USA) LLC; UBS Securities LLC; and Wells Fargo Securities LLC.

An Accounting Side Note

From an accounting standpoint, every transaction must satisfy a balance between assets and liabilities. A balance sheet is an accounting/financial report, where essentially all assets and liabilities are listed on a "sheet." Its very name suggests this balancing act between assets and liabilities. If a transaction leads me to increase my assets by x-dollars, then to keep my balance sheet balanced, I must either: 1) lose an equal amount of x-dollars of a different asset or 2) increase my liabilities in an equal x-dollar amount.

For example, after a full accounting of all my assets, imagine all I have is $10,000 in cash. If I run to the dealership and I buy myself a car I would lose my asset of $10K cash in exchange for a different asset, a car worth $10K. I gained an asset (a car) and lost an asset (cash) in equal amounts. My balance sheet remains balanced.

If I decided to save my $10K but wanted to buy the car anyway, I could do so on credit. For example, I run to my dealership and buy the $10K car with my credit card, then my assets increase by one car worth $10K. But now I am liable for $10K debt on my credit card. When I buy on credit, instead of losing an asset on the other side of the transaction, I "gain" a liability. So, I gain $10K worth of assets and I "gain" $10K worth of liabilities. My balance sheet remains balanced.

Case A: Fed's open market purchase

The Fed buys $1 million worth of Treasury bills from Wells Fargo. Remember treasuries are an asset to the holder and a liability to the issuer (the U. S. Treasury). This means the Fed would be adding $1 million worth of Treasury bills on the asset side of its own balance sheet and Wells Fargo would be losing (deducting) $1 million worth of assets from its balance sheet.

So far so good. But how is the transaction fulfilled? No representative from the Fed would put $1 million in cash in a bag and walk it over across the street to the Manhattan Branch of Wells Fargo in New York City. Which is to say, how does the Fed purchase those treasuries from Wells Fargo?

The Fed buys the treasuries with reserves. So it credits Wells Fargo with $1 million worth of reserves, which means the Fed is adding $1 million worth of reserves as a liability on its own balance sheet. All of this is reflected on Figure 2.6, which shows a T-account for the whole banking system and the T-account for the Fed:

BANKING SYSTEM

Assets		Liabilities
Securities	−$1 million	
Reserves	+$1 million	

FEDERAL RESERVE SOMA

Assets		Liabilities	
Securities	+$1 million	Reserves	+$1 million

Figure 2.6: Example of an open market purchase.

This open market transaction means Wells Fargo bank is out one asset ($1 million of treasuries) and gains another asset ($1 million of reserves). Wells Fargo's balance sheet remains balanced. On the other side of the transaction, the Fed's balance sheet increases its assets by $1 million (worth of treasuries), but it also increases its liabilities by $1 million (of reserves), so the Fed's balance sheet also remains balanced.

Since reserves are part of the monetary base, whenever the Fed purchases x-dollar amount of securities in the open market, it adds x-dollar of reserves in the monetary base.

The monetary base increases dollar-for-dollar by the same amount of a Fed's open market purchase

Case B: Fed's open market sale

An open market sale by the Fed reverses all the results from an open market purchase. When the Fed sells $1 million worth of Treasury bills to Wells Fargo, the Fed would be draining $1 million worth of Treasury bills from the asset side of its own balance sheet, while Wells Fargo at the same time would be adding $1 million worth of assets to its balance sheet. The transaction takes assets in the amount $1 million of reserves from Wells Fargo's balance sheet, which means the Fed's liabilities to Wells Fargo (and therefore the banking system) decrease by $1 million worth of reserves.

All of this is reflected in Figure 2.7, which shows a T-account for the whole banking system and the T-account for the Fed:

BANKING SYSTEM			
Assets		**Liabilities**	
Securities	+$1 million		
Reserves	−$1 million		

FEDERAL RESERVE SOMA			
Assets		**Liabilities**	
Securities	−$1 million	Reserves	−$1 million

Figure 2.7: Example of an open market sale.

This open market transaction means Wells Fargo bank is out one asset ($1 million of reserves) and gains another asset ($1 million of treasuries). Wells Fargo's balance sheet remains balanced.

On the other side of the transaction, the Fed's balance sheet decreases its assets by $1 million (worth of treasuries) but it also decreases its liabilities by $1 million (of reserves), so the Fed's balance sheet also remains balanced.

Since reserves are part of the monetary base, whenever the Fed sells x-dollar amount of securities in the open market, it drains x-dollar of reserves from the monetary base.

The monetary base decreases dollar-for-dollar by the same amount of a Fed's open market sale

So, one way for the Fed to control the monetary base is to conduct open market operations (purchases and sales of securities). This is the most common tool and possibly the most powerful tool, but there are others.

Case C: Fed's discount loans

A discount loan is a reserves loan made by the Fed directly to a commercial bank. This is a different way to supply reserves to the banking system. Instead of supplying reserves through outright purchases/sales, the Fed supplies reserves by lending them to a willing bank and charging them a specific interest rate, called the discount rate. The discount rate is not a market rate but a managed rate (i. e., set exclusively by the Fed).

Discount loans generate reserves that are being borrowed by banks. Therefore, discount loans alter bank reserves. For example, an increase in discount loans affects both sides of the Fed's balance sheet: $1 million of discount loans increases bank reserves and the monetary base by $1 million. This is reflected in Figure 2.8.

FEDERAL RESERVE SOMA			
Assets		**Liabilities**	
Discount loans	+$1 million	Reserves	+$1 million

BANKING SYSTEM			
Assets		**Liabilities**	
Reserves	+$1 million	Discount loans	+$1 million

Figure 2.8: Example of a discount loan (step 1).

If banks repay $1 million in discount loans to the Fed, the preceding transactions are reversed. This can be seen in Figure 2.9.

Comparing open market operations and discount loans reveals a few interesting facts. Both change the monetary base, but the Fed has greater control over open market operations. The Fed holds exclusive control over its own balance sheet, so it enjoys good control over its own open market operations. On the other hand, the Fed sets the discount rate—the interest rate the Fed charges on discount loans.

FEDERAL RESERVE SOMA			
Assets		**Liabilities**	
Discount loans	−$1 million	Reserves	−$1 million

BANKING SYSTEM			
Assets		**Liabilities**	
Reserves	−$1 million	Discount loans	−$1 million

Figure 2.9: Example of a discount loan (step 2).

The discount rate differs from most interest rates because it is set by the Fed, whereas most interest rates are determined by demand and supply in financial markets. Even if the Fed can control the discount rate, it cannot force banks to take discount loans—the Fed cannot effectively force banks to borrow from it. This means the tool of open market operations is more effective, and more powerful, than the discount loan tool.

The monetary base (MB) includes what is called nonborrowed reserves (NBR), which are reserves that come from open market operations (so they are not borrowed). It also includes borrowed reserves (BR), which come from discount loans.

$$MB = NBR + BR.$$

Again, the Fed has better control over the nonborrowed part of the monetary base.

The monetary base increased sharply in the fall of 2008 and stayed at high levels through 2019, before beginning a slow decline that ended in March 2020 with the onset of COVID-19, when it rose again. Most of these increases occurred because of an increase in the bank reserves component, not the currency in circulation component of the monetary base.

The Fed's holdings of Treasury securities actually fell while the base was exploding. As the Fed began to purchase private debt connected with Bear Stearns and AIG during the 2007 Financial Crisis, the asset side of its balance sheet expanded, and so did the monetary base. Early in 2020, the Fed resumed purchases of U. S. treasuries at a fast pace in response to the COVID-19 shock.

Conclusion: Whenever the Fed purchases assets of any kind (whether treasuries or private debt), the monetary base increases

The first step in the money supply determination is the monetary base. We have established the Fed can control the monetary base through open market operations and through discount loans. Both open market operations and discount loans can exert a quantitative impact on the monetary base. Can the public's liquidity preference impact the monetary base?

The answer is not likely. The public's preference for currency relative to checkable deposits does not affect the monetary base. For example, assume households and firms decide to withdraw $1 million from their checking accounts. Should this not affect the monetary base? Well, it may affect the composition but not the quantity of the monetary base. This results from the fact that one component of the monetary base (reserves) would fall along with deposits, while the other (currency in circulation) would rise by the same amount—a full offset in the monetary base. This is shown in Figure 2.10.

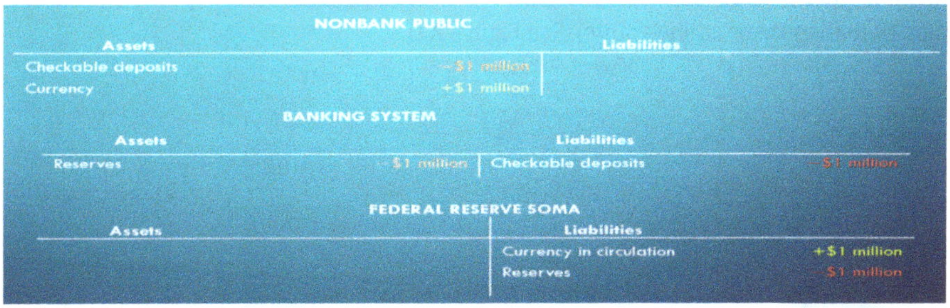

Figure 2.10: Example of a discount loan (step 3).

2.6 The Money Multiplier

The monetary base includes two tools of monetary policy the Fed can use: open market operations and discount loans. The Fed can conduct monetary policy by managing the monetary base. But the monetary base alone does not determine the money supply. The money multiplier is the other determinant of our money supply model—the middle box in Figure 2.3.

The money multiplier will combine with the monetary base to help us arrive at an aggregate money supply. We will show later that the Fed can influence the money multiplier with another tool of monetary policy we have already discussed: interest on reserves (IOR). But importantly, the Fed alone cannot control the money multiplier. This is because the money multiplier is determined by the actions of three actors in the economy: the Fed, the nonbank public, and banks.

Before we can understand the money multiplier, we must first discuss another concept: the multiple deposit expansion. Expansion in deposits generates a deposit multiplier—which relates directly to the money multiplier—and helps us understand the final step in the money supply determination.

The idea is simple. In a fractional reserve system, as that of the U. S. and all other industrialized economies, a commercial bank keeps only a fraction of reserves in its "vault" or its account with the central bank and typically loans the rest. A loan then becomes a new deposit, a fraction of which is kept by the next bank, which then issues more loans, which become more deposits… rinse and repeat.

Let's return to our previous example. Imagine now that the Fed buys $100K worth of U. S. treasuries from Wells Fargo. Recall the Fed buys them by crediting Wells Fargo's balance sheet with $100K in reserves, so the monetary base has increased by $100K. Now imagine that Wells Fargo chooses to use these reserves to issue a $100K loan to Belle, a Wells Fargo customer. So, Wells Fargo credits Belle's checking account with the $100K loan. This transaction keeps Wells Fargo's balance sheet balanced. Wells Fargo's assets increase by $100,000 worth of loans (which should be paid back with interest in the future), and its liabilities increase by $100,000 worth of checkable deposits (now Belle's money to dispose of as she wants). See Figure 2.11.

WELLS FARGO			
Assets		**Liabilities**	
Securities	−$100,000	Checkable deposits	+$100,000
Reserves	+$100,000		
Loans	+$100,000		

Figure 2.11: Example of a bank loan (step 1).

Now, imagine Belle does not borrow the $100K to simply keep them in her checking account at Wells Fargo. Let's say she spends the loan proceeds by writing a check for $100,000 to buy ovens from Ashley's Bakery Equipment. Ashley sells the equipment to Belle and deposits the $100,000 payment in her own bank, say PNC. This means Wells Fargo loses $100,000 worth of checkable deposits and PNC gains those $100,000 of checkable deposits. After PNC has cleared the check and collected the funds from Wells Fargo, both banks T-accounts look like Figure 2.12.

WELLS FARGO			
Assets		**Liabilities**	
Securities	−$100,000	Checkable deposits	$0
Loans	+$100,000		
Reserves	$0		

PNC BANK			
Assets		**Liabilities**	
Reserves	+$100,000	Checkable deposits	+$100,000

Figure 2.12: Example of a bank loan (step 2).

Notice that this transaction—Belle purchasing bakery equipment from Ashley— does not impact the monetary base. The original $100K injection of reserves remains in the banking system, it simply has transferred from Wells Fargo to PNC, both part of the Federal Reserve System. In addition, notice the money supply has not changed either. This is because $100K worth of deposits were deducted from Wells Fargo and added to PNC. Essentially, $100K worth of reserves in the banking system substantiates $100K worth of deposits in the money supply.

Now, imagine PNC makes a calculated bet that Ashley will not close her account and will only demand a portion of her checking account from time to time for the foreseeable future. So, PNC decides to take a fraction of the $100 reserves and loan them out. This will garner PNC some interest rate returns in the future. Suppose that PNC makes a $90,000 loan to Sam's Printing who writes a check in that amount for equipment from Computer Universe, who has an account at SunTrust Bank.

Something important is happening here! What was a new loan to Sam became a new deposit to Computer Universe's account at SunTrust Bank. The total amount of reserves in the system remains unchanged at $100K in the banking system. But because the process of loaning a fraction of reserves creates more loans, reserves are being redistributed within the banking system, multiplying the amount of deposit generated. This can be seen more specifically in the T-accounts of PNC and SunTrust in Figure 2.13.

PNC BANK				
Assets			**Liabilities**	
Reserves	+$10,000		Checkable deposits	+$100,000
Loans	+$90,000			
SUNTRUST BANK				
Assets			**Liabilities**	
Reserves	+$90,000		Checkable deposits	+$90,000

Figure 2.13: Example of a bank loan (step 3).

The total amount of reserves from the original Fed injection is still $100K. Originally, the whole $100K of reserves was sitting in Wells Fargo's reserve account. Now $10K sits in PNC and $90K sits at SunTrust. Now imagine, SunTrust decides to take the same calculated risk as PNC did before.

After conducting its analysis and due diligence, SunTrust decides it wants to keep $9K in reserves and loan its excess reserves of $81,000 to Val's Barber Shop to use for remodeling. If the proceeds of the loan to Val's Barber Shop were deposited in another bank, checkable deposits in the banking system would rise by another $81,000. See Figure 2.14.

Therefore, while reserves in the banking system would remain the same at $100K ($10K in PNC, $9K in SunTrust, and $81K in some other bank), checkable deposits would have increased by $100K (in PNC) plus $90K (in SunTrust) plus $81K (in some third bank). Therefore, through the loan process, an injection of $100K worth of reserves has given rise to $271K of deposits in our example. This is called the multiple deposit creation. This

PNC BANK			
Assets		**Liabilities**	
Reserves	+$10,000	Checkable deposits	+$100,000
Loans	+$90,000		

SUNTRUST BANK			
Assets		**Liabilities**	
Reserves	+$9,000	Checkable deposits	+$90,000
Loans	+$81,000		

Figure 2.14: Example of a bank loan (step 4).

multiple deposit creation is part of the money supply process, in which an increase in bank reserves results in rounds of bank loans and generation of checkable deposits. See Figure 2.15.

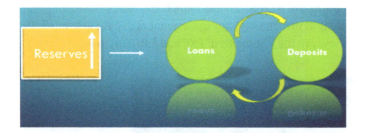

Figure 2.15: The deposit multiplier.

As a result, an increase in the money supply is a multiple of the initial increase in reserves. Note that the multiple deposit creation process depends on the ability and will-ingness of banks (like SunTrust and PNC and others) to use a fraction of their reserves to issue loans. And it also depends on the nonbank public's (people like Sam and Val and others) willingness to borrow. But we mentioned earlier that three agents helped deter-mine the multiplier (and by extension the multiple deposit creation process): Banks, the nonbank public, and the Fed.

How does the Fed impact the multiple deposit creation process? With the new tool of monetary policy that we have already partially discussed: Interest on Reserves (IOR).

2.7 The Last Tool of Monetary Policy: IOR Impact on the Money Multiplier

Many banks may demand reserves for two purposes: to loan some of their excess re-serves and to voluntarily keep a portion of reserves and collect the IOR from the Fed to remain well capitalized.

The amount of reserves demanded by banks must be inversely related to market rates, since these rates constitute the opportunity cost of holding reserves. Every dollar kept "in the vault" does not collect a market rate. As the interest rate gets lower, the opportunity cost of holding reserves lowers as well, which is reflected as a downward movement along the banks' demand curve for reserves, as shown in Figure 2.16.

Presumably, as banks accumulate more and more reserves, interest rates could be driven unnaturally low.

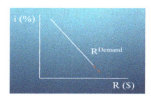

Figure 2.16: The demand curve for bank reserves.

If market rates for federal funds reach levels below IOR, banks would be happier keeping reserves on hand and collecting IOR than lending those reserves to collect a lower rate. Therefore, IOR acts as a floor against interest rates on loans. When market rates reach the IOR, the bank should hold reserves (perfectly elastically) while collecting the IOR. See Figure 2.17.

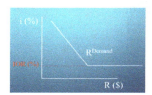

Figure 2.17: The demand curve for bank reserves (continued).

Prior to 2020, banks kept a reserve ratio that was ("required") set by the Fed. After 2020, any given bank began to keep a reserve ratio that was ("voluntary") set by itself. This means that the bank may dispose of its excess reserves by loaning a portion (and collecting a market rate) and voluntarily holding a portion (and collecting IOR). So, after 2020, the new equation for a bank's demand (R^D) for reserves is given by

$$R^D \, (\$) = \text{LOANS} \, (\$) + \text{VR} \, (\$).$$

Since the optimal level of voluntary reserves (VR) is subjective and varies from bank to bank, voluntary reserves are very difficult to model. We now make the following strong simplifying assumptions about voluntary reserves:

1. The bank keeps an idiosyncratic "rule of thumb" in its own desired VR. So, we assume banks keep a voluntary reserve ratio (vrr), which is held fixed (at a constant %) for a given IOR.
2. Competition drives all banks to choose the same voluntary reserve ratio (vrr).
3. Banks increase their vrr if IOR increases and decrease their vrr if IOR decreases.

As an example, imagine that at an IOR of 1%, the bank keeps a vrr of 10%. This means that the bank volunteers to hold 10% of its reserves to collect a 1% return (IOR = 1%) from the Fed, and loans 90% of its reserves to collect other rates from the market. See Figure 2.18.

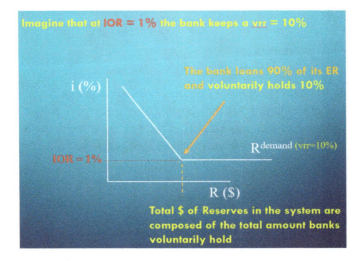

Figure 2.18: The demand curve for bank reserves with IOR = 1%.

These 90% of reserves being loaned out will generate more deposits, which will generate more loans and more deposits again... in the process of multiple deposit creation we saw in the previous section.

Let's say the Fed feels that this deposit creation is too large and would like to tamp down all this loan activity. The Fed could use its IOR tool of monetary policy to do so. In order to persuade banks to loan less, the Fed could raise the IOR and reward banks with a higher interest rate for keeping more reserves on hand. In our example, assume the Fed raises the IOR (from 1%) to IOR = 3%.

Banks would then (independently) demand more reserves for any level of the interest rate. This would shift the demand curve to the right. The total amount of reserves in the system would now be larger because banks would voluntarily hold more, incentivized by the higher IOR. But more reserves in the system means reduced loans, because banks are now loaning a smaller fraction of their reserves at a higher IOR than before (when the reward for holding reserves was lower). See Figure 2.19.

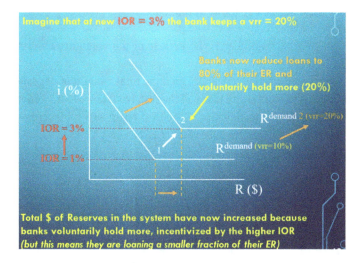

Figure 2.19: An increase in the demand for reserves at a higher IOR.

So, even if a higher IOR increased reserves in the system, it would ultimately be a contractionary policy action, because fewer loans lead to fewer deposits, which lead to a reduction of the money supply.

To see this, let's take our example out to its logical conclusion. Remember the original injection of reserves in the previous sections? The Fed had purchased $100K of treasuries from Wells Fargo, which then ended up at PNC. At an IOR of 1% PNC would loan out 90% of reserves and voluntarily keep 10%.

But the story does not stop there. If PNC lends out (1 − vrr ∗ R = 0.9 ∗ $100K), the $90K loan becomes a new deposit in SunTrust. If SunTrust voluntarily keeps 10% ($9K) and lends the rest, the $81K loan becomes a new deposit at a third bank, and so on. If every bank voluntarily keeps 10%, the total amount of reserves in the banking system remains equal to the original injection of $100K of reserves.

But the multiple deposit creation process suggests a magnification of deposits, and an increase in the money supply ensues as a result of the loan creation process.

The *simple deposit multiplier* (dm) is the ratio of the amount of deposits created by banks (ΔD) to the amount of new reserves (ΔR). In our example, the initial deposit was $100K, the second was $90K, the third $81K, etc.... So, the total amount of new deposits created is given by

$$\Delta D = \$100K + [(0.9) * \$100K] + [(0.9 * 0.9) * \$100K] + [(0.9 * 0.9 * 0.9) * \$100K] + \cdots,$$

which simplifies to $\Delta D = \$100K * [1 + 0.9 + 0.9^2 + 0.9^3 + \cdots]$.

An infinite series $[1 + 0.9 + 0.9^2 + 0.9^3 + 0.9^4 + \cdots]$ reduces to $1/(1 - 0.9)$. If we apply this result for an infinite series to the amount of new deposits created, it results in:

$$\Delta D = \$100K * [1/0.1] = \$1 \text{ million.}$$

This means the simple deposit multiplier is the inverse of the voluntary reserve ratio dm = 1/vrr.

So, in our example, if vrr = 10% when IOR is 1%, then the total amount of deposits generated if every bank keeps (vrr = 10%) and loans all the rest, would be $900K! Added to the original deposit, would mean that an injection of $100K of reserves would increase the money supply by a factor of 10 to $1 million. See Figure 2.20.

Bank	Increase in deposits	Increase in reserves	Increase in loans
PNC Bank	$100,000	$10,000	$90,000
SunTrust Bank	90,000	9,000	81,000
Third Bank	81,000	8,100	72,900
Fourth Bank	72,900	7,290	65,610
Fifth Bank	65,610	6,561	59,049
.	.	.	.
.	.	.	.
.	.	.	.
Total increase	$1,000,000	$100,000	$900,000

Figure 2.20: An example of deposit creation.

Now if the Fed wanted to conduct a contractionary monetary policy and contract the money supply, one way to do it would be to raise the IOR. If the Fed raised the IOR from 1% to 3% and this led banks to raise their own vrr from 10% to 20%, then the deposit multiplier (recall dm = 1/vrr) would decrease from $[1/0.1] = 10$ to now $[1/0.2] = 5$. See Figure 2.21.

This means that when the Fed raised IOR to 3%, which led banks to increase the vrr so that vrr = 20%, the same injection of reserves of ΔR = $100,000 would generate a lower amount of deposits ΔD = $500,000 since the multiplier is now smaller at a higher vrr. ΔD = $100,000 * [1/0.2] = $500K. And this makes sense, if each bank is voluntarily keeping more reserves each time a new deposit is brought in; even if the number of loan-deposit rounds remains the same, fewer dollars are being lent and deposited each time. Now, in order to build a complete account of the money supply process, we augment the concept of the simple deposit multiplier in three ways:

Bank	Increase in deposits	Increase in reserves	Increase in loans
PNC Bank	$100,000	$20,000	$80,000
SunTrust Bank	80,000	16,000	64,000
Third Bank	64,000	12,800	51,200
Fourth Bank	51,200	10,240	40,960
Fifth Bank	40,960	8,192	32,768
	.	.	.
	.	.	.
	.	.	.
Total increase	$500,000	$100,000	$400,000

Figure 2.21: An example of deposit creation when the multiplier is reduced.

1. In addition to the link between reserves and deposits, we need a link between the monetary base and the money supply.
2. We need to include the effects of changes in the nonbank public's liquidity preference (the desire to hold currency relative to checkable deposits). The more currency the nonbank public holds relative to checkable deposits, the smaller the multiplier deposit creation process.
3. We need to include the effects of changes in banks' voluntary reserve ratio. The more reserves banks hold relative to their checkable deposits, the smaller the multiplier deposit creation process.

We make two key assumptions for deriving the money multiplier. First, banks hold a fixed amount of reserves. Second, the nonbank public keeps a fixed holding of currency. In the same way that the deposit multiplier links deposits and reserves (in rates) as we have seen:

$$\Delta D = dm * \Delta R,$$

where $dm = \frac{1}{vrr}$. We need a money multiplier that links the money supply and the monetary base (in levels).

$$M1 = (mm) * MB.$$

Recall M1 includes currency (C) and deposits (D)—and, since 2020, D contains both checking and savings deposits. We assume deposits (D) are less liquid than currency (C), so that M1 = C + D.

Now recall the monetary base (MB) includes currency (C) and reserves (R). Before 2020, the relationship used to be R = ER + RR, but since 2020, RR = 0, so all reserves are now voluntarily held by banks.

Substituting the money supply equation (M1 = C + D) and the monetary base equation (MB = C + R) into the money multiplier equations (mm = M1/MB) gives us:

$$mm = \frac{M1}{MB} = \frac{C + D}{C + R}.$$

Multiplying and dividing this expression by 1/D gives us:

$$mm = \frac{M1}{MB} = \frac{\frac{C}{D} + 1}{\frac{C}{D} + \frac{R}{D}}$$

This multiplier gives us some insight into the money supply determination. The money supply equation

$$M1 = \left[\frac{\frac{C}{D} + 1}{\frac{C}{D} + \frac{R}{D}} \right] * MB. \tag{2.1}$$

This equation suggests that every one dollar increase in the monetary base will ultimately generate more than one dollar in the money supply, if the multiplier in the brackets is greater than 1.

For example, assume C = $500 bn; D = $1,000 bn; and R = $250 bn. Then, the multiplier would be mm = 2, which means for every $1 added to the MB, there's ultimately a $2 increase in M1.

Now imagine that banks begin to hoard reserves (increasing their vrr) and this leads to fewer loans and an increase in reserves (all else being equal). If R increased to $1,000 bn, the multiplier would decline. The new multiplier would be mm = 1.

On the other hand, if C = $500 bn decreased to C = $200 bn; D = $1,000 bn; and R = $250 bn, then the multiplier would increase from mm = 2 to mm = 2.7, which means for every $1 added to the monetary base, there's ultimately a $2.7 increase in M1 due to the reduced liquidity preference of the public. This increased multiplier effect makes sense because reducing currency in circulation by depositing it in banks should lead to a larger deposit-loan feedback.

Summarizing, the Federal Reserve can affect the money supply by controlling the monetary base. The Fed can ostensibly do this through open market operations. When the Fed buys treasuries in the open market it does so with reserves. An increase in reserves raises the monetary base and, therefore, raises the money supply, according to equation (2.1). This is a purely quantitative effect.

In addition, the Fed can also influence the money supply through the multiplier in equation (2.1). Through its management of IOR, the Fed can make reserves more or less attractive for banks to hold.

But as we saw at the beginning of the chapter, the Fed is not the only agent who influences the money supply. For example, if banks (perhaps enticed by higher levels of IOR) voluntarily choose to hold more reserves so that vrr increases, then this would decrease the money creation process. When banks hoard more reserves, they issue fewer loans, which leads to fewer rounds of deposits-loans. So if vrr increases, the multiplier in equation (2.1) goes down, which effectively contracts the money supply.

Related to this, if banks reserve-to-deposit ratio increases, then the value of the money multiplier would fall, reducing the loan-deposit expansion and leading to a reduction in the money supply.

Finally, one more agent can have an impact. Namely, the nonbank public. If individuals idiosyncratically prefer higher levels of liquidity and draw down from their bank deposits or close their bank accounts, this removes reserves from the banking system. In other words, if the currency-to-deposit ratio were to increase, the multiplier in (2.1) goes down, effectively contracting the money supply through the ensuing reduction of the deposit-loan expansion.

Thinking About It…

The Federal Reserve (Fed) operates as America's central bank, established in 1913 with three main objectives: maximum employment, price stability, and moderate long-term interest rates. Unlike commercial banks, the Fed a nonprofit institution serving the public interest. The Fed measures and influences the money supply through two main metrics: M1 containing more liquid assets (currency, checking accounts), and M2: a broader measure including savings deposits.

Note that in 2020, savings deposits were moved from M2 to M1, significantly changing these measures. The Fed controls the money supply through three main tools:
1) Open Market Operations: Buying/selling securities to control the monetary base.
2) Discount Loans: Lending directly to banks.
3) Interest on Reserves (IOR): Paying interest on bank reserves (replaced reserve requirements in 2020).

The money supply is determined by three key factors:
1) The monetary base (currency + bank reserves).
2) The money multiplier (how banks create money through lending).
3) The public's behavior (preferences for holding currency vs. deposits).

A key concept is the money multiplier, which shows how an initial increase in reserves leads to a (typically) larger increase in the money supply through bank lending. This process is influenced by: banks' voluntary reserve ratios, the public's preference for holding cash vs. deposits, and the Fed's monetary policy decisions.

Importantly, there are two ways of measuring money.

Simple-sum aggregates (the Fed's traditional approach). This is problematic if various monetary assets are not close substitutes.

Divisia aggregates (a weighted approach, accounting for different levels of liquidity). This method is consistent with proper indexation methods and it is a far better descriptor of the money supply and a better indicator of monetary policy.

These tools and measures help the Fed manage the money supply to achieve its economic objectives. However, the Fed's control over the money supply is not absolute, as both banks and the public influence the final outcomes.

2.8 Glossary

Balance Sheet A financial statement showing assets and liabilities, crucial for understanding how Fed operations affect the monetary base and banking system.

Bank Reserves Deposits that commercial banks keep in their accounts with the Fed plus vault cash, serving as assets for banks and liabilities for the Fed.

Currency in Circulation The total amount of paper money and coins held by the nonbank public.

Discount Loans Direct loans from the Fed to commercial banks, with interest charged at the discount rate, serving as a tool for supplying reserves to the banking system.

Divisia Aggregate A weighted measure of the money supply that accounts for the different degrees of "moneyness" or liquidity of various monetary assets. Developed by William A. Barnett in 1980, it provides a more accurate picture of monetary conditions than simple-sum aggregates in that it assigns different weights according to the liquidity and monetary services each component provides.

Federal Funds Rate The interest rate that banks charge each other for overnight loans of reserves.

Federal Reserve (Fed) The central bank of the United States, established in 1913, charged with conducting monetary policy with objectives of maximum employment, price stability, and moderate long-term interest rates.

Interest on Reserves The interest rate the Federal Reserve pays banks on their reserve balances. Introduced in 2008 and became a primary monetary policy tool in 2020 when reserve requirements were eliminated. Acts as a floor for other interest rates and influences banks' decisions about holding versus lending reserves.

Liquidity The ease with which an asset can be converted into cash without significant loss of value. Cash is the most liquid asset.

Monetary Base The sum of bank reserves and currency in circulation. Often called "high-powered money," it serves as the foundation for money supply expansion in the banking system. The Federal Reserve can directly influence the monetary base through open market operations.

Money Multiplier The ratio showing how much the money supply increases for each unit increase in the monetary base through the banking system's lending activities.

Money Supply The total amount of monetary assets available in an economy at a specific time. The Fed measures it by simply summing up assets together into an M1 monetary aggregate and an M2 monetary aggregate (which is a broader measure).

Multiple Deposit Creation The process by which an initial deposit leads to multiple rounds of lending and new deposit creation, expanding the money supply.

Nonborrowed Reserves Reserves that come from open market operations rather than discount loans, representing the portion of reserves over which the Fed has more direct control.

Open Market Operations The buying and selling of government securities by the Federal Reserve to control the monetary base. When the Fed buys securities, it increases bank reserves dollar-for-dollar; when it sells securities, it decreases reserves by the same amount.

Primary Dealers Selected banks and securities firms authorized to trade directly with the Fed and participate in Treasury auctions.

Simple-Sum Monetary Aggregate The traditional method of measuring money supply by simply adding up all monetary components, assuming perfect substitutability between different types of money. This can often lead to large measurement error.

System Open Market Account (SOMA) The Fed's portfolio of securities used for conducting monetary policy through open market operations.

Voluntary Reserve Ratio (vrr) The percentage of deposits that banks choose to hold as reserves after the elimination of required reserves in 2020.

Part II: **Time, Probability, and Risk**

3 Time Value of Money

Contents

In this chapter, we discuss the relationship that money and debt have with time. The crucial point connecting monetary measures and time is the concept of the interest rate. Think of interest rates as a time machine that allows us to place value on monetary assets at different times by bringing them backward or forward in time to a time when they can be compared. Interest rates are important because they affect: the level of consumer expenditures on durable goods; investment expenditures on plant, equipment, and technology; the way that wealth is redistributed between borrowers and lenders; the prices of such key financial assets as stocks, bonds, and foreign currencies, etc.

For our purposes, we will use "interest rate" and "yield" interchangeably throughout this chapter. We will be more specific in future chapters. For now, we want to begin with some basic calculations about interest rates.

3.1 Valuing Assets Over Time

Often, financial instruments yield different payouts at various times. Payments come due at different time periods. And different investments promise returns on different dates. How do we make sense of it all? We must learn how to calculate and compare rates of return on different financial instruments.

Generally speaking, one dollar today is worth more than one dollar at a future date. This is because a dollar today can earn interest and be worth more than one dollar in the future. This will generally hold even if there is no change in the purchasing power of that dollar so long as the interest rate is above zero, which is almost always the case. This also works in reverse. This means that one dollar at a future date is generally worth less than one dollar today.

There are two general concepts that allow us to understand whether the promise to make a payment on one date is more or less valuable than the promise to make it on a different date. Namely, the concepts of future value and present value. We discuss both in turn below.

https://doi.org/10.1515/9783111193120-005

3.2 Future Value

Future value (FV) is the value on some future date of an investment made today. This is useful to understand the return we will enjoy on an investment at some future date. For example, if we deposited $100 today in a savings account and our bank promised a 5% interest rate if we kept the $100 in the account for one year, at the end of the year we would have $105.

How do we come up with that number? We would get back our original $100 amount of savings. But we would also collect a return from having saved the amount at an interest rate of 5%. The interest return is $5 since $100 \times (0.05) = $5.

Therefore, $100 invested today at 5% interest gives $105 in a year. We can say that the future value of $100 today at 5% interest is $105 one year from now. The initial $100 yields $5, which is why interest rates are sometimes called yields. This scheme is like a simple loan of $100 for a year at an interest rate of 5%. So, in the present time, the value of this investment is $100, which in the future has a value of $105. Altogether, this is calculated as $100 + $100 * (0.05) = $100 * (1 + 0.05) = $105. This gives us some insight into our first equation:

$$FV = PV * (1 + i),$$

where the future value (FV) of the present value (PV) of $100 investment—when the interest rate (i) promised for the next year is 5%—equals $105.

What if we left the $105 for another year with the interest remaining unchanged at 5%? This question can be restated as: "What is the FV one year from now of $105 at present at an interest rate of 5%?"

Applying the formula shows we would have $110.25 next year. FV = $105 * (1 + 0.05) = $110.25. This was the answer to our decision to reinvest the $105 once we collected it from our initial $100 investment the previous year.

What if we had made that plan from the beginning? If we wanted to know how much would we have in two years if we invest $100 today at an interest rate of 5%?

In two years, we would get our $100 back, plus the interest earned in the first year $100 * (0.05), plus the interest earned on the investment the second year (another $100 * 0.05). But after year one we would have collected $5 in interest earnings. That interest earning would also collect interest on the second year (this type of interest accruing interest is called compound interest), which would amount to $5 * 0.05.

Another way to ask the question would be: What will the future value of $100 be in two years when the interest rate is kept fixed at 5%? The future value would be $100 + $100 * (0.05) + $100 * (0.05) + $5 * (0.05) = $110.25, the same answer we had before. But this could easily be rewritten as $100 * (1 + 0.05) * (1 + 0.05).

So while the equation above holds for the FV if we only invest for one year, if we invested it for two years, the formula becomes FV $= $ PV $\times (1 + i)^2$. So, in general, the future value (FV) of a current investment at an arbitrary number of years in the future (n) at a fixed interest rate (i) is given by:

$$FV = PV * (1 + i)^n.$$

Table 3.1 gives the future values of $100 investment at a fixed interest rate of 4% for various years into the future.

Table 3.1: Future value calculations.

Years into the future	Calculation	Future value
1	$100(1.04)	$104.00
2	$100(1.04)^2	$108.16
3	$100(1.04)^3	$112.48
5	$100(1.04)^5	$121.66
10	$100(1.04)^{10}	$148.02

3.3 Compounding

Interest earned on the original principal is called simple interest (SI). Interest earned on interests already paid is called compound interest (CI). Total interest is the sum of the two. In the example above, total interests are $10.25 after two years. In that example, $SI = 100 * 5\% * 2 = \$10$ and $CI = 10.25 - 10 = \$0.25$.

We notice SI is much larger in this case ($10) and CI is much smaller ($0.25). But this is because we invest over a small number of periods. Investing or saving in the short term, we find SI is always larger than CI. However, while SI grows linearly, CI grows exponentially. Therefore, the power of compounding clearly becomes more important as time passes.

To make this point clear, take the following example. On May 24, 1626, Peter Minuit purchased Manhattan Island from the Canarse Native Americans for about $24 worth of trinkets, beads, and knives. The purchase took place at what is now Inwood Hill Park in upper Manhattan, New York. Consider the following thought experiment. If the tribe had taken the cash value, instead of the goods, and invested it to earn 6% per year, how much would the tribe have in present day, about 387 years later?

This can be easily calculated to be roughly $267 bn with a FV equation in Python.

```
FV_Manhattan = 24 * (1 + .06)**(2024-1626)
print("{:,.2f}".format(FV_Manhattan))
```

The total interest that would have been earned is, in essence, the FV of the investment scheme minus the original $24 invested, which in Python code can be expressed as:

```
Total_interest = FV_Manhattan-24
print("{:,.2f}".format(Total_interest))
```

But how much of this total interest is earned simply from the original amount invested? Will it be more or less than the interest earning interest? In other words, how much of this is gained from SI and how much from CI?

The amount of SI 387 years later is a miserly $572.

```
Simple_interest = 24 * .06 * (2024-1626)
Simple_interest
#Simple interest collected is negligible
#compared with compound interest
```

The rest of the $267 bn is earned with CI!

The assumption we have been making so far is that interest rates are paid/earned once a year. What if interest rates were paid monthly? Converting n from years to months is easy, but converting the interest rate is a bit harder. If the annual interest rate is 5%, what is the monthly rate? Assume i^m is the one-month interest rate and n is the number of months, then a deposit made for one year ($n = 12$) will have a future value of:

$$FV = \$100 * (1 + i^m)^{12}.$$

Since we know that in one year the future value is $100(1.05), we can solve for i^m:

$$(1 + i^m)^{12} = (1.05) \leftrightarrow (1 + i^m) = (1.05)^{1/12} = 1.0041.$$

Therefore $i^m = 1.0041 - 1$, or 0.0041. These fractions of a percentage point are called basis points (or bps). One basis point is one one-hundredth of a percentage point, 0.01 percent. On a monthly basis, the FV of $100 one year from now at an annual rate of 5% would be 41 basis points.

Another common question for an investment proposition would be: If we invest $100 at 5% annual interest, how long will it take to double our money? A rough approximation can be obtained with what is known as *the Rule of 72*. We divide the annual interest rate (in percentage points, not decimals) into 72.

If the interest rate remained fixed at i%, the approximate time to double the investment is 72/i, independently of the amount.

In our example, the interest rate was 5% so it would take (72/5 =) 14.4 years to approximately double our investment.

To verify this, suppose we save $5,000 today at an interest rate of 5%. After 14.4 years, we would have

$$\$5,000 * (1 + 0.05)^{14.4} = 10,094$$

essentially doubling our initial investment.

3.4 Present Value

The present value (PV) is the opposite side of the coin of our concept of future value. And it is quite useful in finance because PV is like a time machine that allows us to place a value on payments that will be received in the future in today's dollars. In fact, according to the *classical theory of asset prices*, the price of a financial or monetary asset equals the present value of the expected asset income that it promises in the future. Asset prices depend on people's expectations of future asset income, and PV is the tool we use to compare the desirability of different investment schemes, even if they only promise payments in the future and do not deliver anything now.

Since many financial instruments, pension schemes, and investment opportunities promise future cash payments, we need to know how to value those payments without having to wait until they are actually made.

Present value (PV) is the value today (in the present) of a payment that is promised to be made in the future. Or, alternatively, it is the amount that must be invested today in order to realize a specific amount on a given future date. Mathematically, we can simply solve the FV formula for PV as follows:

$$PV = \frac{FV}{1+i},$$

which is just the future value calculation inverted. We can generalize the process for arbitrary n periods in the future, as we did for the future value, to answer the following question:

What is the PV of a future payment made n years in the future, at a fixed interest rate i?

This can be answered with the following equation:

$$PV = \frac{FV}{(1+i)^n}.$$

We can conclude a few things from this equation. First, the higher future value of the payment, the higher its present value.

Second, the longer into the future we have to wait for a future payment to be made, the less valuable it is today. That is, the PV decreases as n (the time to payment) increases. This is because the longer we have to wait for the payment, the longer we are effectively discounting it.

Third, the present value of a future payment goes down as the interest rate increases. Think of the interest rate as the reward we would be getting for holding an alternative asset that promises it. The higher the interest rate, the more interest return we are forgoing had we invested in the alternative asset that pays it. Therefore, the higher the interest rate, the faster we discount the future value. This lowers the present value.

Doubling the future value of the payment, without changing the time of the payment or the interest rate, doubles the present value. This is true for any percentage.

Table 3.2: Present value calculations.

Interest rate	1 year	5 years	10 years	20 years
1%	$199.10	$951.50	$905.30	$819.50
2%	$980.40	$905.70	$820.30	$673.00
3%	$970.90	$862.60	$741.10	$553.70
4%	$961.50	$821.90	$675.60	$456.40
5%	$952.40	$783.50	$613.90	$376.90
6%	$943.30	$747.30	$558.40	$311.80
7%	$934.60	$713.00	$508.30	$258.40
8%	$925.90	$680.60	$463.20	$214.50
9%	$917.40	$649.90	$424.40	$178.40
10%	$909.10	$620.90	$385.50	$148.60
15%	$869.60	$497.20	$247.20	$61.11

Table 3.2 shows the PV of a $1,000 payment. Higher interest rates are associated with lower present values, regardless of size or time of payment. As we select a given interest rate in a given row, and we travel rightward across the columns, we can also see that at any fixed interest rate, an increase in the time reduces its present value. The longer we have to wait, the more we discount the future payment, and the higher the interest rate, the faster we discount the future payment.

Present value is the single most important relationship in our study of financial instruments. One reason PV calculations are so useful is because they allow us to compare different payment options in time.

For example, Annie just won a lottery worth $5 million. The lottery will pay her over a period of 5 years (i. e., $1 million per year for 5 years). *How much did she really win today?*

In order to answer that question, she needs one piece of crucial information: what is the prevailing interest rate in the market?

This will be important for Annie to make her decision. If the interest is high, she would be missing out on interest gains while she waits to get paid, because she cannot collect interest on money she does not yet have. This means waiting longer is more costly when interest rates are high. If the interest rate is low, future payments are discounted more slowly, so she might prefer to wait as the opportunity cost she is faced with is low when interest rates are low.

Suppose that the interest rate is 2% and she is given two choices: take $1 million every year for the next 5 years (this is an installment plan) or take $4 million now (this is a lump-sum payment). How could she compare the two options? She knows the PV of $4 million today is $4 million. What is the PV of the installment plan?

She needs to compare the $4 million payoff with the PV of the other option of the installment payment. Whichever plan offers her the highest PV should be the more desirable option.

The installment plan involves the same cash flow of $1 million at an interest rate of 2%. The first one must be discounted one period ($n = 1$), the second payment in two years must be discounted two periods ($n = 2$), and so on. We must apply our PV formula for each annual payment and then add them all up. The following bit of Python code will reveal the PV of the proposed installment is $4.7 million. Therefore, the installment plan is worth more than the lump sum payment.

```
CF=1000000; n=5;
#This is the constant cash flow over the next 5 years (n=5)
```

But we are missing one last piece of information: the prevailing interest rate in the market. We can code it into Python as follows:

```
i=.02
#Let's say the interest rate is 2%
```

```
CF=1000000; n=5;
#This is the constant cash flow over the next 5 years (n=5)
```

The following code defines a PV equation that calculates the present value of this plan is $4,713,459.51:

```
# The PV of the proposed payment plan is:
PV = CF/(1+i) + CF/(1+i)**2 + CF/(1+i)**3 + CF/(1+i)**4 + CF/(1+i)**5
print("{:,.2f}".format(PV))
```

In this case, at an interest rate of 2%, the present value of the five-year payment stream is $4.7 million, which is greater than the $4 million lump-sum payment so Annie might take the annual payment option.

But what if the interest rate was substantially higher, say 9%?

This means that future payments would be discounted faster. If Annie got the money now, she could deposit it in a bank account that would pay her 9%. Not having the money now to deposit is costing her a potential 9% return. This means she might be less patient and less willing to wait for future payments if the interest rate is this high. So the question is: Should she take the $1 million annual payment for five years at a fixed interest rate of 9% or the lump-sum payment of $4 million today?

In Python code, we can easily compute the PV of this payment as:

```
CF=1000000; n=5; i=.09;
PV = CF/(1+i) + CF/(1+i)**2 + CF/(1+i)**3 + CF/(1+i)**4 + CF/(1+i)**5
print("{:,.2f}".format(PV))
```

which comes out to be $3,992,710.04. Now, the present value of the payment stream is less than the lump-sum payment, so Annie would probably take the one-time (lump-sum) payment.

But this should make sense. A much higher interest rate means the opportunity cost of holding cash right now is higher. Having to wait to get paid means Annie would be forgoing a higher return on her cash. Therefore, the value of the annuity is discounted faster.

Consider a second example. Let's say Annie has a cousin named Paul. Paul wants to borrow $10,000 from Annie today and promises to pay her back in 20 years at an interest rate of 6%. This means that the future value of the loan—what Paul will need to pay her back in 20 years—is $32,071.36. Both Annie and Paul can make this FV calculation. They both agree that waiting 20 years is too long to pay off the loan and choose an installment plan.

Paul proposes dividing the FV equally among the 20 years to make an annual installment payment every year for the next 20 years. While the proposal may sound fair, Annie wants to know if Paul is correctly valuating the present value or whether he would be overpaying or underpaying what is owed. They both know the PV of the $32,071.36 loan in 20 years time is $10,000 today. The question is: *What is the PV of Paul's proposed installment plan?* In the previous example, we knew the payment amounts, the number of years, and the interest rate, and we wanted to calculate the PV.

In this example, we know the PV, the number of years, and the interest rate, and what we want to know now is the actual payment amount—the cash (C) disbursement to be made every year. We apply the PV formula as follows:

$$\$10,000 = \frac{C}{1 + 0.06} + \frac{C}{(1 + 0.06)^2} + \frac{C}{(1 + 0.06)^3} + \cdots + \frac{C}{(1 + 0.06)^{20}}.$$

Annie and Paul want to know what C will be. Will it really be $1,603.57? This can be easily calculated in a few lines of Python code.

Instead of writing the PV equation every time and redefining our values (CF, n, i) each time, we could automate our analysis by defining a function that calculates the PV when supplied with inputs.

The snippet of code below defines a function called *PV_simple* to calculate the PV of a single cash flow (CF).

```python
def PV_simple(CF, i, n):    #PV_simple is our first user-defined function
    PV = CF / (1 + i)**n
    return print("{:,.2f}".format(PV))
```

The code above defines the PV function. Once that function is instantiated by entering into memory in Python, it can be called simply by entering values for CF, i, and n. We can then call the function with the appropriate values to verify the PV of the loan is $10,000.

```
PV_simple(32071.36, .06, 20)
```

Now we need to calculate the PV of the installment plan. We need a different equation than *PV_simple*. We first define an equation to calculate the PV of an installment plan paid yearly, which is generally termed an annuity.

```
#np.set_printoptions(formatter={'float': '{: 0.3f}'.format})
def PV_annuity(CF, i, n):
    beg=1; end=n+1; PV=0;
    for t in range(beg, end):
        PV += CF[t-1] / (1 + i) ** t
        #np.set_printoptions(formatter={'float': '{: 0.2f}'.format})
        #np.set_printoptions(formatter={'int_kind': '{:,}'.format})
    return (print("{:,}".format(PV)))
```

This is a very similar equation to *PV_simple*, but instead of taking a single value of a cash flow, it will take multiple values (a range) of cash flows. Paul's proposed plan has 20 payments of $1,603.57. The following lines of code instantiate the payment plan:

```
this_is_a_list=[1603.57];
pmnt = 20 * this_is_a_list
pmnt
```

which outputs the following list of values:

```
[1603.57,
 1603.57,
 1603.57,
 1603.57,
 1603.57,
 1603.57,
 1603.57,
 1603.57,
 1603.57,
 1603.57,
 1603.57,
 1603.57,
 1603.57,
 1603.57,
 1603.57,
 1603.57,
 1603.57,
```

```
1603.57,
1603.57,
1603.57]
```

We can convert a list of values to a numpy array, which makes it easier to work with as follows:

```
#work with arrays instead of lists
import numpy as np

#This converts list to array
ins_pmnt=np.array(pmnt)

ins_pmnt
```

which outputs the following:

```
array([1603.570000, 1603.570000, 1603.570000, 1603.570000, 1603.570000,
       1603.570000, 1603.570000, 1603.570000, 1603.570000, 1603.570000,
       1603.570000, 1603.570000, 1603.570000, 1603.570000, 1603.570000,
       1603.570000, 1603.570000, 1603.570000, 1603.570000, 1603.570000])
```

Applying this 20-year installment plan and the relevant information to the *PV_annuity* function we defined earlier allows us to find out that at $18,392.82 the PV of the proposed payment plan is almost twice as much as the $10,000 that is owed.

The PV of the loan is $10,000 yet the PV of the proposed payment is $18,393. This means each year Paul would be overpaying almost twice what the correct amount should be. *What would be the correct annual payment to guarantee a $10,000 PV under these terms?*

Again, the correct payment (C) solves the following equation:

$$\$10,000 = \frac{C}{1+i} + \frac{C}{(1+i)^2} + \frac{C}{(1+i)^3} + \cdots + \frac{C}{(1+i)^{20}},$$

which in Python, can be solved with:

```
Correct_pmnt = 10000*((rate*(1 + rate)**periods)/((1 + rate)**periods - 1))
Correct_pmnt
```

which shows the correct payment of this installment plan should be $871.85. At $871.85, the payment is roughly half what Paul proposed. Annie wants to verify this by calculating the PV of 20 annual payments of $871.85 at an interest rate of 6%.

Applying our defined formula, she can verify the PV is indeed $10,000 up to a rounding error.

```
#We can check whether this correct payment is fair:
Correct_pmt=[871.85];
pmnt = 20 * Correct_pmt;
corr_ins_pmnt=np.array(pmnt);
corr_ins_pmnt
```

```
print(PV_annuity(corr_ins_pmnt, rate, periods))
```

This is an example of a fixed payment loan. However, all this analysis can extend to a variable payment loan where the cash flow (C) changes over time. This is important because many securities are claims on future payments, which may vary. This allows us to employ the PV calculation to evaluate prices of securities. In general, the price of any security can be obtained as the present value at a given interest rate or yield of the future payments expected to be made by the security issuer. The same equation can be used where the payments, instead of being fixed cash flows (C), might be variable payments (R), as follows:

$$PV = \frac{R_1}{1+i} + \frac{R_2}{(1+i)^2} + \frac{R_3}{(1+i)^3} + \cdots + \frac{R_n}{(1+i)^n}.$$

3.5 Time Variation and Risk

Thus far we have assumed interest rates (i) are fixed. But the fact that future payments may vary over time introduces some uncertainty as to the amount of a future payment or whether the payment will be made at all. This introduces some measure of risk. In the face of uncertainty, investors will generally want to be compensated for taking on risk. This is called a risk premium. This premium typically takes the form of a yield that is added above and beyond the prevailing interest rate (i). A risk-adjusted PV equation takes the following form:

$$PV = \frac{R_1}{1+i+\psi} + \frac{R_2}{(1+i+\psi)^2} + \frac{R_3}{(1+i+\psi)^3} + \cdots + \frac{R_n}{(1+i+\psi)^n},$$

where ψ represents what is commonly known as the risk premium. As investors demand higher compensation for taking the risk associated with the uncertainty of a future return that is not guaranteed, the value of that future payment is further discounted above the prevailing interest rate. In other words, as risk of a future payment becomes riskier, investors demand a higher risk premium (a higher ψ), reducing the present value of the investment lower than it would have been had the future payment been guaranteed.

Thinking About it...

Interest rates act as a "time machine" for comparing monetary values across different time periods. The time value techniques of PV and FV, which we cover in this chapter, can be used to price financial instruments and securities.

FV shows what an investment today will be worth at a future date. It incorporates both simple interest (earned on principal) and compound interest (earned on previously earned interest). It demonstrates the power of compound interest through examples, like how $24 invested in 1626 at 6% would be worth billions today.

PV can be used to compare different payment options (like lump sum vs. installment payments). For a given payment scheme, PV decreases as interest rate increases (faster rate of discounting), or when the time to payment increases (longer period of discounting).

PV and FV are useful because securities differ in their future payments. For example, bonds generally have fixed payments and U. S. government bonds have no default risk, while corporate bonds are often subject to default risk. On the other hand, stocks have uncertain payments and they are also subject to default risk.

The bigger the risk premium or the higher the yield or interest rate, the lower the price of a security. In order to understand risk, we must quantify it. This is done with the mathematics of probability theory, which we cover in the next chapter.

3.6 Glossary

Amortization The process of gradually paying off a debt over time through regular payments that include both principal and interest. Each payment reduces the principal amount owed.

Annuity A series of equal payments made at regular intervals over a specified period, often used in loans, mortgages, or retirement planning.

Basis Points (bps) A unit of measurement for interest rates, where one basis point equals 0.01% (one one-hundredth of a percentage point). Used to precisely describe small changes in interest rates.

Capital Gain The profit realized from the sale of an asset when its selling price exceeds its purchase price or original investment.

Classical Theory of Asset Prices A theory in the field of finance that posits that the price of a financial or monetary asset equals the present value of the expected asset income that it promises in the future.

Compound Interest (CI) Interest earned on previously earned interest, rather than just the principal. While smaller than simple interest in the short term, it grows exponentially over time and can lead to significant wealth accumulation over long periods.

Default Risk The possibility that a borrower will be unable to make required payments on their debt obligations. This risk often influences the interest rate charged on loans.

Discount Rate The interest rate used to determine the present value of future cash flows. Often reflects both the time value of money and risk considerations.

Future Value (FV) The value of an investment at a future date, calculated by accounting for the initial amount (principal) plus any accumulated interest over time.

Interest Rate (i) A measure that acts as a financial "time machine," allowing comparison of monetary values across different time periods. It represents the rate at which money grows when invested or the cost of borrowing money.

Net Present Value (NPV) The difference between the present value of cash inflows and outflows over a period of time. Used to analyze the profitability of an investment or project.

Numpy Array Numpy is a Python library that is used for numerical calculations. A numpy array is a type of data formatted in Python that can be organized in vector or array form, which facilitates calculations.

Present Value (PV) The current value of a future payment or series of payments, discounted back to the present using an interest rate.

Principal The original amount of money invested or borrowed, before interest begins accruing.

Real Return The return on an investment after adjusting for inflation, representing the actual increase in purchasing power.

Risk Premium An additional return demanded by investors above the basic interest rate to compensate for uncertainty in future payments. The higher the risk, the higher the premium required, which results in a lower present value of future payments. This compensation investors demand for taking on added risk is typically expressed as a percentage.

Rule of 72 A quick method to estimate how long it will take for an investment to double at a given interest rate. Divide 72 by the interest rate percentage to get the approximate number of years.

Simple Interest (SI) Interest earned solely on the original principal amount invested. It grows linearly over time and is typically larger than compound interest in the short term but is overtaken by compound interest over longer periods.

Time Value of Money The concept that money available now is worth more than the same amount in the future due to its potential earning capacity through interest.

Yield Used interchangeably with interest rate in basic calculations, representing the return on an investment over a specific period.

4 Primer on Probability Theory

Contents

Risk is ubiquitous in financial markets. Future outcomes are uncertain. Risk may be unavoidable but, as it turns out, possibly useful. In order to mitigate risk and possibly gain an advantage over uncertainty, we must attempt to assess it first. Assessing risk involves finding ways to quantify it. In this chapter, we consider a brief primer on the concepts of probability. Probability allows us to quantify the likelihood of future outcomes. These concepts can then be leveraged to quantify risk in financial markets.

4.1 The Basics

There are three main axioms of working with probabilities that are attributed to the Soviet mathematician Andrey Kolmogorov. The three main Kolmogorov axioms are:

1. *Axiom 1*: Probability can be represented as a real number greater than or equal to zero and less than or equal to one.
2. *Axiom 2*: Total probability of some event is equal to 1.
3. *Axiom 3*: Probability of mutually exclusive events is the sum of probabilities.

Probability can be thought of as an area. We use $P(A)$ to denote the probability of event A, or the area of A. The first axiom suggests $0 \leq P(A) \leq 1$. Zero means A occupies no area and 1 means A occupies the whole area.

Probabilities of events can also be added up. For example, $P(A, B) = P(A) + P(B)$ represents the probability that event A and event B occur.

The probability of an event can also be thought of as the frequency with which that event occurs. Take a fair-sided dice, which means each side is equally likely, with six possibilities. If x denotes a given side of the dice, say 1, then its probability is given by $P(x) = \frac{1}{6}$. This is an example of discrete probability, because each roll of the dice is a discrete and independent event.

A continuous probability refers to a process where events are not easily separable at discrete intervals. One way to generate a continuous probability is to repeat a single discrete event (e. g., throwing a dart) many many times, so that the event is so frequent that it is difficult to separate any given outcome from the other. Throwing 10 darts at a board could be modeled as a discrete probability, whereas throwing 10 million darts could be more easily thought of a continuous probability.

https://doi.org/10.1515/9783111193120-006

Let's say we want to throw a dart at a circular target inside a square with two meters on each side. Each throw is an independent event. See Figure 4.1.

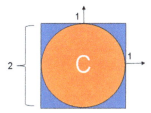

Figure 4.1: A target for many dart throws.

What would be the probability of hitting the orange target C? The area of C is π, and the area of the square that contains it is 4 (2 m × 2 m). Now, if we divided the target in four quadrants, what would be the probability of hitting the top right (northeast) quadrant?

The probability of hitting the orange target in that upper right quadrant should be $\frac{\pi}{4}$. We can verify this with a simple simulation. First, we note that each dart throw is an independent event. We are going to simulate it as a random event. The following snippet of Python code simulates 1,000 throws. It draws the portion of the throws that would land inside and outside the target and graphs them.

```
darts2 = np.random.random((1000, 2))
radius2 = np.sqrt(np.power(darts2, 2).sum(axis=1))
inside = radius2 <= 1
fig, ax1 = plt.subplots(figsize=(10, 5))
plt.plot(darts2[inside].T[0], darts2[inside].T[1], '*')
plt.plot(darts2[~inside].T[0], darts2[~inside].T[1], '.')
plt.show()
```

This Python snippet carries out a simulation that generates 1,000 throws out of which 796 land in the orange target.

Figure 4.2 looks somewhat sparse given we have only 1,000 simulated values. But we could really generate a much larger simulation. If we do this again for 100,000 throws, we get something closer to the theoretical value of $\frac{\pi}{4}$. The following snippet shows a similar figure, now filled in with many more simulated dart throws. All we need to change is to substitute 1K for 100K in the first line. See Figure 4.3.

```
darts2 = np.random.random((100000, 2))
radius2 = np.sqrt(np.power(darts2, 2).sum(axis=1))
inside = radius2 <= 1
fig, ax1 = plt.subplots(figsize=(10, 5))
plt.plot(darts2[inside].T[0], darts2[inside].T[1], '*')
```

```
plt.plot(darts2[~inside].T[0], darts2[~inside].T[1], '.')
plt.show()
```

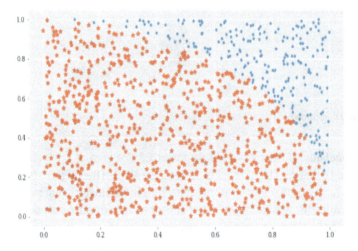

Figure 4.2: A Python simulation of 1,000 dart throws.

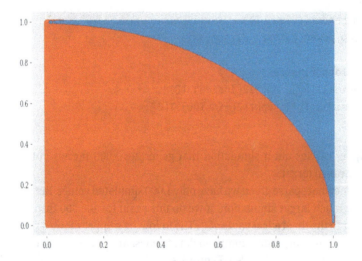

Figure 4.3: A Python simulation of 100,000 dart throws.

The following command

```
len(darts[inside])/len(darts)
0.78557
```

demonstrates that our simulation provides a rough approximation to the measurement of $\frac{\pi}{4}$. This technique is known as Monte Carlo integration and is very commonly used when we are interested in estimating values of complex functions.

Comparing the two simulations reveals the 1,000 throw simulation yields $P(\text{1K throws}) \equiv 0.796$, whereas the 100,000 throw simulation shows $P(\text{100K throws}) \equiv 0.7872$, which is closer to the theoretical value of $\frac{\pi}{4}$. Increasing the number of simulated throws provides a better approximation.

4.2 Combinatorics

What if instead of a single event, we have a sequence of events? If the events happen in sequence, but are otherwise independent of each other, we simply multiply the probabilities. For example, in a fair-sided dice, if the probability of getting a three is $\frac{1}{6}$, then the probability of first getting a three and then getting a two is:

$$P(3,2) = P(3) * P(2) = \frac{1}{6} * \frac{1}{6} = \frac{1}{36}.$$

Similarly, the probability of getting an odd value on the first roll and an even value on the second roll would be:

$$P(\text{even, odd}) = \frac{3}{6} * \frac{3}{6} = \frac{1}{4},$$

which also works in reverse order of throws:

$$P(\text{odd, even}) = \frac{3}{6} * \frac{3}{6} = \frac{1}{4}.$$

The general methodology involves three steps: first, we enumerate all possible outcomes; second, we calculate the "area" of each outcome; and third, the probability of each outcome is calculated as the fraction of the total area it occupies. To enumerate all possible outcomes, it is useful to borrow ideas from combinatorics.

Permutations are the total number of possible sequences of n different elements, which are given by a concept that is known as "factorial", which is denoted by the ! sign, where $n!$ means:

$$n! = n * (n-1) * (n-2) * (n-3) * \cdots * 1.$$

Another concept of combinatorics is *Combinations*. They show the total number of ways of grouping N elements into two groups of size k and $N - k$.

$$C_k^N = \frac{N!}{k! * (N-k)!}.$$

With these two concepts, we can easily calculate the number of possible outcomes in many situations. For example, the number of possible playing card shuffles (possible permutations) is 52! = 8.065e67 in scientific notation, a very large number. Another example is the number of ways of getting three tails and two heads in five coin flips (combining three tails and two heads in five flips) is given by

$$C_3^5 = \frac{5!}{3! * (5-3)!} = \frac{5 * 4 * 3 * 2 * 1}{3 * 2 * 1 * 2 * 1} = \frac{120}{12} = 10.$$

There are three useful tools to explain probabilities:
1. *Histograms*: Summarize the observed frequency of each outcome $N(X)$.
2. *Probability Distributions*: Show the probability associated with each possible outcome $P(X)$.
3. *Cumulative Probability Distributions*: Show the probability associated with outcomes smaller or equal to each outcome $P(X \leq x)$.

Can we calculate the probability distribution of the outcome of flipping five coins that come out heads with probability p?
    The probability of flipping N_h heads and $N - N_h$ tails is given by $p(N, N_h) = p_h^N *$ $(1-p)^{N-N_h}$, since we need to get N_h heads with probability p each time and $N - N_h$ tails with probability $1 - p$ each time. As we saw earlier from combinatorics, we also know the number of ways of getting N_h heads out of a total N flips is given by:

$$C_{N_h}^N = \frac{N!}{N_h! * (N - N_h)!}.$$

Therefore, combining the two equations allows us to compute the probability distribution of getting N_h heads out of a total N as:

$$p(N, N_h) = \frac{N!}{N_h! * (N - N_h)!} * p_h^N * (1-p)^{N-N_h}.$$

The following one line of Python code applies this equation to the probability of three heads in five throws.

```
prob = np.array([np.math.factorial(5)/(np.math.factorial(i)
*np.math.factorial(5-i))*np.power(0.5, i)*
np.power(0.5, 5-i) for i in range(6)])
```

Let's simulate the probability distribution in Python. The snippet below defines a simple function to generate coin flips where Heads = 1, Tails = −1. We can specify how many coins we want to flip at each step and how many steps we want and what the probability of flipping heads is.

```python
def flip_coin(n_coins, n_times, p=0.5):
    return 2*(np.random.random((n_times, n_coins))<p)-1
```

We can call this function to flip a single coin five times and assign it to a variable called "coins" as follows:

```python
coins = flip_coins(1,5)
coins
```

```python
array([[-1],
       [1],
       [-1],
       [1],
       [1]])
```

We can always turn the numerical value to a label heads or tails with the following snippet of code:

```python
for ij in range(len(coins)):
    if coins[ij]==1:
        print("Heads")
    else:
        print("Tails")
```

```
Tails
Heads
Tails
Heads
Heads
```

A *histogram* is a tool that summarizes the distribution of numerical data. The term was first introduced by the statistician Karl Pearson. To construct a histogram, the first step is to divide the entire range of values into a series of intervals—and then count how many values fall into each interval, called bins, which are placed next to each other.

A *probability* mass function is a tool that can be used to calculate histograms. The following snippet of Python code defines a probability mass function:

```python
def pmf(values, normed=False):
    counts = Counter(values.flatten())
    output = np.array(sorted(counts.items(),
    key=lambda x: x[0]), dtype='float')
```

```
if normed:
    norm = output.T[1].sum()
    output.T[1] = output.T[1]/norm

return output
```

Let's say we want to figure out the number of ways to get three heads and two tails by flipping five coins. We would need to flip five coins at once, record the result and repeat it again. Once we toss the five coins a large number of times, we may become more assured we have covered all possible combinations. We can do this in Python by simulating flipping five dice 10,000 times and construct the probability distribution of the simulation and compare it to the theoretical probability distribution with a histogram.

```
#Flip five coins 10K times
values = flip_coin(5, 10000)

#This sums the total across the 2nd dimension (cols)
total = values.sum(axis=1)
np.shape(total)
total
#This finds on net how many heads or tails all five die
#each throw

array([ 1,   1,   1, \ldots,   1, -1, -5])
```

These next lines produce the probability distribution of the 10,000 simulated flips and calculate the theoretical probability of getting three heads and two tails (or two tails and three heads) in five flips, as well as producing graphs of the results:

```
dist = pmf(total, normed=True)

prob = np.array([np.math.factorial(5)/(np.math.factorial(i)*np.math.factorial(5-i))
                *np.power(0.5, i)*np.power(0.5, 5-i) for i in range(6)])

plt.bar([-5, -3, -1, 1, 3, 5], prob, label="exact")
plt.plot(dist.T[0], dist.T[1], 'b-', label="simulation")
plt.legend()
plt.show()
```

By graphing both, we can conclude that the simulation approximates the exact distribution closely. See Figure 4.4.

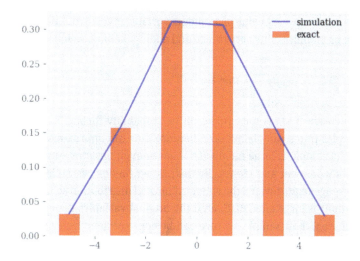

Figure 4.4: Probability distributions of three heads and two tails in five flips.

Naturally, we expect the curve to be symmetric as there are exactly as many ways of having three heads and two tails as there are of having three tails and two heads. There are many different types of probability distributions—some of which may be symmetric and some of which may not be.

4.3 Averages, Expectations, and the Central Limit Theorem

An n-sided dice has a uniform probability $1/n$ of landing on any of its sides. After, say, 10 rolls of a fair dice, we might have: $x = [6, 5, 4, 3, 5, 1, 1, 5, 2, 4]$. The behavior of this x variable is stochastic, which is another word for probabilistic. But what about a function of this random variable (like the average)? The equation for the average is given by:

$$\hat{x} = \frac{1}{n} \sum_{i=1}^{n} x_i.$$

In this specific example, the average is 3.5, as expected. But if, say, the sixth and the seventh rolls had come out sixes instead of ones, the average would have been 4.5.

We could throw the dice 10,000 times and we could find an average. But if we repeated the experiment 10 times, we would find 10 different averages, so what would be the correct value of the average?

For any given set of dice rolls, we are only approximately estimating the true value. In general, the higher the number of rolls in a given realization, the better our estimate of the average. The true, or expected value, is the one obtained after an infinite (or at least, very large) number of realizations.

The "true average" or the expected value of a random variable involves multiplying each outcome times the probability of its occurrence and adding them up as follows:

$$\mu_x = \sum_{i=1}^{n} p_i * x_i.$$

The central limit theorem (CLT) is a useful result in probability theory. It allows summarizing large samples into a sample average, because they can approximate the true expected value if the sample is large enough (if it has enough observations). The CLT advances that for independent and identically distributed random variables, the standardized sample average tends toward the standard normal distribution so long as the number of observations is large enough. Even if the original variables themselves are not normally distributed, their sample average can be approximated by a normal (also known as a Gaussian) distribution.

Let's say we obtain a large sample of observations that are independent from each other—each generated observation does not depend on the values of the other generated observations—and we compute their sample average (or arithmetic mean). If we repeat this procedure many times, resulting in a collection of observed averages, the CLT says that if the sample size was large enough, the probability distribution of these averages will closely approximate a normal distribution.

The probability of observing a random value of x from N observations drawn from a normal distribution centered at its mean μ_x and with variance σ^2 is given by:

$$P_N(x, \mu_x, \sigma^2) = \frac{1}{\sqrt{2\sigma^2}} e^{-\frac{(x-\mu_x)^2}{2\sigma^2}}.$$

The mean value is given by $\mu_x = \frac{1}{N}\sum_{i=1}^{N} x_i$ and the variance is $\sigma^2 = \frac{1}{N-1}\sum_{i=1}^{N}(x_i-\mu_x)^2$. If the sample size N is large enough, it can be approximated by a normal distribution.

The CLT is a key concept in probability theory because it implies that probabilistic and statistical methods that work for normal distributions can be applicable to many problems involving other types of distributions.

Thinking About It...

Imagine we are standing in a trading pit in a financial exchange like the New York Stock Exchange (NYSE), watching investors buy and sell securities. Each of those securities have uncertain returns. How can traders price those securities if their returns are not fixed and guaranteed? A way to do this is to think probabilistically, starting with the fundamental rules laid down by mathematician Andrey Kolmogorov.

Kolmogorov teaches us that we can think of probability like measuring the area of possibility—it can't be negative, and it can't exceed the whole space of what's possible.

We can think about simple and countable events (like throwing a single dart on a dartboard or buying a single share of stock once). However, financial markets are rarely built on a single transaction, so it requires the complex world of continuous probability. Imagine throwing one dart at a target—that's discrete. Now imagine throwing ten million darts—suddenly the individual throws blur together into a continuous pattern. Combinatorics help parse out large amounts or flows of transactions.

A single transaction may look random. And when combining it with may other random transactions, the complexity may look chaotic. However, the remarkable central limit theorem (CLT) principle tells us that when we look at enough random events together—whether they are dart throws, stock prices, or interest rates—their average behaviors tend to follow a predictable pattern. Probability and statistics can be leveraged for coping with the inherent uncertainty of financial markets.

4.4 Glossary

Axiom A fundamental principle or self-evident truth on which other statements are based. In probability theory, there are three main Kolmogorov axioms that form the foundation of probability theory.

Central Limit Theorem (CLT) A fundamental principle stating that for independent, identically distributed random variables, their standardized sample average tends toward a normal distribution as the sample size grows larger.

Continuous Probability Probability distribution where events are not easily separable into distinct intervals. Emerges when discrete events are repeated so frequently that individual outcomes blend together (like millions of dart throws).

Correlation A statistical measure that expresses the extent to which two variables are linearly related, ranging from −1 to +1.

Cumulative Probability Distribution A function that shows the probability associated with outcomes smaller than or equal to each possible outcome.

Discrete Probability Probability that deals with separate, countable events where each outcome is distinct and independent (like dart throws or coin flips). Each event has a specific, separate probability.

Expected Value The "true average" of a random variable, calculated by multiplying each possible outcome by its probability and summing these products. Represents the long-term average after infinite trials.

Kolmogorov Axioms The three fundamental principles of probability theory: probabilities are non-negative numbers between zero and one, total probability equals 1, and the probability of mutually exclusive events is the sum of their individual probabilities.

Law of Large Numbers A theorem stating that as the number of trials increases, the sample average tends to converge to the expected value.

Monte Carlo Integration A technique using random sampling to obtain numerical approximations of complex mathematical functions and probabilities.

Mutually Exclusive Events Events that cannot occur simultaneously, where the occurrence of one event prevents the occurrence of the other.

Normal Distribution A symmetric, bell-shaped probability distribution defined by its mean and variance, which often emerges as the limiting distribution in real-world phenomena explained by the central limit theorem.

Null Hypothesis A statistical hypothesis that assumes no significant difference exists in a set of given observations.

Population The complete set of all items or individuals that are of interest for a particular statistical study.

Probability Distribution A mathematical description showing the probability associated with each possible outcome of an event. It can be visualized as a graph or formula.

Probability $P(A)$ A numerical measure between zero and one that represents the likelihood of an event occurring. Can be thought of as the "area" of possibility that an event occupies within the total space of possible outcomes.

Sample Average The arithmetic mean of a set of observations, calculated by summing all values and dividing by the number of observations.

Sample Size The number of observations or data points in a statistical sample, important in determining the reliability of statistical estimates and the applicability of the central limit theorem.

Stochastic Another term for probabilistic, referring to random variables or processes that can be analyzed statistically but not predicted precisely.

Uniform Probability A probability distribution where all possible outcomes have equal likelihood of occurring, such as in a fair die.

Variance A measure of variability in a dataset, calculated as the average of squared deviations from the mean.

5 The Fundamentals of Risk

Contents

According to the Merriam-Webster Dictionary, risk is "the possibility of loss or injury." For outcomes of financial and economic decisions, we need a different definition. Risk is a measure of uncertainty about an investment's future payoff. Risk is a relative concept. It is always assessed over some time horizon and compared to a benchmark. In this chapter, we familiarize ourselves with the concept of risk and the mathematics necessary to quantify risk.

5.1 Measuring Risk: Expected Value

Risk is an abstract concept, but it can be quantified. Generally speaking, the riskier the investment, the less desirable and the lower the price. Risk arises from uncertainty about the future. We do not know which of many possible outcomes (economists call this "states of the world") will follow in the future. Because risk has to do with the future payoff of an investment, we must imagine all the possible payoffs and the likelihood of each.

The definition of risk refers to uncertainty over an investment or group of investments. Since what constitutes an investment can be broad and not very specific, the concept of risk is often described very broadly. However, there are two main tenets that always apply to risk. One, risk must be assessed over some time horizon. In general, risk over longer periods is higher. Two, risk must be measured relative to some benchmark—not in isolation. A good benchmark can be the performance of a group of experienced investment advisors, money managers, or even the market index itself.

In order to quantify risk, we need to familiarize ourselves with the mathematical concepts surrounding random events and probabilities. One important concept borrowed from probability theory is that of expected value, which summarizes a given investment's return out of all possible values.

To understand investment returns, we need to list all the possible outcomes and figure out the chance of each one occurring.

Probability is a measure of the likelihood that an event will occur. It is always between zero and one. It can also be stated in terms of frequencies.

https://doi.org/10.1515/9783111193120-007

Example 1. Assume we have an investment that can rise or fall in value. Let's say that for a $1,000 investment in the stock market, the value of our stock can rise to $1,400 or fall to $700. The amount we could get back is called the investment's payoff. We can construct a payoff table and determine the investment's expected value—the average or most likely outcome.

Table 5.1: A payoff table for investing $1,000 (Case 1).

Possibilities	Probability	Payoff	Payoff × Probability
#1	0.5	$700	$350
#2	0.5	$1,400	$700

Expected Value = Sum of Probabilities × Payoffs = $1,050.

Table 5.1 shows a probability payoff for investing $1,000 based on two states of the world with equal (0.5) probability. This table shows that a $1,000 investment has an expected value of $1,050. This does not mean the investment guarantees a payoff of $1,050. Indeed, if we invested only once, we could never get $1,050 back; we would either get $700 or $1,400. The expected value shows the average of most likely outcome of the investment if we were to repeat it many times.

Repeating the investment multiple times, sometimes we would receive the $700 payoff and sometimes we would receive the $1,400 payoff, which would average to $1,050—particularly if we ran the investment enough times for the central limit theorem (CLT) to apply.

Let us now imagine we have a different investment scheme where a $1,000 investment may lead to more possible outcomes. Let's say our $1,000 investment could rise in value to $2,000, with a probability of 0.1, or could rise in value to $1,400, with a probability of 0.4, or could fall in value to $700, with a probability of 0.4, or could fall in value to $100, with a probability of 0.1. This information can be summarized in the following payoff table.

Table 5.2: A payoff table for investing $1,000 (Case 2).

Possibilities	Probability	Payoff	Payoff × Probability
#1	0.1	$100	$10
#2	0.4	$700	$280
#3	0.4	$1,400	$560
#4	0.1	$2,000	$200

Expected Value = Sum of Probabilities × Payoffs = $1,050.

Table 5.2 shows a probability payoff for investing $1,000 based on four states of the world with varying probabilities. Multiplying the payoff times its corresponding probability and summing these across all possibilities reveals the expected value of this second investment scheme is also $1,050. Using percentages allows comparison of returns regardless of the size of initial investment. The expected return in both cases is $50 on a $1,000 investment, or 5%.

If both investment strategies (Case 1 and Case 2) yield the same return of 5% on an initial investment of $1,000, does this mean the two investments are equivalent?

Not necessarily. We note that Case 1 has only two possible outcomes, whereas Case 2 has more outcomes. The possibility of more outcomes gives rise to more uncertainty on what return an investment will yield. This means that while the expected value gives important information about the desirability of a given investment strategy, we must turn to another concept to measure the uncertainty or risk associated with a given investment strategy.

5.2 Measuring Risk: Variance and Standard Deviation

It seems intuitive that the wider the range of outcomes, the greater the risk. A risk-free asset is an investment whose future value is known with certainty (a single state of the world and a single outcome with a probability of one) and whose return is the risk-free rate of return. This means the received payoff is guaranteed and cannot vary. Neither Case 1 nor Case 2 above are free of risk, because the payoff can vary across states of the world (two for Case 1 and four for Case 2).

But their expected values do not give us an insight on how risky these two investment strategies are. To quantify their risk, we must come up with a measure of their spread. Measuring the spread in payoffs allows us to measure investment risk.

One measure of spread is given by the variance. The variance is the average of the squared deviations of all the possible outcomes from their expected value, weighted by their probabilities. This means the variance can never be a negative number. The smallest value a variance can take is zero. An investment with a variance of zero is an investment with a constant payoff (one that never varies). This means the payment is guaranteed and it is, therefore, an investment with a risk-free return. As the variance rises above zero, the risk of investment increases. The higher the variance, the higher the risk.

An equation for the variance is:

$$\sigma^2 = \sum_{i=1}^{n} p_i * (x_i - \mu_x)^2.$$

Therefore, the steps to compute the variance are:

1. *Compute the expected value*: We can compute the expected value as: $\mu_x = 0.5 * \$700 + 0.5 * \$1,400 = \$1,050$.

2. *Subtract expected value from each of the possible payoffs and square the result:*
   $1,400 – $1,050 = ($350) = 122,500 (dollars)^2; $700 – $1,050 = ($350) = 122,500 (dollars)^2.

3. *Multiply each result times the probability and add up the results:* 0.5 * [122,500 (dollars)]^2 + 0.5 * [122,500 (dollars)^2] = $122,500 (dollars)^2.

This gives us that the variance of the investment for Case 1 is not zero, so this investment scheme is not free of risk. The question is whether this variance is large or small relative to alternative investment schemes. One issue with the concept of variance is that the units of measurement may be difficult to interpret. We do not know what the square of a dollar really is! So an alternative measure is called *standard deviation,* which is simply the square root of the variance. The standard deviation is more useful because it deals in normal units, not squared units (like dollars-squared). Also, we can calculate standard deviations into a percentage of the initial investment, so it can be more readily interpreted.

The standard deviation is given by:

$$\sigma = \left[\sum_{i=1}^{n} p_i * (x_i - \mu_x) \right]^{\frac{1}{2}},$$

which in Case 1 is simply $\sqrt{122,500 \text{ (dollars)}^2}$ = $350. This means the standard deviation of the initial investment of $1000, is $350 or 35%. Let us now calculate the standard deviation of Case 2. See Table 5.3.

Table 5.3: Calculating the standard deviation of investment $1,000 (Case 2).

Probability	Payoff	Payoff-expected value	(Payoff-expected value)^2
0.1	$100	($100 – $1,050) = –$950	$902,500 (dollars)^2
0.4	$700	($700 – $1,050) = –$350	$122,500 (dollars)^2
0.4	$1,400	($1,400 – $1,050) = $350	$122,500 (dollars)^2
0.1	$2,000	($2,000 – $1,050) = $950	$902,500 (dollars)^2

Variance = $278,500 (dollars)^2.

The variance can be calculated as:

$$0.1 * \$902,500 \text{ (dollars)}^2 + 0.4 * 122,500 \text{ (dollars)}]^2 + 0.4 * 122,500 \text{ (dollars)}^2$$
$$+ 0.1 * \$902,500 \text{ (dollars)}^2 = \$278,500 \text{ (dollars)}^2.$$

The standard deviation of the initial of $1,000 for Case 2 is $\sqrt{\$278,500 \text{ (dollars)}^2}$ = $528. This means that standard deviation of the initial investment of $1,000 is $528 or

53%. The greater the standard deviation, the higher the risk. Case 1 has a standard deviation of $350 and Case 2 has a standard deviation of $528. Case 1 has a lower risk. We can also see this in Figure 5.1.

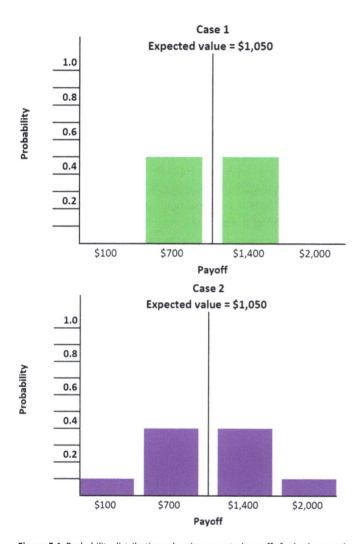

Figure 5.1: Probability distributions showing expected payoffs for both scenarios.

We can see Case 1 is more clustered around the expected value of $1,050 with a standard deviation of 35%, whereas Case 2 is more spread out around the same expected value of $1,050 with a standard deviation of 53%. Case 2 has higher standard deviation, therefore it carries more risk.

5.3 Measuring Risk: Value at Risk (VaR)

Sometimes we are less concerned with spread over possible outcomes from an investment strategy and we are more concerned with what the worst possible outcome may
be. Sometimes, we may just want to assess an outcome with a small likelihood of a very
large loss. Examples might include: What is the probability that a bank fails? What is
the probability of a large loss in the stock market? What is the probability of defaulting
on a variable versus a fixed-rate mortgage?

If we are holding stock in a company, the worst-case scenario might be that the
company goes bankrupt and its price crashes. This means we take a large loss (this is
typically called a "blowout"). The expected value and standard deviation of the price of
the stock do not really tell us the risk we face, in this case. VaR answers the question:
how much will I lose if the worst possible scenario occurs?

Sometimes this is the most important question we want answered. The following
snippet of Python code calculates the maximum loss that could be expected in the next
month from a stock portfolio worth $150,000. Two assumptions are required to make the
calculation: 1) the variance (volatility) of the portfolio must be assumed or estimated;
and 2) we must assume that no further trading takes place within the month.

```
#set up confidence level
Conf_lvl = 0.99;


#Set up how many days of trading to allow for
Trading_Days = 252;


#Notional Portfolio Value
NPV = 150000;


#Set up portfolio volatility
volatility = 0.305;


# Estimate VaR for 1 month (21 business days) into the future
t = 21;


#
cutoff = norm.ppf(Conf_lvl)



#The VaR equation
VaR = NPV * volatility * np.sqrt(t/Trading_Days) * cutoff
print("At {:.2f} confidence level, the loss will not exceed
    ↪  {:,.2f}".format(Conf_lvl, VaR))
```

```
print("This is consistent with a move of {:.2f} standard deviations
  ↪   below the expected return".format(cutoff))
```

```
At 0.99 confidence level, the loss will not exceed 30,723.81
This is consistent with a move of 2.33 standard deviations below the
  ↪   expected return
```

This shows with 99% confidence that the largest loss that could be expected within the month from the $150,000 portfolio is just shy of $31,000.

5.4 The Trade-offs Between Risk and Returns

Many people are averse to risk—they do not like risk and will pay to avoid it. Insurance is a good example of this. For most buyers, the expected return of their insurance is negative. This means they will pay insurance premiums over their lifetime and never collect a return. However, many find value in insuring against a worst-case scenario by collecting a negative return (in other words, paying) in exchange for minimizing risk.

A risk-averse investor will always prefer an investment with a certain return to one with the same expected return but any amount of uncertainty. Often, investors require compensation for taking on added risk. The compensation investors require to hold the risky asset is called the *risk premium*. Typically, the riskier the investment, the higher the risk premium. See Figure 5.2.

Figure 5.2: Risk premium and expected returns.

5.5 The Basics of Risk Management

There are two main types of risk: *idiosyncratic risk* and *systemic risk*.

Idiosyncratic risk refers to that type of risk only affecting a small number of people, a small number of firms or a small sector of industry. These risks are unique to a small portion of an economy. Another type of idiosyncratic risk is a risk that may be bad for one sector of the economy but good for another. For example, a rise in oil prices could be good for the energy industry, while being bad for the car industry.

On the other hand, systemic—or economy-wide risks—are those types of risks that affect a very large swath or even the whole economy. There is a manifest trade-off between risks and returns. Conventionally, chasing higher returns connotes having to deal with higher levels of risk. Therefore, investors must come up with strategies to mitigate risk and plans for responding to both idiosyncratic and systemic risk.

Some investors take on so much risk that a single big loss can wipe them out. Traders call this "blowing up." Risk can be reduced through a process called diversification, which is the principle of holding more than one risk at a time. Diversification comes in two varieties: hedging and spreading. One can hedge risks or spread them among many investments. If done correctly, these can help reduce the idiosyncratic risk an investor bears.

Hedging is the strategy of reducing idiosyncratic risk by making two investments with opposing risks. Even if one industry is volatile, the payoffs may yet be kept relatively more stable. For example, let us say we have three strategies for investing $100: A—Invest $100 in Exxon (an energy company); B—Invest $100 in Toyota (an automotive company); C—Invest $50 in each company. We will assume oil prices have an equal chance or rising and falling. When oil prices rise, owners of Exxon receive $120 for every $100, while Toyota prices fall to $96. On the other hand, when oil prices fall, owners of Toyota receive $120 for every $100, while Exxon prices fall to $96.

Table 5.4: A payoff table for investing $1,000.

Probability	Expected payoff	Standard deviation
Exxon only	108	$12
Toyota only	108	$12
Half-and-half	108	$0

Table 5.4 shows the expected value and standard deviation for each of the three investment strategies. The expected payoff for Exxon-only investment is the same is the same as Toyota's only, which is $(0.5 * \$120) + (0.5 * \$96) = \$108$. And the standard deviation for either investment is also the same, that is:

$$\sqrt{0.5 * (\$120 - \$108)^2 + 0.5 * (\$96 - \$108)^2} = \$12.$$

What is the expected payoff for hedging with the half-and-half strategy? Instead of investing $100 in either, hedging in this case involves investing $50 in Exxon and $50 in Toyota. Recall there are two states of the world with equal probability: oil prices go up or oil prices go down.

The expected payoff of $50 investment in Exxon is $(0.5 * \$60) + (0.5 * \$48) = \$54$ and the expected payoff of $50 investment in Toyota is also $(0.5 * \$60) + (0.5 * \$48) = \$54$, so the total expected payoff of the hedging strategy is also $(\$54 + \$54) = \$108$. However, the standard deviation of the hedging strategy is zero:

$$\sqrt{0.5 * (\$60 + \$48 - \$108)^2 + 0.5 * (\$48 + \$60 - \$108)^2} = \$0.$$

Importantly, while hedging has effectively eliminated risk from 12% ($12 standard deviation of a $100 investment in our example) in the real world, correct hedging will likely reduce, but will rarely completely eliminate risk.

Investments do not always predictably move in the opposite direction in response to an economic or financial event. Therefore, correct hedging may not always be possible. An alternative risk management approach is to diversify by spreading risk around multiple investments. While hedging required finding investments with opposite risks, this type of diversification requires finding investments with unrelated payoffs to spread the underlying risk.

Let's now consider a different investment scheme consisting of three strategies for investing $100: A—Invest $100 in American Express (a credit card company); B—Invest $100 in IBM (a technology company); C—Invest $50 in each company. We will assume prices of American Express and IBM move independently. In this case there are four states of the world with equal probability, 25%, of each occurring. Investing $100 in American Express has a 25% probability of returning $120 in state 1, $120 in state 2, $100 in state 3, and $100 in state 4. Investing $100 in IBM has a 25% chance of returning $120, a 25% chance of returning $100, a 25% chance of returning $120, and a 25% of returning $100 in each of the four respective states of the world.

Applying the formulas for expected value and standard deviation that we have seen before, the following snippet of Python code reveals that investing $100 in either company yields the same expected return and the same standard deviation.

```
AXP_exp_payoff=(0.25)*120+(0.25)*120+(0.25)*100+(0.25)*100
AXP_exp_payoff
110.0
IBM_exp_payoff=(0.25)*120+(0.25)*100+(0.25)*120+(0.25)*100
IBM_exp_payoff
110.0
AXP_sd=( (0.25)*(120-110)**2+(0.25)*(120-110)**2+(0.25)*(100-110)**2+(0.25)*(100-110)**2 )**0.5
AXP_sd
10.0
IBM_sd=( (0.25)*(120-110)**2+(0.25)*(100-110)**2+(0.25)*(120-110)**2+(0.25)*(100-110)**2 )**0.5
IBM_sd
10.0
```

If we invest $100 in American Express, the expected value is $110 and the standard deviation is 10%. Similarly, if we invest $100 in IBM, the expected value is $110 and the standard deviation is 10%. Both strategies yield the same expected return of 10% (the expected payoff of $10 from a $100 investment). However, they both have some level of risk, 10%. What if we diversified and invested $50 in each company? The payoff table for the diversified strategy looks as follows:

Table 5.5: Calculating the standard deviation of investing $1,000.

State of the world	Probability	AMEX	IBM	Total payoff
#1	0.25	$60	$60	$120
#2	0.25	$60	$50	$110
#3	0.25	$50	$60	$110
#4	0.25	$50	$50	$100

Table 5.5 shows the expected payoff table of the diversified option of investing $50 in American Express and $50 in IBM. According to the table, the expected total payoff of investing $50 in each company is $(0.25) * \$120 + (0.25) * \$110 + (0.25) * \$110 + (0.25) * \$100 = \$110$. In this case, diversifying does not alter the expected payoff. Therefore, investing $100 in American Express, investing $100 in IBM, or investing $50 in each yield the same expected payoff.

However, the standard deviation of the diversification strategy is lower than investing in either company, as can be seen below:

$$\sqrt{0.25 * (\$120 - \$110)^2 + 0.25 * (\$110 - \$110)^2 + 0.25 * (\$110 - \$110)^2 + 0.25 * (\$100 - \$110)^2} = \$7.07.$$

The diversified portfolio has a lower standard deviation, so while diversification does not necessarily affect expected payoffs, in this case it reduces risk (from 10% to 7.07%). This can also be seen in Figure 5.3.

Figure 5.3: Diversification chart.

The more independent sources of risk held in a portfolio, the lower the overall risk. As we add more and more independent sources of risk, a much lower standard deviation may be achieved, although expected payoffs may also decrease. Diversification through the spreading of risk is the basis for the insurance business, personal financial planning, and investment banking.

Thinking About It...

Risk is defined as uncertainty about an investment's future payoff. It must be assessed over a time horizon and compared to a benchmark. Risk-free assets have guaranteed returns with no uncertainty.

Expected value of an investment is calculated by summing all possible outcomes multiplied by their probabilities, and it shows the average outcome. However, it does not indicate risk level, so two investments can have the same expected value but different risk levels.

Risk can be better reflected by measures of scatter around the expected value. The variance measures the spread of possible outcomes around the expected value, but the standard deviation (which is the square root of the variance) is more practical as it uses more understandable units of measurement. Higher standard deviations indicate higher risk, and they can be used to compare risk levels between investments.

Risk can be managed through *hedging* and *diversification*. Hedging can mitigate risk by making investments with opposing risks. Diversification can help reduce risk by spreading investments across multiple unrelated assets. Proper diversification may reduce overall portfolio risk without necessarily reducing expected returns. Diversification is the foundation for insurance, financial planning, and investment banking.

There is a trade-off between risk and returns. Higher risk typically demands higher expected returns (risk premium). Risk-averse investors prefer certainty, even with lower returns. There are two types of risk: idiosyncratic, affecting specific investments; and systemic, affecting the entire market.

5.6 Glossary

Blowout A severe loss scenario where an investment dramatically decreases in value, such as when a company goes bankrupt. Also known as "blowing up" in trading terminology.

Confidence Level In risk analysis, particularly value at risk (VaR) calculations, the statistical probability that a potential loss will not exceed a specified value over a given time period.

Diversification A risk management strategy that involves spreading investments across different assets or asset classes to reduce overall portfolio risk. Effective diversification requires investing in assets whose returns are not perfectly correlated.

Expected Value The weighted average of all possible outcomes of an investment, where each outcome is weighted by its probability of occurrence. It represents the most likely or average outcome if the investment were repeated many times.

Hedging A risk management strategy where an investor takes an offsetting position in a related investment to reduce risk exposure. The goal is to protect against adverse price movements by having investments that move in opposite directions under the same conditions.

Idiosyncratic Risk Also known as unsystematic risk, it refers to risk that affects only a specific asset, company, or small sector of the economy. This type of risk can be reduced through diversification.

Independent Payoffs Investment returns that are not correlated with each other, important for effective risk spreading in diversification strategies.

Insurance Premium The cost paid to transfer risk to an insurance company, typically resulting in a negative expected return for the buyer in exchange for protection against worst-case scenarios.

Notional Portfolio Value (NPV) The total value of a portfolio used as the base for risk calculations, particularly in value at risk (VaR) analysis.

Payoff The actual return or value received from an investment in a particular state of the world.

Payoff Table A structured presentation showing all possible investment outcomes and their associated probabilities, used to calculate expected values and risk measures.

Portfolio Volatility A measure of how much a portfolio's value fluctuates over time, often expressed as a standard deviation and used in risk calculations.

Risk-Free Asset An investment whose future value is known with certainty and provides a guaranteed return. Government securities are often considered the closest approximation to risk-free assets.

Risk Horizon The time period over which investment risk is assessed, with longer periods generally associated with higher risk.

Risk Management The process of identifying, analyzing, and taking steps to reduce or control risk in an investment portfolio through strategies like diversification, hedging, and spreading.

Risk Premium The additional return an investor expects to receive as compensation for taking on extra risk compared to a risk-free investment. Generally, the riskier the investment, the higher the risk premium investors demand.

Standard Deviation A statistical measure of the dispersion of possible investment outcomes around their expected value. It provides a standardized way to quantify risk by showing how much returns typically deviate from the average. Higher standard deviation indicates greater risk.

State of the World A possible future scenario or outcome that could occur, each with an associated probability and payoff in risk analysis.

Systemic Risk Also called systematic or market risk, it represents risk that affects the entire market or economy simultaneously. This type of risk cannot be eliminated through diversification alone.

Time Horizon The duration of time over which an investment or risk analysis is conducted, crucial for proper risk assessment and management strategies.

Value at Risk (VaR) A statistical measure that quantifies the maximum potential loss an investment portfolio could face over a specific time period at a given confidence level. It answers the question "How much could I lose in a worst-case scenario?"

Variance A statistical measure that quantifies the spread of possible outcomes around the expected value by averaging the squared deviations from the mean. It is the square of standard deviation and serves as a fundamental measure of investment risk.

Volatility A statistical measure of the dispersion of returns for a given investment, often used interchangeably with standard deviation in financial contexts.

Part III: **Financial Markets**

6 The Bond Market

Contents

In previous chapters, we discussed simple loans (for example, a loan to our cousin) and fixed-payment loans (for example, an auto loan). Whether we are expecting a single future payment or a sequence of future payments, we need the concept of present value to evaluate their worth. And this calculation implies an important connection between security prices and interest rates. In this chapter, we will extend these concepts to the bond market.

6.1 Discount Bonds

Alexander Hamilton, the first Secretary of the U. S. Treasury, brought bonds to the U. S. One of his first acts was to consolidate all debt from the Revolutionary War, resulting in the first U. S. government bonds. Many features of original bonds are the same, even with a more complex bond market.

A bond is a promise to make a series of payments on specific future dates. Bonds create obligations, and are therefore thought of as legal contracts that require the borrower to make payments to the lender, and specify what happens if the borrower fails to do so. Who makes this promise to pay? Governments and firms. Governments at various levels: local (city level/municipality level), subnational (regional level, state level), and national (often called treasury bonds). Firms also make this promise to pay. These are called corporate bonds.

Governments and firms create new bonds (this is called "issuing") to sell them to the public. An original seller of a bond is called the issuer and the buyer of the bond is called the holder. For example, when the U. S. Treasury issues a new bond, it is selling a claim for a future payment that the Treasury promises to fulfill sometime in the future. Who does it sell it to? Private citizens, foreigners, businesses, other governments, and financial firms. The buyers of the bond are called *bond holders*. They pay for the bond now in exchange for a future payment. The bond is considered an instrument of debt.

The *bond issuer* is selling an instrument of debt, so in essence it becomes a borrower. The *bond holder* is buying an instrument of debt, so the holder becomes a lender.

Bonds come in two types: *coupon bonds* and *discount bonds*. Discount bonds are sometimes called zero-coupon bonds, because they promise no interim payments be-

https://doi.org/10.1515/9783111193120-009

tween the date when the bond is issued and the date when the final payment is due. When an issuer of a discount bond sells it, it enters into a legal contract with the holder, whereby the seller promises to make a future payment, the amount of which is called the *principal, face value* (FV), or *par value*, of the bond. The contract also specifies when the payment is due, which is called the maturity date or the term to maturity.

What incentivizes the investor/lender to buy the discount bond is that it is sold at a discount—where the price is below the face value. This is because the face value is paid sometime in the future and the value of that future payment must be discounted to the present with a present value calculation.

The U. S. Treasury issues Treasury bills (T-bills), which are a type of discount bond with a maturity of up to one year. If FV denoted the face value of a discount bond, n is the time to maturity and i is the interest rate, the price of a discount bond (P_{DB}) is given by:

$$P_{DB} = \frac{FV}{(1+i)^n}.$$

Say, we have a T-bill that represents a promise by the U. S. government to pay $1,000 on a fixed future date. If the interest rate were 5%, the price of a one-year T-bill would be $952.38. If the bond had a shorter maturity, we would discount fewer periods, which would increase the price of the bond. So the price of a six-month T-bill with a face value of $1,000 and an interest of 5% would be:

$$P_{DB} = \frac{\$1,000}{(1+0.05)^{\frac{1}{2}}} = \$975.90.$$

This is slightly higher than $952.38. The following snippet of Python code defines the equation to calculate the value of a discount bond.

```
# We can define a function to calculate the Price of a discount bond
def Price_db(FV, i, n):    #PV_simple is our first user-defined function
    Price_db = FV / (1 + i)**n
    return print("{:,.2f}".format(Price_db))
```

Applying this formula, we can see that on a $1,000 bond at an interest rate of 5%, the price value declines the longer we have to wait for the final payment of the face value of the bond.

```
i = .05;     #Today's interest rate
FV = 1000;   #Principal of Face Value of the bond
n = 1;       #To be paid in one year

# So the price of a bond that promises $1K five years when the interest
↵   is 5% would be...
```

```
Price_db(FV, i, n)
952.38
```

When the maturity of this bond increases to two or three years, the price of the bond decreases.

```
n = 2;Price_db(FV, i, n)
907.03
```

```
n = 3;Price_db(FV, i, n)
863.84
```

Our first takeaway is: The price of the discount bond is inversely related to its maturity. Incidentally, if the discount bond were redeemable immediately, there would be no periods to discount the face value. No discounting means the price of the bond would exactly equal the cash value of the promised principal.

```
n = 0;Price_db(FV, i, n)
1,000.00
```

In addition to the term to maturity, another crucial factor that impacts the price of a discount bond is the interest rate. As we have seen in previous chapters, if the prevailing rate increased from 5% to, say, 7% or 10%, the discount bond would be discounted faster.

```
#Returning to our example
i = .05;    #Today's interest rate
FV = 1000;  #Principal of Face Value of the bond
n = 3;      #To be paid in three years
```

Keeping the maturity fixed at three periods, what happens to the price of the bond as the interest rate increases?

```
i=0.05;Price_db(FV, i, n)   # At 5%
863.84
```

```
i=0.07;Price_db(FV, i, n)   # At 7%
816.30
```

```
i=0.10; Price_db(FV, i, n) # At 10%
751.31
```

At any fixed maturity (n), as the interest rate increases, we are discounting the face value faster, so the price decreases. Similarly, if the interest rates decreases, future payments are discounted more slowly, which serves to appreciate the value of the contract promising the payment, thereby raising its price. The following Python snippet shows the price of a three-year bond goes up as the interest rate decreases.

```
i=0.04;Price_db(FV, i, n)   # At 4%
889.00
```

```
i=0.02;Price_db(FV, i, n)   # At 2%
942.32
```

```
i=0.01;Price_db(FV, i, n)   # At 1%
970.59
```

Our second takeaway is: The price of the discount bond is inversely related to its yield or interest rate.

An implicit assumption we are making here is that market interest rates are non-negative. While, technically, there is no upper bound on yields, it is believed there is a zero-lower-bound (ZLB) on (nominal) interest rates below which they cannot go. However, in the late 2000s and early 2010s, some negative yields were reached for a small number of financial instruments in a few countries. If this were the case for bonds, it begs the question: What would be the price of a discount bond with a negative yield?

In that case, the denominator in the price formula would be smaller than one, which would render the price of the bond even larger than its face value. For example, the price of a three-year bond with a face value of $1,000 and a yield of –1% would actually be $1,030, which is higher than its face value.

```
i=-0.01;Price_db(FV, i, n)   # At -1%
1,030.61
```

In other words, if a lender were to pay $1,030.61 today for a $1,000 payment in three years, this bond would not be sold at a discount, but it would actually be sold at a premium. This is clearly an unusual proposition. Why would anyone pay more today for the privilege of receiving a lower cash payment in the future?

There could be some tax implications or some unusual carrying costs of cash to explain this somewhat aberrant behavior. In any case, some yields have, on rare occasions, become slightly negative, but it is highly unlikely that they will ever be largely, or even moderately, negative. This would lead to what is known as a *liquidity trap problem* with an instrument in infinite supply and zero demand...the market would most likely break!

In summary: 1. The price of the discount bond is inversely related to its maturity. We will see that this rule can be extended to any type of bond. 2. Prices and yields of discount bonds are inversely related. This will hold for any type of bond. 3. Discount bonds are also called zero-coupon bonds (meaning they do not make any coupon payments)–the only payment is the face value at maturity. Most notable examples of discount bonds are issued by government institutions such as the U. S. Treasury.

6.2 Coupon Bonds

A second type of bond is known as coupon bonds. Coupon bonds are somewhat more common than discount bonds. When an issuer of a coupon bond sells it, the issuer enters into a legal contract with the holder, whereby the issuer/borrower is required to make annual payments, called coupon payments. The contract specifies: the annual interest the borrower pays (i_c), which is known as the coupon rate; the date on which the payments stop and the loan is repaid (n), which is called the maturity date or term to maturity; and the final payment to be made when the bond matures, which is the principal, face value, or par value of the bond. Therefore, what distinguishes coupon bonds from discount bonds is that the former actually makes periodic payments even before the bond matures—before paying back the face value—while the latter makes a single face value payment at maturity. As with discount bonds, *it must also be the case that, say, a coupon bond with a $100 face value payment at a future date is worth less than 100 dollars cash today.*

What would be the value of a coupon bond's $100 principal to be paid in five years at an interest rate of 3%? This would require the exact same calculation we used before for a discount bond. In fact, the price of this coupon bond would be exactly the same as the price of a discount bond (P_{DB}) with a five year maturity with the same principal of $100 and the same interest rate of 3%.

$$P_{DB} = \frac{\$1,000}{(1 + 0.03)^5} = \$862.61.$$

So, if we let (P_{DB}) denote the price of the bond's principal, the price of a coupon bond's $1,000 principal with maturity of five years at an interest rate of 3% would also be $862.61.

$$P_{BP} = \frac{\$1,000}{(1 + 0.03)^5} = \$862.61.$$

So, does this represent the full price of the coupon bond? Not necessarily. We need to remember that the coupon bond promises regular future payments between the date that it is issued and the date that it matures. While these payments are made periodically at regular intervals, they are also made some time in the future. Therefore, we need to discount this stream of future coupon payments to the present. Since these payments add value to the bond, they must also be reflected in its price.

The fact that coupon payments are made on regular intervals allows us to model them as an annuity. Luckily, we have discussed how to calculate the present value of an annuity in previous chapters.

The price of a stream of coupon payments (P_{CP}) can be calculated generally as the sum of the present values of each coupon payment as follows:

$$P_{CP} = \frac{C}{(1+i)} + \frac{C}{(1+i)^2} + \cdots + \frac{C}{(1+i)^n}.$$

These resemble fixed loan payments, where C is the fixed amount of a coupon payment. This present value expression gives us a general formula for the string of yearly coupon payments made over n years. This formula can be easily written into Python as follows:

```python
#The PV of a stream of coupon payments
def PV_coup(C, i, n):
    beg=1; end=n; PV_cpn=0;
    for t in range(beg, end+1):
        PV_cpn += C / (1 + i) ** t
    return (print("{:,}".format(PV_cpn)))
```

... taking as inputs the fixed amount of the coupon payment (C), the number of periods until maturity (n) and the interest rate (i). With this equation defined, we can now call it to calculate the present value of any collection of coupon payments.

For example, what is the PV of a string of five ($n = 5$) coupon payments in the amount of $100 at an interest rate of three percent ($i = 0.03$)?

```python
Coupon=100;rate=.03;maturity=5;
PV_coup(Coupon, rate, maturity)
457.97
```

If the amount of the coupon payment were to increase, the bond would be more valuable so its price would also increase. In fact, the increase is one-to-one, meaning that—while keeping all other terms unchanged—if the coupon payment were to double, the price of the bond would also double. The snippet below shows that if the interest rate and maturity remained the same, but the coupon payment were to double from $100 to $200, the present value of the coupon bond would double as well, from $457.9 to $915.9.

```python
Coupon=100; Coupon=200;
PV_coup(Coupon, rate, maturity)
915.94
```

Keeping everything else constant, the present value of a stream of coupon payments would decrease if the interest rate were to increase. This is because each future coupon payment would be discounted faster at a higher interest rate. The following snippet of Python code shows that the present value of a $200 coupon bond, paid once a year for the next five years, would decrease from $915.9 if the interest rate were to rise from 3% to 7%.

```
Coupon=200;maturity=5;rate=.03;rate=.07;
PV_coup(Coupon, rate, maturity)
820.03
```

This means that the present value of a stream of coupon bonds decreases as the interest rate increases. This should also make sense. At higher interest rates, we could collect more returns on deposits that we hold now. But if we are holding a coupon bond, we cannot collect returns now on payments that are not made yet. Since we are waiting to be paid that coupon payment, waiting is more costly at higher interest rates, because there are potentially higher returns that we are not collecting while we wait. In other words, there is an opportunity cost of holding a coupon bond and that opportunity cost is higher at higher interest rates. So, a higher interest rate generally makes the coupon bond less valuable, all else being equal.

Finally, what happens to the present value of a coupon bond as it promises more payments (as n increases)?

All else being equal, a coupon bond that promises more payments will be more valuable. For example, if at an interest rate of 7%, the maturity of a $200 coupon bond were to increase from five years to eight years (meaning, it would make eight payments instead of five), the present value of that bond would increase from $820 to $1,194.

```
Coupon=200;rate=.07;maturity=5;maturity=8;
PV_coup(Coupon, rate, maturity)
1194.25
```

Given that a coupon bond provides two sources of revenue—a stream of coupon payments and the bond principal at maturity—the price of the coupon bond must reflect both factors. Specifically, the price of the coupon bond (P_{CB}) adds up the price of the coupon payments (P_{cp}) and the bond's principal (P_{BP}), or the face value of the bond.

$$P_{CB} = P_{CP} + P_{BP} = \frac{C}{(1+i)} + \frac{C}{(1+i)^2} + \cdots + \frac{C}{(1+i)^n} + \frac{FV}{(1+i)^n}.$$

The following lines of code define a Python function to calculate the price of the coupon bond:

```python
def P_cb(FV, C, i, n):
    beg=1; end=n+1; PV_cpn=0;
    for t in range(beg, end):
        PV_cpn += C / (1 + i) ** t
    P_cb = np.round(PV_cpn + FV / (1 + i)**n,1)
    return (print("{:,}".format(P_cb)))
```

This formula allows us to answer questions such as: What is the price of a five-year coupon bond with a face value of $1,000 and $100 coupon payment at an interest rate of 10%?

The price of a coupon bond may not always equal its face value. However, in this case, the price of this particular coupon bond would be $1,000, the same as its face value of $1,000.

```python
FV=1000;C=100;i=.10;n=5;
P_cb(FV, C, i, n)
$1,000.00
```

Why is it the case here that the price of this bond equals its face value? We can answer this by noticing that this bond pays $100 coupon payments out of $1,000 FV, which means that the return from a coupon payment is 10% (= $100/$1,000). This is called the coupon rate (cr). The coupon rate equals the coupon payment divided by the face value of the bond.

$$cr = \frac{C}{FV}.$$

Any time the coupon rate equals the interest rate (cr = i), the price of the coupon bond equals its face value (P_{CB} = FV). This holds whether the bond has a short or a long maturity. This also holds independently of the amount of the face value or coupon payment or interest. We can verify this by applying the formula to a much longer coupon bond with 30 year maturity (n = 30) that has a much larger face value ($30,000) with coupon payments of $600 at an interest rate of 2%.

```python
FV=30000;C=600;i=.02;n=30;
P_cb(FV, C, i, n)
30,000
```

The price of this coupon bond also equals its face value of $30,000 even when it has a much longer maturity than five years. This is because its coupon rate of 2% equals the prevailing interest rate of 2%.

Let's get back to our five-year coupon bond with a $1,000 face value and coupon payments of $100 at an interest rate of 10%.

$$P_{CB} = \frac{100}{(1+0.1)} + \frac{100}{(1+0.1)^2} + \cdots + \frac{100}{(1+0.1)^5} + \frac{1,000}{(1+0.1)^5} = 1,000.$$

Some of the same conditions we learned about the discount bond also apply to the coupon bond. For example, if the face value increases, all else being equal, the bond's price increases. This makes sense, because the bond is more desirable when it promises a higher future payment.

On the other hand, when the amount of the coupon payment declines, so does the value and, therefore, the price of the coupon bond. This also follows the same reasoning, that there is a direct relationship between coupon payments, face value, and the price of a coupon bond.

Finally, when we examined discount bonds before, we learned that higher interest rates lead to lower bond prices, because with higher interest rates, investors incur higher opportunity costs of holding these bonds, so they discount the future faster, making the wait for the future payment at maturity less desirable today. This also holds generally for coupon bonds. However, when we are pricing coupon bonds, we now must contend with not just one but two rates: the coupon rate (cr) and the prevailing market rate (i).

We have seen that any time the coupon rate and the interest rate are equal, the price of the coupon bond equals its face value. What happens to the price of the coupon bond when the interest rate is higher than the promised coupon rate? If the coupon rate is lower than prevailing rates in the market ($cr < 10\%$), this must mean that the opportunity cost of holding the coupon bond outweighs the benefit of coupon payments, which makes the coupon bond less valuable. Therefore, whenever the interest rate is above the coupon rate, the price of the coupon bond is lower than its face value.

In the previous example, if the coupon payments promised decreased from $100 to $40, the coupon rate would decrease from 10% to 4%. Therefore, at an interest rate of 10%, the price of a five-year $1,000 face value coupon bond with a coupon rate of 4% would be $772—which is lower than its $1,000 face value.

$$P_{CB} = \frac{40}{(1+0.1)} + \frac{40}{(1+0.1)^2} + \cdots + \frac{40}{(1+0.1)^5} + \frac{1,000}{(1+0.1)^5} = 772.$$

```
# As the coupon payment decreases so does the price of the bond decrease
FV-1000;i=0.1;C=100;C=40;
P_cb(FV, C, i, n)
772.6
```

Similarly, any time a coupon bond promises a coupon rate above the prevailing interest rate ($cr > 10\%$) the price of the bond is above its face value. For example, if we had another coupon bond with the exact same terms as the previous one, but with a coupon rate of 15% instead of 4%, the price of the bond would increase from $772 to $1,189, which is above its $1,000 face value.

$$P_{CB} = \frac{150}{(1+0.1)} + \frac{150}{(1+0.1)^2} + \cdots + \frac{150}{(1+0.1)^5} + \frac{1,000}{(1+0.1)^5} = 1,189.50.$$

```
# As the coupon payment decreases so does the price of the bond decrease
↪  as well
FV=1000;i=0.1;C=100;C=150;
P_cb(FV, C, i, n)
1,189.5
```

Finally, all else being equal, what happens as the maturity increases? Holding every-thing the same, what if instead of a five-year bond it was a 30-year bond? In this case, we have tension: two forces pulling in opposite directions. The longer we have to wait for maturity, the less the face value means to us today because we are discounting longer. But the more coupons we get in the interim (as we wait), the more valuable the coupon bond is today. However, recall the value of those coupons also declines the longer we have to wait for them.

So as we saw in earlier sections, the price and the time to maturity are inversely related for discount bonds. The longer in the future we have to wait for the face value payment, the lower the price of the discount bond today. The relationship is not as clear for coupon bonds because of this tension between coupons and time. In other words, longer maturities may affect the price of the bond, but this effect is factored by the rela-tionship between the coupon rate and the prevailing interest rate.

For example, as we saw earlier, if the bond has a coupon rate that equals the pre-vailing interest rate (cr = i), maturity will not impact the price of the bond. Whether it is a five-year, a thirty-year or any other maturity, the price of the bond equals its face value.

$$P_{CB} = \frac{100}{(1+0.1)} + \frac{100}{(1+0.1)^2} + \cdots + \frac{100}{(1+0.1)^5} + \frac{1,000}{(1+0.1)^5} = 1,000,$$

$$P_{CB} = \frac{100}{(1+0.1)} + \frac{100}{(1+0.1)^2} + \cdots + \frac{100}{(1+0.1)^{30}} + \frac{1,000}{(1+0.1)^{30}} = 1,000.$$

```
FV=1000;C=100;i=.10;n=5;
P_cb(FV, C, i, n)
1,000.00
```

```
FV=1000;C=100;i=.10;n=30;
P_cb(FV, C, i, n)
1,000.00
```

On the other hand, we saw that if the coupon rate was above the prevailing interest rate (cr > i), the price of the coupon bond will be above face value. For this type of bond, as the maturity increases, the return from coupon payments outweigh the opportunity cost at each period, for more periods. Therefore, a coupon bond that is priced above its face value would experience an increase in price at longer maturities.

For example, at an interest rate of 10%, a $1,000 face value coupon bond with a coupon rate of 15% at five years would have a price above $1,000 and at 30 years would have an even higher price.

```
#Return to our benchmark
FV=1000;C=150;i=.10;n=5;
P_cb(FV, C, i, n)
1,189.5
```

```
#If maturity was 30 years instead of
#five (the rest of the bond terms remain the same)
FV=1000;C=150;i=.10;n=30;
P_cb(FV, C, i, n)
1,471.30
```

Conversely, if the coupon rate stood below the market rate (cr < i), the price of the bond would be below its face value. In that case, if the maturity were to increase, the opportunity cost of holding that bond would be higher than the expected return from the coupon payment each period... for more periods. This effect would compound at longer maturities, decreasing the price of the coupon bond. For example, at an interest rate of 10%, the price of a coupon bond with a coupon rate of 8% that pays a $1,000 face value in five years would be $924. Holding everything else the same, increasing the maturity would lower the price further below its face value. If instead of five years, the bond had a maturity of 30 years, its price would go down to $811.

```
#Return to our benchmark
FV=1000;C=80;i=.10;n=5;
P_cb(FV, C, i, n)
924.2
```

```
#If maturity was 30 years instead of five (the rest of the bond terms
⌐  remain the same)
FV=1000;C=80;i=.10;n=30;
P_cb(FV, C, i, n)
811.50
```

In summary: 1. The price of a coupon bond is directly related to its coupon payments and face value. All else being equal, if either the price or the coupon payment increases, so does the price. 2. The price of zero-coupon bonds always lies (at a discount) below its face value. This is not necessarily the case for coupon bonds. 3. Whenever the coupon rate equals the market rate, the price of the coupon bond equals its face value. If the coupon rate is above the market rate, the coupon bond is priced above its face value. And if the coupon rate is below the market rate, the price of the coupon bond lies below its face value.

6.3 Interest Rates, Yields, and Bond Prices

The relationship between bond prices and interest rates is important. Bonds promise fixed payments at future dates, so generally the higher the interest rate, the lower their present value. The value of a bond varies inversely with the interest rate used to calculate the present value of the promised payment.

Suppose a bond has four years until maturity. Its face value is $1,000, which means it pays $1,000 at maturity with annual coupons of $50. If the interest rate were 5%, the price of this bond would be $1,000—the same as its face value.

$$P = \frac{50}{(1 + 0.05)} + \frac{50}{(1 + 0.05)^2} + \cdots + \frac{50}{(1 + 0.05)^5} + \frac{1,000}{(1 + 0.05)^5} = 1,000.$$

If the interest rate were to increase from 5% to 6%, the price of the bond would decrease from $1,000 down to $965.34.

$$P = \frac{50}{(1 + 0.06)} + \frac{50}{(1 + 0.06)^2} + \cdots + \frac{50}{(1 + 0.06)^5} + \frac{1,000}{(1 + 0.06)^5} = 965.34.$$

This is the case because the interest increased, and at 6% it is now higher than the coupon rate of 5%. It is often the case that interest rates may depart from coupon rates. This is because a coupon rate is generally fixed at origination—when the bond is newly issued. The amount of the coupon payment is guaranteed not to change over the life of the bond. Short of a payment default by the issuer, the coupon bond makes the same payment at the prescribed time. These terms are contractually guaranteed at issuance. So, while coupon rates are fixed at issuance and do not change over the life of bond, interest rates vary daily.

Once a newly minted bond has been sold, it can be resold again at any time before maturity in a secondary market. The terms of the bond, such as the coupon rate and the face value, never change since they are fixed at issuance. But the prevailing rate may certainly fluctuate from day to day. Generally, bonds are traded daily. Every trading day, there are two bond markets: one for "newly minted" bonds and one for "second-hand" bonds, where these bonds are bought and sold. Even if the terms that give fundamental value to the bond like the face value and coupon rate are fixed, the prevailing rate may change daily and, therefore, the price of the bond may change daily.

The current yield (cy) is the measure of the proceeds the bond holder receives for making the loan (purchasing the bond). The current yield measures that part of the return from buying the bond that arises solely from the coupon payments. When we buy a

coupon bond today, the coupon payments are agreed upon and fixed at that time. Therefore, as we purchase the bond, we know what it currently yields because we know what
the coupon payments will be.

$$cy = \frac{C}{P}.$$

For example, what is the current yield of a one-year coupon bond with a face value
of $100 and a coupon rate of 5% selling for $98?

$$cy = \frac{C}{P} = \frac{5}{98} = 0.0510.$$

Its current yield would be 5.1%. Notice the current yield of 5.1% is above the coupon
rate of 5% because the $98 price of the bond is below its face value of $100.

The most useful measure of the return from holding a bond is called the yield to
maturity (*YTM*). *This is the yield bond holders receive if they hold the bond to its maturity
when the final principal payment is made.* In other words, the YTM equals the coupon
rate when the bond is sold. One way to think about this is that when we buy a bond, we
need to know the interest rate that prevails currently in the market.

If the interest rate is high today, the price of the bond is low today, which means we
get a face value in the future for a relatively low price today. If the interest rate is low
today, the price of the bond is relatively high, which means we get a face value in the
future for a relatively high price today. Therefore, the market interest rate (i) gives as
a sense of what the current bond price should be (e. g. is the bond's value high or low?)
today. Then, comparing the price to the promised coupon rate from the bond gives us insight into what the bond currently yields at purchase. Importantly, if the bond is held to
its maturity, then the current yield is what the bond eventually yields at maturity. Therefore, the YTM equals the current yield (at purchase) if the bond is held to its maturity.

Since the YTM is the yield bond holders receive if they hold the bond to its maturity
when the final principal payment is made, it must be equal to the interest rate (i) that
solves the equation for the present value of the coupon bond. Let's return to our example. Say we have a one-year coupon bond with a face value of $100 and a coupon rate of
5% selling for $98. We calculated the current yield of this bond is 5.1%. What is its YTM?
We need to solve the following equation for the interest rate i

$$P = \frac{C}{(1+i)} + \frac{FV}{(1+i)} = 98 = \frac{5}{(1+i)} + \frac{100}{(1+i)}.$$

Solving the equation for i reveals the YTM for this bond is 7.07%. Therefore, we find
that this bond has a coupon rate of 5%, a current yield of 5.1% and yield to maturity
of 7.1%.

We will find that it is always the case that for a bond that is priced below its face
value, its coupon rate is below its current yield, which in turn is below its yield to maturity.

Take another example. Say we have a $1,000 face value coupon bond that pays $50 coupon payments, matures in four years, and the prevailing interest rate is 5%. We already know how to calculate the price of this coupon bond. The snippet below shows the price is $1,000.

```
FV=1000; C=50; n=4; i=.05;
P_cb(FV, C, i, n)
1,000.00
```

We know the coupon rate is cr $= \frac{C}{FV} = \frac{50}{1,000} = 5\%$ and the current yield is the same, since we now know the price and the face value equal each other cy $= \frac{C}{P} = \frac{50}{1,000} = 5\%$. What is the YTM of this bond? The following Python snippet provides a definition:

```
def YTM(FV, P, C, n):
    num=(FV-P)/n
    den=(FV+P)/2
    i=(C+num)/den
    return (print("{:,}".format(i)))
```

Calling this function with the details of this bond reveals that the YTM is also 5%, as shown in the following code snippet

```
# YTM equation
FV=1000;P=1000; C=50; n=4;
YTM(FV, P, C, n)
0.05
```

The table below summarizes what we have learned about the relationship between the coupon rate, the current yield, and the yield to maturity.

In summary:
1. *When Bond Price < Face Value: Coupon rate < Current Yield < Yield to Maturity.*
2. *When Bond Price = Face Value: Coupon rate = Current Yield = Yield to Maturity.*
3. *When Bond Price > Face Value: Coupon rate > Current Yield > Yield to Maturity.*

For a fixed coupon rate, the YTM is always inversely related to the price of the bond. Table 6.1 shows the YTM of various bonds with 10% coupon rates.

When the YTM equals the cr, the price of the bond equals its face value. As the yield to maturity increases above the coupon rate, the price of the bond decreases. When the coupon bond is priced at its face value, the yield to maturity equals the coupon rate. The yield to maturity is greater than the coupon rate when the bond price is below its face value. Therefore, the price of a coupon bond and the yield to maturity are negatively related.

Table 6.1: YTM s for 10-year bonds with coupon rates of 10% and a face value of $100.

Yield to maturity (%)	Bond price ($)
7.13%	$120
8.48%	$110
10.00%	$100
11.75%	$90
13.81%	$80

6.4 Rates of Return

There are two possible sources of earning a return from holding a coupon bond: the coupon payments collected at regular intervals and the face value collected at maturity. For example, if we paid $95 for a one-year coupon bond with a $100 face value and a coupon rate of 10%, we would get two returns. The 10% coupon rate means we would get a $10 coupon payment. This is a dollar return obtained from holding the bond. And if we held this bond to its maturity, we would get $100 when the bond expires.

Since we paid $95 for the bond, we would also be collecting an extra ($100−$95 =)$5. The rise in value from an investment is referred to as a capital gain and it is part of the return on our investment from holding the bond. On the other hand, if the price of the bond was above the face value, the holder would incur a capital loss at maturity. In this particular example, we would be getting a $10 coupon payment plus a $5 capital gain from holding a bond that we paid $95 for. Therefore, the total return from holding this bond to maturity would be ($15/$95 =) 15.8%.

Since we have two sources of returns from holding a coupon bond, its rate of return must reflect both. This is an equation for the rate of return (RoR):

$$\text{RoR} = \frac{C}{P} + \frac{FV - P}{P}.$$

The first term in the sum is what the bond currently yields (cy $= \frac{C}{P}$) and the second term is the capital gain ($\frac{FV-P}{P} > 0$) or capital loss ($\frac{FV-P}{P} < 0$) from selling the bond.

As we discussed in the previous section, if we buy a multi-period coupon bond for a price that exactly equals its face value and hold it to its maturity, then the current yield, the coupon rate, and the yield to maturity we get from the bond are the same. We are now prepared to draw some insight into the relationship between all of these rates (cy, cr, YTM) and the rate of return (RoR).

For example, imagine that with a prevailing interest rate of 6% ($i = 0.06$), we buy a 10-year coupon bond that promises a 6% coupon rate (cr $= 0.06$) and a principal payment of $1,000 at maturity. We know that since (cr $= i$), the price of this coupon bond should be equal to its $1,000 face value.

$$P_{CB} = \frac{60}{(1+0.06)} + \frac{60}{(1+0.06)^2} + \cdots + \frac{60}{(1+0.06)^{10}} + \frac{1,000}{(1+0.06)^{10}} = 1,000.$$

Since the price of the bond equals its face value, if we hold this bond to maturity, we know its coupon rate is 6% (cr $= \frac{C}{FV} = \frac{\$60}{\$1,000} = 6\%$) and its current yield is also 6% (cy $= \frac{C}{P} = \frac{\$60}{\$1,000} = 6\%$), which also equals to a YTM = 6%.

So if we hold this coupon bond to its maturity, what return do we get? Since we are holding to maturity, we should be able to sell it back to the issuer for its face value, and since the face value exactly equals what we originally paid for it, we will incur neither a capital gain nor a capital loss. The rate of return equation tells us we also get a 6% rate of return from holding this bond.

$$\text{RoR} = \frac{C}{P} + \frac{FV - P}{P} = \frac{\$60}{\$1,000} + \frac{\$1,000 - \$1,000}{\$1,000} = 6\%.$$

Since we are holding this bond to its maturity, what we really get from this bond is its coupon rate (cr = 6%), which is equal to what the bond currently yields at any given time (cy = 6%), which equals its yield to maturity since we are holding it to its maturity (YTM = 6%), which is ultimately the return we get from holding it (RoR = 6%).

The following snippet of Python code calls the various equations we defined and applies the terms of this coupon bond:

```
FV=1000; P=1000; C=60; n=10


current_yield=C/P; coupon_rate=C/FV;


print('A ten-period bond with Face value'); print(FV); print('sells
↵  for'); print(P)
print('========================================')
print('current yield');print(round(current_yield,4))
print('========================================')
print('coupon rate');print(round(coupon_rate,4))
print('========================================')
print('YTM');print(YTM(FV, P, C, n))
print('========================================')
print('There is no capital gain from holding it to maturity
↵  (FV-P=)');(FV-P)/P



A ten-period bond with Face value
1000
sells for
1000
```

```
=====================================
current yield
0.06
=====================================
coupon rate
0.06
=====================================
YTM
0.06
None
=====================================
There is no capital gain from holding it to maturity (FV-P=)
0.0
```

We can conclude that if we buy a coupon bond with the intention of holding it to its maturity as an investment vehicle, the rate of return from holding the bond to its maturity equals its yield to maturity, or its current yield, or its coupon rate. Remember that while we hold this bond for the 10 years, interest rates, prices, and coupon rates promised by other bonds may fluctuate daily. But this will not have any bearing on the fundamentals of the bond we are holding, since the coupon rate and face value are locked in and guaranteed (so long as the issuer does not default on its promise to pay them).

This often leads to the conclusion that high interest rates are good for financial investors because they imply high rates of return. But this is not always the case. If we buy coupon bonds as a long-term investment vehicle and we hold them to their maturity, then yes... the highest the yield (cr, cy, or YTM), the highest the rate of return from holding the bond, all else being equal.

However, even if we have all the intention of a "buy-and-hold" strategy, we may not be able to hold on to a particular coupon bond until it matures. In that case, we will need to consider the holding period return as the return to holding a bond and selling it before maturity. In the cases of selling ahead of maturity, the holding period return can differ from the yield to maturity.

For example, let's say that we buy the previous bond we discussed for $1,000 today, planning to hold it for its maturity of 10 years. Every year we will collect a coupon payment of $60 and in 10 years we will collect the $1,000 face value by selling it back to the issuer. We know that we should be able to receive a 6% rate of return from holding this bond to its maturity, which is what the bond yields to its maturity. However, let's say that shortly after collecting the first annual coupon payment of $60 next year, we get into a small car accident leading to some unforeseen medical expenses. Unfortunately, we are not insured, we don't have credit cards, and the hospital will not accept bonds as payment. We know we have a $1,000 principal payment coming, but the hospital is not willing to wait nine years to be paid.

This bond we are holding is a financial instrument that has value. It has already made a $60 payment, but the bond certainly has residual value, because it should make nine future payments of $60 over the next nine years. Moreover, in nine years' time, it will make a 1,000 payment to whomever is holding it. So we are going to re-enter the bond market looking to sell this bond in a process that is called "liquidation." We would have liked to keep the bond to its maturity and collect the 6% yield to maturity, but we are going to convert this bond into cash now so that we can pay our medical expenses.

We want to calculate the holding period return. *What is the return from holding the bond for one year and selling it with nine years left before its maturity?* We know we have already been enjoying a current yield of 6% ($60/$1,000), but we do not know what the holding period return is until we find out what is the price we can sell our bond for. Since we are re-entering the bond market with a 10-year bond that has nine years until it matures, we now have to compete with other bonds that may promise other coupon rates in a market where prevailing interest rates may be different from when we originally purchased our bond. All of this will likely impact the price that our bond will fetch.

Let's say that at the time we want to sell the bond, interest rates have gone down. This sounds like it's a bad turn for us because we concluded earlier that maybe lower interest rates mean lower rates of return. But this is actually the opposite. If yields are lower now than when we first bought the bond, this is very good news for us!

Let's assume that the prevailing interest rate today is 5% and brand-new coupon bonds with various maturities (of 10 years, nine years, five years…) now promise lower coupon payments. If the average 10-year coupon bond today promises a coupon rate of 5% ($50 coupon payments for the next 10 years and $1,000 at the end), the 10-year bond we are holding is more valuable than the competition (since it promises a 6% coupon rate and the $1,000 principal back in nine years). Since we are holding a more valuable bond than the competition, the price of the bond should be higher.

In fact in our example, the price will be higher than what we bought it for. Since it promises a 6% coupon rate when the prevailing interest rate is 5%, the bond's future payments (higher than the competition) will be discounted at a slower pace, which leads to an increased price today. The price of our bond that we sell under these conditions would be $1,071 today.

This is the price when we bought the bond:

$$P_{CB} = \frac{60}{(1+0.06)} + \frac{60}{(1+0.06)^2} + \cdots + \frac{100}{(1+0.06)^{10}} + \frac{1,000}{(1+0.06)^{10}} = 1,000.$$

And this is the price if we sell today with nine years left in the life of the bond:

$$P_{CB} = \frac{60}{(1+0.05)} + \frac{60}{(1+0.05)^2} + \cdots + \frac{60}{(1+0.05)^{10}} + \frac{1,000}{(1+0.05)^{10}} = 1,071.$$

Here is the calculation in Python code:

```
#If the market rate (i) fell from 6% at contract to 5% next year,
#I would be selling a bond that has 9 years left of

#$60 coupon payments with a lower interest rate (i=5%)
FV=1000;C=60;i=.05;n=9;
P_cb(FV, C, i, n)
1,071.1
```

If we sold the bond for $1,071, we would be incurring a capital gain. Since we originally bought the bond for $1,000, selling the bond would net us a 7.1% capital gain. This would also be a return from the bond above and beyond the 6% we were getting the first year we held it. Therefore, the holding period return from buying this bond and selling it with nine years left of its maturity for a higher price would be

$$\text{RoR} = \frac{C}{P} + \frac{FV - P}{P} = \frac{\$60}{\$1,000} + \frac{\$1,071 - \$1,000}{\$1,000} = 13.1\%.$$

In this example, we had to liquidate our bond because of our emergency, and we were lucky that interest rates were lower at the time we had to sell. This led to an appreciation in value of the bond we were holding and we were able to collect a capital gain. The holding period return from our bond is higher than the return we would have derived had we kept the bond to maturity. In other words, by selling early, the rate of return is higher than the yield to maturity of the bond.

While we may have invested in bonds as a long-term investment, this turn of events resulted in a profitable proposition. This brings up another motive for investing in the bond market, namely speculation. Some investors enter the bond market with little intention of holding bonds to their maturity. Instead, they might chase higher returns than what the bonds yield to their maturity by speculating on future interest rate movements that might propitiate capital gains from selling early. Specifically, if interest rates decline after a bond has been purchased, the value of the bond increases, generating a higher holding period return by selling ahead of maturity. However, speculation is risky, and it requires taking a calculated risk because interest rates could increase rather than decline, and this would generate capital losses when selling the bond ahead of maturity.

Here is a different scenario facing the same bond. Three years ago, we bought a 10-year bond promising $60 coupon payments when the interest rate stood at 6% ($i = 0.06$). We held the bond for three years and now we are contemplating selling it. Does it make sense to sell it?

To answer the question, we may want to calculate the current yield, the yield to maturity, the holding period rate of return, and the price the bond might fetch if we sell. However, to make all of these calculations, we need to know one crucial bit of information. What is the prevailing market rate today? Let's say the interest rate increased from the 6% we bought at up to now 7%. The following bit of Python code defines a function that calculates the rate of return of a coupon bond:

```
def RoR_pcnt(P_buy, C, i_buy, i_sell, tim2mat):
    beg=1; end=tim2mat; PV_cpn=0;
    for t in range(beg, end+1):
        PV_cpn += C / (1 + i_sell) ** t
    P_sell = PV_cpn + P_buy / (1 + i_sell)**tim2mat
    RoR_pcnt = 100* (C/P_buy + (P_sell-P_buy)/P_buy)
    return (print("{:,}".format(RoR_pcnt)))
```

Given the price (P_{buy}) and interest rate (i_{buy}) at the time of the purchase, the coupon payment specified at the bond's issuance, the prevailing market interest rate at the time we want to sell the bond (i_{sell}), and the time left until the bond matures (tim2mat), we can now make all the necessary calculations. Calling these functions, we defined in Python, with the appropriate information reveals the rate of return from selling this bond early when the interest increased from 6% to 7% would be a low 1.2%, which is much lower than the 6% return we would get if we held the bond to its maturity.

```
FV=1000; P_buy=1000; i_buy=0.06; C=60; n=10; i_sell=0.07; tim2mat=6;


current_yield=C/P_buy; coupon_rate=C/FV;


print('A ten-period bond with Face value '); print(FV); print('is
↪    initially purchased for '); print(P_buy)
print('=======================================')
print('its current yield is ');print(round(C/P_buy,4))
print('=======================================')
print('its coupon rate is ');print(round(C/FV,4))
print('=======================================')
print('its YTM');print(YTM(FV, P_buy, C, n))
print('=======================================')
print('Given a rise in i to 7% at the end of year 3, the price of the
↪    bond would be');print(P_cb(FV, C, i_sell, 6))
print('=======================================')
print('Selling at this price at the beginning of year 4, the RoR of this
↪    bond would be');print(RoR_pcnt(FV, C, i_buy, i_sell, tim2mat))


A ten-period bond with Face value
1000
is initially purchased for
1000
=======================================
its current yield is
0.06
```

```
===========================================
its coupon rate is
0.06
===========================================
its YTM
0.06
```
None
```
===========================================
```
Given a rise in i to 7% at the end of year 3, the price of the bond
⏎   would be
952.3

None
```
===========================================
```
Selling at this price at the beginning of year 4, the RoR of this bond
⏎   would be
1.233

None

The interest rate increasing from 6% to 7% in our example leads to a reduction in the price of the bond so that, if sold, it incurs a reduction in the rate of return. Our example considered a modest increase in the interest rate. However, had the interest rate increased more dramatically, the rate of return might turn out to be negative if the bond sold incurs a capital loss rather than a gain.

Interest rate changes matter greatly for the ultimate period returns on bonds. However, how far in the future we need to wait for the bond to mature will also affect holding period returns. Table 6.2 shows what happens to the rate of return of various bonds that promise the same yield (10%) and have the same face value ($1,000), but differ in their maturities, if the prevailing market interest rate increases.

Table 6.2: Rates of returns of bonds with various maturities when interest rates increase from 10% to 20%.

(a) Years to maturity at purchase	(b) Initial current yield (%)	(c) Initial price ($)	(d) Price next year ($)	(e) Rate of capital gain ($)	(f) Rate of return (b + e) ($)
1	10	1,000	1,000	0.0	+10
2	10	1,000	917	−8.3	+1.7
5	10	1,000	741	−25.9	−15.9
10	10	1,000	597	−40.3	−30.3
20	10	1,000	516	−48.4	−38.4
30	10	1,000	503	−49.7	−39.7

Table 6.2 shows that if the interest rate rose from 10% to 20% at the end of year one, the price of those bonds that have not matured yet would all decrease.

Looking at the first row of the table shows the treasury with one year maturity would come due, returning the face value of $1,000 to the holder. The holder in this case would have held the one-year treasury to its maturity so she would have collected the coupon rate of 10%, which equals the current yield and the yield to maturity. The price of the bond would be $1,000 at the end of the year. Purchasing the bond for $1,000 and collecting the $1,000 face value back when it matures affords the holder neither a gain nor a loss. In this case, the rate of return on this one-year bond is the sum of the 10% current yield in column (b) plus the 0% capital gain in column (e). This is a case, where cr = cy = YTM = RoR.

However, the interest rate increase at the end of year one will affect the rates of return of all those bonds that have not yet matured by then. These are all shown in the second to the sixth row of the table.

As we discussed earlier, interest rates and bond prices are inversely related. We can see that as the interest rate doubles, the price of all these bonds from the two-year to the 30-year decline. However, the longer we have to wait for the bond to mature, the more heavily that bond's price is discounted.

As the interest rate doubles, we can see on the second row that the price of the two-year bond decreases from $1,000 down to $917. This is because this bond has only one year left before it matures, so it requires a relatively short wait.

Comparatively, the thirty-year bond on the last row experiences a much larger decline from $1,000 down to $503. This is because there are a lot more periods left (29) to discount the $1,000 principal to its present value. Therefore, the longer we have to wait for the bond to mature, the larger the capital loss as a result of an interest rate increase, or the larger the capital gain as a result of an interest rate reduction.

Generally, there is no interest rate risk for any bond whose time to maturity matches the holding period. However, since bonds are not always held to their maturity, prices and returns for long-term bonds are more volatile than those for shorter-term bonds. This introduces the concept of risk in the bond market, which we discuss in the next section.

6.5 Bond Risk

Bonds are promises to pay a certain pre-specified dollar amount sometime in the future. How can that be risky?

Essentially, risk arises if the promised payment were to be reneged on. Alternatively, risk could arise if the value of the payment were eroded even if the promised payment itself were fulfilled. Finally, unforeseen movements in interest rates might bring about risk if a bond is sold before maturity. Therefore, the risk of holding bonds falls under three main categories: *1) default risk, 2) inflation risk, and 3) interest rate risk.*

Default risk refers to the probability that the bond's issuer may not fulfill the payment. Inflation risk refers to uncertainty in future inflation, which might make uncertain the real return of the payments made. Interest rate risk refers to the chance that unforeseen increases in the interest rate could mean capital losses.

Some bonds have low or near zero default risk. They fulfill payments with such high levels of certainty that the interest rate they pay is called the risk-free rate. These are typically treasury bonds of financially sound economies such as Treasury bonds of the U. S. or Sterling Bonds of the U. K. They promise a safe or risk-free interest rate, which is the rate that savers can receive with certainty.

But other types of bonds may not be so safe. Other types of bonds, most notably corporate bonds, may carry some default risk. We can use the risk-free rate from treasuries as a reference (a benchmark) to understand how risky other corporate bonds might be. Since interest rates are used to determine the present value of future payments, they should reflect an asset's riskiness. If future payments are not certain, an asset is risky, and that risk should reduce the present value of future income.

The risk premium (ψ) is a payment on an asset that compensates the owner for taking risk, and it is typically measured as a percentage.

The present value of a certain future payment is determined using the risk-free interest rate (i_{safe}). But the present value of a riskier future payment is determined using an interest rate that includes a risk premium (ψ) reflecting the riskiness of the asset. This risk premium can be added to the YTM that the bond would typically promise if the bond were held to its maturity (i. e., no interest rate risk) and the face value were redeemed with certainty (i. e., no default risk).

For example, imagine the risk-free rate treasury rate offered today is 5%. Let's say the Microsoft corporation offers its own one-year corporate bond that also promises 5% with a face value of $100. If Microsoft's bond were free of risk, the price of the bond would be the present value of $105 in one year. This means if we bought Microsoft's bond today at a price of $100, we would collect a 5% coupon rate, which is what the bond currently yields ($i_c = 5\%$), and we would redeem it at maturity (selling it back to Microsoft) for its $100 face value, thereby collecting no capital gain/loss. Our return from this investment would have been 5%, which is what the bond yielded to its maturity. Without risk, the YTM for this bond would be 5%.

```
# YTM equation
FV=100;P=100; C=5; n=1;
YTM(FV, P, C, n)
0.05
```

Now imagine there is a 10% chance that Microsoft would go bankrupt before paying back the bond, bringing about some degree of default risk. So, there are two possible payoffs: $105 or $0. Now that the value of the bond at its maturity is not certain, we must formulate an expectation of its value. Rather than the certain $105 payment in a year, now the expected payment in a year is $94.50.

Why? Because in the presence of future uncertainty, formulating an expected value involves multiplying the probability and the amount of each expected payoff, and summing up all the outcomes. In our example, the expected value of our bond would be:

$$E(V) = (0.9) * \$105 + (0.1) * \$0 = \$94.50.$$

But this is the expected value of the bond in one year, so it needs to be discounted to the present. The price of the one-year coupon bond today would be:

$$P_{CB} = \frac{C + FV}{(1 + i)} = \frac{\$94.50}{(1 + 0.05)} = \$90.$$

Recall that in the absence of risk, the YTM of this one-year Microsoft bond was 5%. But now with some risk of default, the YTM will increase.

How? Well, since there is some risk of default now, the price of that bond today is discounted to $90 (when it would have been $100 absent risk). This means that while the coupon rate is still guaranteed at 5% (cr = $\frac{\$5}{\$100}$ = 5%), the bond's current yield has now increased to 5.6% (cy = $\frac{\$5}{\$90}$ = 5.6%). Moreover, the yield to maturity would be much higher because—were Microsoft not to default on its payment—the bond would also render a capital gain:

```
#What if the price of the bond was above the face value?
FV=100; P=90; C=5; n=1

current_yield=C/P; coupon_rate=C/FV;
YTM(FV, P, C, n);
0.157

print('A one-period bond with Face value'); print(FV);
print('sells for'); print(P)
print('=====================================')
print('current yield');print(round(current_yield,4))
print('=====================================')
print('coupon rate');print(round(coupon_rate,4))
print('=====================================')
print('YTM');print(YTM(FV, P, C, n));

A one-period bond with Face value
1000
sells for
1010
```

```
========================================
current yield
0.0495
========================================
coupon rate
0.05
========================================
YTM
0.03980099502487562
None
```

Notice that as we contend with some probability of default, the price of the bond would decline from $100 to $90 and its yield would increase from 5% to 15.8%. With higher risk, investors would demand a higher risk premium, which would lead to further yield increases and a deeper erosion in the price of bonds.

Thinking About It...

There are different types of bonds: Discount and coupon bonds. Discount bonds (zero-coupon bonds) only pay face value at maturity, whereas coupon bonds make regular coupon payments plus face value at maturity.

There are a few fundamental concepts about bond prices. The price of discount bonds is inversely related to maturity and to interest rates. Discount bonds are always sold below face value (except in rare negative interest rate scenarios). For coupon bonds, their price can be above, below, or equal to face value. Bond prices and yields are always inversely related. Treasury bonds are typically considered "risk-free" and used as benchmarks.

Bonds can be held to maturity or traded before maturity. Trading before maturity introduces interest rate risk. Longer-term bonds have more price volatility. Risk premiums increase yields and decrease prices. Understanding the relationship between prices, yields, and risks is crucial for bond investment decisions.

The chapter emphasizes the fundamental inverse relationship between bond prices and yields, and how different factors like maturity, coupon rates, and risks affect bond valuations.

6.6 Glossary

Bonds A financial instrument representing a promise to make a series of payments on specific future dates, creating a legal contract between the borrower (issuer) and lender (holder).

Capital Gain/Loss The difference between the selling price and purchase price of a bond, realized when a bond is sold before maturity.

Corporate Bonds Bonds issued by companies, which typically carry more default risk than government bonds.

Coupon Bond A bond that makes regular coupon payments throughout its life and returns the face value at maturity.

Coupon Payment Regular, fixed payments made by the bond issuer to the bond holder at specified intervals, typically annually or semi-annually, calculated as a percentage of the face value.

Coupon Rate (cr) The annual coupon payment expressed as a percentage of the bond's face value, fixed at issuance.

Current Yield (cy) The annual coupon payment divided by the bond's current market price, representing the return from coupon payments relative to the bond's price.

Default Risk The probability that a bond issuer will fail to make promised coupon payments or repay the face value at maturity.

Discount Bond (Zero-Coupon Bond) A type of bond that makes no interim payments between issuance and maturity, sold at a price below its face value and paying the full face value at maturity.

Face Value (FV) / Par Value / Principal The final payment amount promised by the bond at maturity, representing the principal amount that will be repaid to the bond holder.

Holder The buyer of a bond who becomes a lender by purchasing the debt instrument.

Holding Period Return The total return earned from holding a bond for a specific period, including both coupon payments received and any capital gains or losses.

Interest Rate Risk The risk that changes in market interest rates will affect the value of a bond, particularly relevant when selling before maturity.

Issuer The original seller of a bond, typically a government or firm that creates and sells the bond to raise funds.

Liquidity Trap A market situation where an instrument has infinite supply and zero demand, typically associated with negative interest rates.

Maturity Date The specific future date when the bond expires and the issuer must repay the face value to the bond holder.

Risk-Free Rate The interest rate that can be earned with certainty and no risk of default, typically represented by government treasury securities.

Risk Premium (ψ) The additional return required by investors to compensate for taking on risk, measured as a percentage above the risk-free rate.

Term to Maturity The time remaining until a bond's maturity date.

Treasury Bills (T-bills) A type of discount bond issued by the U. S. Treasury with maturity up to one year.

Yield to Maturity (YTM) The total return an investor would receive if they held the bond to maturity, accounting for coupon payments and any difference between purchase price and face value.

Zero-Lower-Bound (ZLB) The theoretical floor below which nominal interest rates cannot go, traditionally thought to be zero.

7 Interest Rates

Contents

In the previous chapter, we discussed the key relationship between interest rates and prices in the bond market. Interest rates are an important signal in our decisions to invest in bonds and other financial instruments. This chapter expands on this point by showing that the prevailing interest rates on bonds are determined by the current forces of supply and demand in the bond market. But they are also heavily affected by expectations of the future.

7.1 Bond Supply and Bond Demand

The forces of supply and demand determine bond prices and bond yields. A bond supply curve is the relationship between the price and the quantity of bonds people are willing to sell, all else being equal. So it is a schedule of prices and quantities. We typically express bond supply as a curve in a two-dimensional space, with bond prices on the vertical axis and bond quantities on the horizontal axis. In that two-dimensional space, the bond supply curve slopes upward. This means that, ceteris paribus, the higher the price of a bond, the larger the quantity supplied. But why is this the case?

There are two main reasons related to each side of the market. The first is from the point of view of the investor (or lender or holder) of the bond and the second is from the issuer (or borrower or seller). Consider the first point of view of a typical bond investor who holds a portfolio of bonds. All else being equal, the higher the price of those bonds, the more tempting it is to sell those bonds ahead of maturity and possibly collect higher capital gains. So, at higher prices, the quantity supplied of second-hand bonds (those originally issued in the past but that are yet to mature) should also increase.

Now consider the second point view of some corporation or government. The higher the price at which they can sell the bond, the lower the yield they have to promise on it. This means that if, say, a company is seeking to finance a project, issuing brand new bonds at high prices is a way to cheaply borrow to finance capital expenditures. So, at higher prices, the quantity supplied of newly issued bonds should also increase. All else being equal, for a $1,000 one-year discount bond, the quantity of bonds supplied will be higher at $950 than it will be at $900. See Figure 7.1.

The bond demand curve is the relationship between the price and the quantity of bonds that investors demand, all else being equal.

https://doi.org/10.1515/9783111193120-010

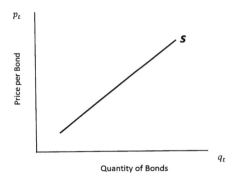

Figure 7.1: A supply schedule for bonds.

Let's now discuss the demand side. Recall from previous chapters that bond prices are inversely related to their yield. Therefore, the higher the yield of a given bond, the lower its price, all else being equal. The lower the price bond holders must pay for a fixed-dollar payment on a future date, the more likely they are to buy a bond.

There are two reasons for this. Since lower prices come hand-in-hand with higher yields, buying inexpensive bonds typically means receiving higher current yields and, importantly, higher YTM were the bonds to be held until maturity (all else remaining the same, particularly risk remaining the same).

Another reason why at lower prices investors might be motivated to buy more is that if prices are low, there may be more room for upward movement in bond prices in the future, which would translate to capital gains were those cheap bonds to be sold before maturity. All else being equal, for a $1,000 one-year discount bond, the quantity of bonds demanded will be lower at $950 than it will be at $900. See Figure 7.2.

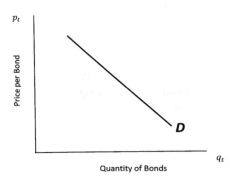

Figure 7.2: A demand schedule for bonds.

When the quantity of bonds supplied (Q_S) and the quantity of bonds demanded (Q_D) equal each other, we say the bond market is in equilibrium, and this point is reflected where both curves meet. In Figure 7.3 below, (P^*) denotes the equilibrium price. What if bonds prices were below equilibrium? Say current bonds prices (P_1) were unusually low. Then, many investors who wish to buy bonds cannot generally get them at a price below equilibrium. This would generate a shortage (an excess demand) of bonds in the market.

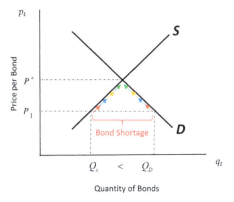

Figure 7.3: A shortage in the bond market.

Bonds are clearly a desirable product. Whenever there is a shortage of a given good that is typically desirable, we tend to see a bidding up of its price.

Therefore, if bond investors cannot find the bonds they wish to hold at the current price P_1, they may begin to bid up the prices they are willing to buy them for. This is reflected by the arrows alongside the demand curve in Figure 7.3.

Bond issuers would be all too willing to supply more bonds at higher prices, which is reflected by the arrows alongside the supply curve. Both of these forces drive up the price of the bond from P_1 toward equilibrium.

In a process called market clearing, this bidding up of prices will shrink the shortage regions (the difference between Q_S and Q_D) until the bond market returns to its equilibrium condition, where $Q_S = Q_D$ when the price reaches P^*.

Conversely, what if bond prices were above equilibrium? Say current bonds prices (P_2) were unusually high. In this case, we would have the opposite scenario, where at a high price bond issuers would be all too happy to supply more bonds. However, it would be difficult to find investors to be willing to pay such a high price. This would generate a surplus (or excess supply) of bonds.

Since at the high price of P_2 suppliers cannot find buyers, bond issuers/sellers will begin to cut prices. Excess supply puts downward pressures on the price (reflected on the downward arrows alongside the two curves in Figure 7.4) until once again markets clear and the quantity supplied equals the quantity demanded.

From this analysis, we can see that any change in the price (and the quantity demanded or supplied) of the bond causes movements alongside the supply and demand curves for bonds. Essentially, any market surprise that impacts the variables in the axes (price and quantity) can be reflected by movements along the curves. In other words,

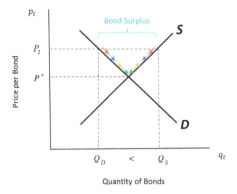

Figure 7.4: A surplus of bonds.

the curves themselves do not change (they do not shift or tilt) in response to shocks to the bond price (or quantity).

This begs the question: what factors will impact (shift) the supply and demand curves? Whatever those factors might be, we know they cannot be the two variables (P and Q) shown on the axes. They must be something else.

Let's first discuss factors that may potentially affect the demand (curve) for bonds. Since demand typically describes the willingness and ability to purchase, if a given factor is to have an impact on bond demand it must be because it affects the willingness or ability to buy it.

One factor is the personal (or institutional) wealth of the investor. Insofar as bonds are generally desirable goods (what economists call normal goods), bond demand should increase when the ability to purchase (wealth) increases. On the other hand, if an investor experiences a sharp reduction in wealth, she can now afford fewer bonds, so, all else being equal, her demand for bonds will decrease.

These shocks affecting the ability to purchase bonds are typically called *an income or wealth effect*, which is often determined by current forces in the market.

While the ability to purchase bonds is generally tied to the current financial health of the investor and current market conditions, the willingness to buy bonds is typically shaped by expectations of the future.

Since inflation often erodes real returns, changes in expected inflation may impact bond demand. For example, if investors expected inflation to increase in the future, the real value of the bond's promised payments would decrease, making it less desirable to purchase today. On the other hand, with declines in inflation expectations, investors would expect an appreciation in the real value of the bond's future payments, making the bonds more desirable to purchase today.

Expectations of future interest rates will also affect the demand curve for bonds. Recall from previous chapters that prices and interest rates are inversely related. Since changes in prices are on the vertical axis of our graphs, they do not affect the demand (curve) for bonds, they only affect the quantity demanded through movements alongside the curve. So, this must also be the case for interest rates or yields.

Changes in current interest rates will not impact (shift) the demand for bonds, but changes in expected future interest rates will. For example, if interest rates were expected to fall, investors would want to buy more bonds now while the yield is higher. Because expected declines in interest rates would foretell expected increases in the price of the bonds—opening opportunities for higher capital gains—bonds would be more desirable to buy now if we expected interest rates to decline.

Conversely, if interest rates are expected to increase, investors might buy fewer bonds now and wait until those expectations materialize to higher yields.

Expected returns work in a similar fashion to expected interest rates in their effect on bond demand. But, while expected interest rate changes affect the willingness to buy the bond, expected returns affect the willingness to buy the bond relative to alternative assets. This is typically called a *substitution effect*.

For example, if relative to alternative assets (e. g., money markets) bond returns were expected to increase in the future, then even on a fixed budget, the investor might sell off (substitute away from) other assets and buy (substitute into) more bonds.

Other examples of factors that determine bond demand through a substitution effect are risk and liquidity. As we discussed in previous chapters, risk is not an absolute, but a relative concept.

For example, if bonds became less risky relative to alternative investment, all else being equal, they would become more desirable, thereby increasing demand for bonds. Furthermore, investors like liquidity, all else being equal. The easier it is to convert a particular bond into cash, the more liquid it is. The more liquid the bond is, the more desirable it is, thereby increasing its demand.

An increase in bond demand means that, independently of prices, more quantity is being demanded. This suggests that whether prices are high, moderate, or low, some factor that serves to increase bond demand would shift the bond demand curve to the right, guaranteeing more quantity demanded at any given price. This is shown in Figure 7.5. Say we begin in the equilibrium point 1, where the S and D curves meet at price P^*, as the market clears to $Q_S = Q_D = Q^*$.

The demand for bonds would increase for any given price if investors: 1) experienced an increase in wealth, 2) expected lower levels of future inflation, 3) expected future interest rates to decrease, 4) expected lower returns in money markets (a substitute for bond markets), or 5) expected more uncertainty/risk in the stock market—all else being equal.

This would lead to a wholesale shift to the right of the demand curve to a new demand curve D_2.

After the rightward shift in Figure 7.5, the old equilibrium point, (Point 1 in the graph) would no longer hold. That is because, while P^* used to imply $Q_S = Q_D = Q^*$, after the curve shifts right, P^* pins down the same quantity supplied (Q_S) from the supply curve as before.

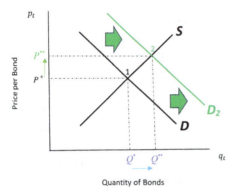

Figure 7.5: An increase in the demand for bonds.

However, Q_D now falls in the new D_2 curve generating a shortage of bonds at the old price P^*. Market forces would bid up the price of bonds to a new equilibrium condition (point 2 in the graph) at a higher equilibrium price P^{**} and higher quantity of bonds sold $Q_S^{new} = Q_D^{new} = Q^{**}$. Table 7.1 summarizes the various factors that would result in the rightward demand shift displayed in Figure 7.5.

In conclusion, all else being equal, any factor that would serve to increase the demand for bonds would eventually increase the quantity sold of bonds, as well as raise equilibrium prices, and lower equilibrium yields in the bond market.

Table 7.1: Factors that affect bond demand and shift the demand curve.

Surprise change in	Effect on bond demand
An increase in wealth increases demand for all normal (non-inferior) assets, including bonds	Bond Demand shifts ⟹ Bond Prices ⇑ Bond Yields ⇓
An increase in expected inflation makes bonds with fixed nominal payments less desirable	Bond Demand shifts ⟸ Bond Prices ⇓ Bond Yields ⇑
An increase in expected returns on bonds relative to substitute financial instruments makes purchasing bonds more attractive now	Bond Demand shifts ⟹ Bond Prices ⇑ Bond Yields ⇓
An increase in the risk of bonds relative to substitute assets makes purchasing bonds less attractive now	Bond Demand shifts ⟸ Bond Prices ⇓ Bond Yields ⇑
An increase in the liquidity of bonds relative to the liquidity of alternative assets makes purchasing bonds more attractive now	Bond Demand shifts ⟹ Bond Prices ⇑ Bond Yields ⇓

Let's now discuss factors that may potentially affect the supply (curve) for bonds. Recall, the bond supply curve is the relationship between the price and the quantity of bonds that institutions supply, all else being equal. Factors that may shift the supply curve of bonds may fall under two main categories: those that affect the institution that issues the bonds (idiosyncratic factors) and those that affect the economy (systemic or economy-wide factors).

Institutionally, any change in a government's borrowing needs will impact the supply of bonds outstanding, all else being equal. Often, local governments finance expenditures by issuing municipal bonds. When local governments want to increase expenditures on public works (such infrastructure projects as parks, roads, government buildings like City Hall, etc.) or expand on services (as those offered by parks and recreational facilities), new bond issuance will increase.

When central governments want to increase spending (e. g., on national defense) above and beyond what they appropriate in taxes, they may issue treasury bonds. Increases in a central government's spending (Federal spending in the U. S.) lead to new treasury issuance. Any increase in municipal or treasury bond issuance serves to increase the supply of bonds at any price. This shifts the supply curve of bonds to the right.

Another institutional source of bond supply is the issuance of corporate bonds. When firms and corporations want to increase capital spending (higher expenditures on property, plant, and equipment) or invest in research and development, they may finance these expenditures by issuing new corporate bonds. Any increase in corporate bond issuance serves to increase the supply of bonds at any price. This shifts the supply curve of bonds to the right.

There are also economy-wide factors that may also affect the bond supply. For example, a general improvement in business conditions or an increase in confidence about economic conditions may lead firms to become more optimistic about the future and increase investment. This would serve to shift the supply of bonds to the right.

Recall we concluded earlier that changes in expected inflation affect the demand for bonds. They may also affect supply. For example, even if nominal face values and coupon payments may remain unaffected by inflation expectations, when expected inflation rises, the real cost of borrowing falls. Cheaper borrowing costs may spur more borrowing by way of higher bond issuance, which shifts the supply curve of bonds to the right.

An increase in bond supply means that, independently of prices, more quantity is being supplied. This suggests that whether prices are high, moderate, or low, some factor that serves to increase bond supply would shift the bond supply curve to the right, guaranteeing more quantity supplied at any given price. This is shown in Figure 7.6. Say we begin in the equilibrium point 1, where the S and D curves meet at price P^* as the market clears to $Q_S = Q_D = Q^*$.

An increase in government deficits resulting from higher expenditures relative to government revenues and/or an improvement in general business conditions and/or an increase in inflation expectations would all lead to an increase in the supply of bonds

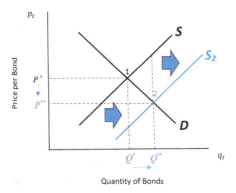

Figure 7.6: An increase in the supply of bonds.

for any given price, leading to a wholesale shift to the right of the supply curve to a new supply curve S_2. After the rightward shift in Figure 7.6, the old equilibrium point, (point 1 in the graph) would no longer hold.

That is because, while P^* used to imply $Q_S = Q_D = Q^*$, after the curve shifts right, P^* pins down the same quantity demanded (Q_D) from the demand curve (D) as before, but the quantity supplied (Q_S) now falls on the new supply curve (S_2) generating a surplus of bonds at the old price P^*.

Market forces would bid down the price of bonds to a new equilibrium condition (point 2 in the graph) at a lower equilibrium price P^{**} and a higher quantity of bonds sold $Q_S^{new} = Q_D^{new} = Q^{**}$. Table 7.2 summarizes the various factors that would result in the rightward shift of the supply curve displayed in Figure 7.6. In conclusion, all else being equal, any factor that would serve to increase the supply of bonds would eventually increase the quantity sold of bonds, reduce equilibrium prices, and raise equilibrium yields in the bond market.

So far, we have discussed different factors that affect the supply or the demand curves for bonds and their ultimate effect on bond yields.

Sometimes, a given factor may affect both supply and demand. In those cases, we need to ascertain whether the effect on both curves lead yields to shift in the same direction or not. If both curves shift in the same direction in response to a given change in a factor, then we have what we call an *augmenting effect*.

An augmenting effect occurs when the effect of a particular shock is compounded due to the similar responses of supply and demand. On the other hand, if the supply and demand for bonds lead yields to move in different directions, then we have what we call an *offsetting* effect.

An offsetting effect occurs when two shocks counteract each other. In these cases, we need to determine which is the dominant shift to effectively understand what the ultimate effect on the bond's yield will be.

For example, an economic downturn would impact both curves. Such a downturn typically erodes consumer confidence. Firms would expect a reduction of consumer de-

Table 7.2: Factors that affect bond supply and shift the supply curve.

Surprise change in	Effect on bond supply
An increase in government deficits where government expenditures outpace government revenues	Bond Supply shifts ⇒ Bond Prices ⇑ Bond Yields ⇓
An increase in expected inflation that reduces the real cost of debt repayment	Bond Supply shifts ⇒ Bond Prices ⇓ Bond Yields ⇑
An increase in the demand for financing capital expenditures by corporations	Bond Supply shifts ⇒ Bond Prices ⇓ Bond Yields ⇑
An increase in market confidence or an improvement in business conditions	Bond Supply shifts ⇒ Bond Prices ⇓ Bond Yields ⇑

mand for the goods they sell. They may respond by reducing their own capital investment, so their demand for financing added capital expenditures would go down and they would issue fewer bonds. An economic downturn may lead to a reduction in the supply of bonds (regardless of price), essentially shifting the bond supply curve to the left.

The other side of this coin is the effect on bond investors. An economic downturn often comes with job separation and reductions of income. So, it often means the economy is experiencing a negative income/wealth effect. When there is an erosion in income, wages, and wealth, investors and households will demand fewer goods, and this may include bonds.

An economic downturn may lead to a reduction in the demand for bonds (regardless of price), essentially shifting the bond demand curve to the left. Both curves shifting left lead to an offsetting effect on bond yields. Therefore, the effect would be ambiguous unless we knew which was the dominant force.

Figure 7.7 shows a scenario where investors are more responsive than bond issuers to an economic downturn. If the demand curve for bonds were the dominant force, then the demand curve would shift to the left more than the leftward shift of the supply curve. Therefore, the new equilibrium price of the bond would go down from point 1 to point 2 on the graph. In this case, bond prices would go down and bond yields would increase in an economic downturn.

Figure 7.8 shows the opposite scenario to the same economic downturn. In this case, if bond issuers responded more than investors during an economic downturn, then it would be the supply curve for bonds that would dominate. In this case the bond supply curve would shift to the left more than the leftward shift of the demand curve. Therefore, the new equilibrium price of the bond would increase from point 1 to point 2 on the

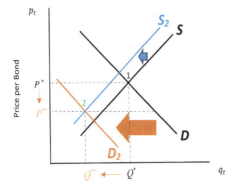

Figure 7.7: Dominant response of bond demand to an economic downturn.

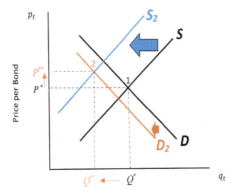

Figure 7.8: Dominant response of bond supply to an economic downturn.

graph, and we would conclude that bond prices would increase and bond yields would go down in an economic downturn.

If we were not clear on whether supply or demand dominates the effect, both curves shifting could give an ambiguous answer in terms of equilibrium bond prices and yields. Even if the theory were ambiguous, the real world is not. The data suggests that in economic recessions, interest rates tend to fall, meaning that bond prices should rise.

7.2 Interest Rate Spreads and Bond Ratings

Changes in bond prices and the associated changes in interest rates can have a pronounced effect on the borrowing costs corporations face. The financial market often experiences simultaneous increases in some interest rates and reductions in others. These gaps—the percent differences among various rates—are called *interest rate spreads*, and economists often look for meaningful market signals arising from interest rate spreads.

For example, an increase in the perceived risk of companies' bonds often leads to declines in prices, which results in interest rate increases and higher corporate borrowing costs. If treasuries remain insulated from this higher risk, this serves to increase the interest rate spread (or simply "spread") between corporate and treasury yields.

We must be able to distinguish between many different types of bonds that are traded in financial markets. In previous chapters, we have already discussed, many factors affecting the price of a bond, such as time to maturity, prevailing interest rates, inflation expectations, perceptions of risk, and so on.

Because default is one of the most important risks a bond holder faces, independent companies (rating agencies) regularly evaluate the creditworthiness of potential borrowers (bond issuers). These companies analyze the financial well-being of bond issuers and estimate the likelihood that a corporate or government borrower will make a bond's promised payments.

The U. S. government has acknowledged a few firms as "nationally recognized statistical rating organizations" (NRSROs). The best known bond rating services are: Moody's https://www.moodys.com/, Standard and Poor (S&P) https://www.spglobal.com/ratings/en/, and Fitch https://www.fitchratings.com/. They monitor the status of individual bond issuers and assess the likelihood a lender will be repaid by the bond issuer. A high rating suggests that a bond issuer will have little problem meeting a bond's payment obligations.

Firms or governments with an exceptionally strong financial position carry the highest ratings, typically referred to as triple A. Since these highly rated institutions are deemed relatively safe from default risk, they can issue the highest-rated bonds with the promise of relatively low yields (e. g. Johnson & Johnson, Microsoft, and the government of Norway).

Figure 7.9 shows the various grades that are available for bonds. The top four categories are considered investment-grade bonds. These are reserved for bonds with little risk of default, typically selected for most government issuers and corporations that are among the most financially sound.

Anything below Baa for Moody's or BBB for Standard & Poor's is considered below investment grade. They are often referred to as speculative or *junk bonds*, because they carry significantly higher risk of default.

The distinction between investment-grade and speculative, non-investment-grade bonds is important. For example, a number of regulated institutional investors are not allowed to invest in bonds rated below investment grade, which is Baa on Moody's scale or BBB on Standard & Poor's scale. This means fewer potential investors can demand these bonds, so companies or governments that are rated below investment grade must promise higher yields to attract demand.

There are two types of junk bonds. *Fallen angels* are bonds that were once investment-grade, but their issuers fell on hard times. There are also junk bonds that begin trading at a junk rating because they may be sold by issuers about which there is little known. Ratings are not fixed. Material changes in a firm's or government's financial con-

Bond Rating			
Moody's	Standard & Poor's	Grade	Risk
Aaa	AAA	Investment	Lowest Risk
Aa	AA	Investment	Low Risk
A	A	Investment	Low Risk
Baa	BBB	Investment	Medium Risk
Ba, B	BB, B	Junk	High Risk
Caa/Ca/C	CCC/CC/C	Junk	Highest Risk
C	D	Junk	In Default

Investopedia

Image by Sabrina Jiang © Investopedia 2020

Figure 7.9: A table of bond ratings.

ditions may precipitate changes in its debt ratings, leading to rating downgrades—which lower an issuer's bond rating—or rating upgrades—which raise an issuer's bond rating.

In addition to corporate and treasury bonds, rating agencies also rate other financial instruments, such as commercial paper.

Commercial paper is a short-term version of a bond, where the borrower offers no collateral, so the debt is unsecured. Commercial paper is issued on a discount basis, as a zero-coupon bond specifying a single future payment with no promise for coupon payments. While commercial paper has typical maturities of less than 270 days, most of it is issued with a maturity of 5 to 45 days and is used, almost exclusively, for short-term financing. A large portion of commercial paper is held by money-market mutual funds.

The rating agencies rate the creditworthiness of commercial paper issuers in the same way they do bond issuers. Almost all commercial paper instruments carry Moody's $P-1$ or $P-2$ rating. P stands for prime grade commercial paper. Speculative-grade commercial paper does exist, but not because it was issued as such.

Ratings agencies have enormous power to affect interest rates and yields. In 2010, the government issued financial reform legislation called the Dodd-Frank Wall Street Reform and Consumer Protection Act, partially to reduce reliance on ratings agencies.

Bond ratings are designed to reflect default risk. The lower the rating, the higher the risk of default. This drives the price of the bond down and the associated yield higher. Because risk is a relative concept, to understand quantitative ratings, it is easier to compare them to a benchmark. Since the U.S. Treasury issued bonds are viewed as having little default risk, they are often used as a benchmark, even globally.

Since U.S. treasuries are a benchmark for many other bonds—and the yield of any given bond is explained in part by the yield of U.S. Treasury—when Treasury yields move, all other yields tend to move along with them in a process that is called *co-movement*.

Figure 7.10: Co-movement in bond yields.
Note: Figure provided by the Federal Reserve Economic Database (FRED) of the Federal Reserve Bank of St. Louis.

Figure 7.10 shows a plot of the risk structure of interest rates. For the vast majority of the postwar experience, the 10-year U. S. Treasury rate, which acts as a reference rate for many corporate bonds, lies below investment-grade corporate yields. Changes in the U. S. Treasury yields account for most of the movement in the Aaa and Baa bond yields.

From 1965 to 2021, the 10-year U. S. Treasury bond yield has averaged 6.27%, about a full percentage point below the average yield on Aaa bonds (7.34%) and two percentage points below the average yield on Baa bonds (8.38%).

Ratings are crucial to corporations' ability to raise financing. A lower rate increases the costs of funding. Since investors clearly must be compensated for assuming risk, the lower the rating of the corporate bond, the higher the risk premium, and, thus, the bigger the spread with the 10-year rate. This explains why the spread between the Aaa and the 10-year U. S. Treasury is smaller than the spread between the Baa and the 10-year U. S. Treasury.

7.3 Term Structure of Interest Rates

In addition to risk, other factors separate different types of bonds. On the other hand, bonds often have similar characteristics. Bonds with the same default rate and tax status but different maturity dates often have different yields. We can think of longer-term bonds as a composite of a series of shorter-term bonds, and their yields depend on what people expect to happen in the future.

The relationship among bonds with the same risk characteristics but different maturities is called the *term structure of interest rates*.

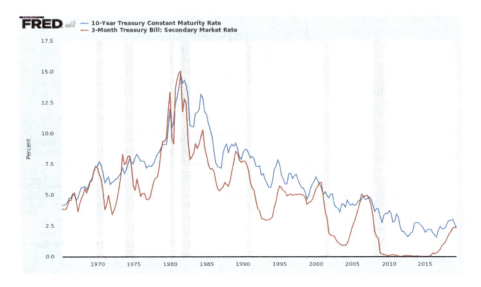

Figure 7.11: Long- and short-term treasury yields.
Note: Figure provided by the Federal Reserve Economic Database (FRED) of the Federal Reserve Bank of St. Louis.

Figure 7.11 compares the three-month and 10-year U.S. Treasury yields in the postwar period. We can see that, while these two treasuries have different maturities, their interest rates tend to move together. We can also see that yields on short-term bonds are somewhat more volatile than yields on long-term bonds. Moreover, long-term yields tend to be higher than short-term yields, as the 10-year treasury rate, generally, tends to be above the three-month treasury yield. Importantly, the gap between the two rates is not fixed. The spread between the 10-year treasury bond and the three-month treasury bill is sometimes wider and sometimes narrower.

A *yield curve* is a popular chart in financial analysis that summarizes the yields of treasuries of various maturities at a specific point in time. Yield curves are a graphical representation of the term structure of interest rates. Figure 7.12 shows the yield curve on May 13, 2018 (source: Wikipedia). The yield curve is typically a snapshot in time where the maturities are shown on the horizontal axis, with short-term bonds on the left and longer-term bonds on the right-hand side.

This yield curve is upward sloping, which means that the short-term bonds had a lower yield than longer-term bonds on that date. While the slope of the yield curve can vary from day to day—and over the months and years—most of the time the yield curve tends to slope upward, as it is shown in Figure 7.12.

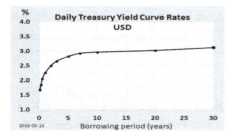

Figure 7.12: An example of a yield curve.

Many theories have been proposed to explain the term structure of interest rates. The first theory we will examine is called the *expectations hypothesis*. This theory focuses on the risk-free interest rate. The risk-free interest rate can be computed, assuming there is no uncertainty about the future. This is an unrealistic assumption, which other theories will relax. For now, we make the assumption of future certainty. Certainty means that bonds of different maturities are perfect substitutes for each other.

For example, if there is no uncertainty, then an investor should be indifferent between holding a single two-year bond or a series of two one-year bonds. The expectations hypothesis implies that the current two-year interest rate should equal the average of the current one-year rate and the one-year interest rate one year in the future. For example, if the current interest rate on the one-year bond is 1% and the future interest rate on the one-year bond is 3%, then the current interest rate on the two-year bond is $(1 + 3)/2 = 2\%$.

When interest rates are expected to rise, long-term interest rates will be higher than short-term interest rates. In these cases, the yield curve will slope up. On the other hand, if interest rates are expected to fall, the yield curve will slope down, and if interest rates are expected to stay the same, the yield curve will be flat. This is shown in Figure 7.13.

Figure 7.13: Possible slopes of the yield curve.

The expectations hypothesis suggests that if bonds of different maturities are perfect substitutes for each other, then we can construct investment strategies that must have the same yields.

For example, Susan, a bond investor, could buy a three-year treasury bond and hold it to maturity. At period t (today), this bond offers a current yield of i_{3t}. If Susan buys this bond and holds it to maturity, one dollar of this bond today yields $(1 + i_{3t})(1 + i_{3t})(1 + i_{3t})$ three years later.

But Susan has another option. She could buy a one-year treasury with a current yield of i_{1t} and, at the end of the year, collect the proceeds and use them to buy the one-year bond again (this is called rollover). Then, at the end of year two she could collect the proceeds from the one-year bond and, again, roll it over into a third year.

Susan can read financial news and gather quotes from many financial assets on offer today. So, she can see the current yields of the one-year and three-year treasury bonds today (at period t). However, today she cannot see what the one-year treasury bond will pay one year from today (at period $t + 1$), or what the one-year treasury bond will pay two years from today (at period $t + 2$).

So, today, Susan can see what the one-year treasury yields i_{1t} trades at, but she cannot see what it will pay a year from today—she cannot see i_{1t+1} today. The best she can do today is formulate an expectation (her own educated guess or forecast) of what the one-year bond will pay a year from today. We will denote this with an superscript e to denote expectation (i_{1t+1}^e).

Similarly, she needs to formulate an expectation today of what the one-year bond will yield in two years (i_{1t+2}^e). If Susan buys this one-year bond with a plan to roll it over twice, one dollar of this bond today yields $(1 + i_{1t})(1 + i_{1t+1}^e)(1 + i_{1t+2}^e)$ three years later, given a rollover plan.

Therefore, Susan, has these two options. She could buy a short-term bond (a one-year treasury) three times in three years; or could buy a single long-term bond (a three-year treasury) and hold it to its maturity. The expectations hypothesis suggests Susan should be indifferent between the two options, which means the returns from the two options should equal each other as follows:

$$(1 + i_{3t})(1 + i_{3t})(1 + i_{3t}) = (1 + i_{1t})(1 + i_{1t+1}^e)(1 + i_{1t+2}^e).$$

Rearranging this equation, we can now write the three-year yield as the average of the current and expected future one-year rates:

$$i_{3t} = \frac{i_{1t} + i_{1t+1}^e + i_{1t+2}^e}{3}.$$

More generally, the expectations hypothesis allows us to write the yield of a long-term bond of arbitrary maturity (n) as an average of current and expected future yields of shorter maturity bonds, so that:

$$i_{nt} = \frac{i_{1t} + i_{1t+1}^e + i_{1t+2}^e + \cdots + i_{1t++n-1}^e}{n}.$$

This equation seems consistent with the co-movement we see in treasury rates, where interest rates of different maturities will move together.

For example, if the current yield on the one-year treasury (i_{1t}) rises, it is clear from the equation that the long-term yield (i_{nt}) also rises, all else being equal.

This equation also suggests that the yields on short-term bonds will be more volatile than yields on long-term bonds. Long-term rates are averages of short-term rates, so changing one short-term rate has little effect on the long-term rate. For example, if the one-year treasury bonds' interest increased by 100 basis points, the thirty-year treasury yield would only go up by 3.3 basis points (100/30).

Similarly, if i_{1t} decreased by 100 basis points, i_{nt} would decrease by 3.3 basis points. This means that a 2% swing in the short-term interest rate comes hand-in-hand with a much smaller swing of 0.07% in the long-term bond.

However, looking at the equation above, the expectations hypothesis cannot explain why long-term yields tend to be higher than short-term yields most of the time. The equation suggests that the yield curve will slope upward only when interest rates are expected to rise.

Since the yield curve normally slopes upward, the expectations hypothesis would suggest that interest rates are expected to rise most of the time. But this is not the case with the data we see. As we saw in Figures 7.10 and 7.11 above, interest rates are just as likely to go up as they are to go down over time.

Therefore, the expectations hypothesis provides a good explanation for two features we see in interest rate data: co-movement and higher volatility in the short term. But it does not explain well the third feature that—though interest rates fluctuate over time— they are not always expected to continuously increase over time.

The expectations hypothesis is quite useful but it falls just shy of explaining all three aspects of interest rate behavior. So, we look for a way to augment the hypothesis. So far, we have abstracted from risk in interest rate determination. We need to extend the expectations hypothesis to include risk.

The yield curve provides a summary of the term structure of interest rates as it is populated by treasuries of different maturities. Even treasuries that are free of default risk, such as U. S. treasuries, carry other types of risk. As we discussed in previous chapters, bond holders face both inflation and interest rate risk. The longer the term of the bond, the greater both types of risk.

Inflation risk refers to the impact that inflation will have on the purchasing power of the nominal returns the investor derives from the bond. Therefore, investing in bonds involves successfully computing real returns from nominal returns, which requires a forecast of expected future inflation. The further we look into the future, the greater the uncertainty of where inflation will be, and, thus, the greater the uncertainty that surrounds the real return of the bond. Therefore, a bond's inflation risk increases with its time to maturity.

As we discussed in previous chapters, there is no interest rate risk for bonds that are held to maturity. Bond holders face interest rate risk when they sell their bonds ahead of maturity. Interest rate risk arises from the mismatch between the investor's investment horizon and a bond's time to maturity. If a bond holder plans to sell a bond prior to maturity, changes in the interest rate generate capital gains or losses. Those gains or losses are magnified with time to maturity. The longer the term of the bond, or the more distant the time to maturity, the greater the price changes for a given change in interest rates and the larger the potential for capital losses. Thus, a bond's interest rate risk increases with its time to maturity.

Since risk increases at longer maturities, investors will require compensation for the increase in risk they take for buying longer-term bonds. So, we can think about bond yields as having two components: one that is risk free—explained by the expectations hypothesis—and one that is a risk premium—explained by inflation and interest rate risk.

These two components are reflected in what is known as the *Liquidity Premium Theory* (*LPT*) of the term structure of interest rates. The LPT essentially augments the expectations hypothesis with an extra term that accounts for the risk premium that investors typically demand in compensation for increased risk.

Just like the expectations hypothesis, the LPT allows us to write the yield of a long-term bond of arbitrary maturity (*n*) as an average of current and expected future yields of shorter maturity bonds. But unlike the expectations hypothesis, the LPT does not require the long-term yield to exactly offset the average of current and expected future shorter-term yields.

Rearranging the expectations hypothesis equation shows the exact offset as follows:

$$i_{nt} - \frac{i_{1t} + i^e_{1t+1} + i^e_{1t+2} + \cdots + i^e_{1t+n-1}}{n} = 0.$$

However, the LPT suggests that the two yields for the long and short terms may not offset each other. If the long-term yield is higher than the current and expected short-term yields, then that difference may arise from a higher risk of holding the long treasury bond.

$$i_{nt} - \frac{i_{1t} + i^e_{1t+1} + i^e_{1t+2} + \cdots + i^e_{1t++n-1}}{n} > 0.$$

Therefore, any positive difference between the long-term yield and the average short-term yields must be explained by a risk premium (rp_n) that compensates the investor for holding the typically riskier long-term bond. The LPT equation becomes:

$$i_{nt} = \frac{i_{1t} + i^e_{1t+1} + i^e_{1t+2} + \cdots + i^e_{1t++n-1}}{n} + rp_n.$$

This equation shows that risk is the key to understanding the slope of the yield curve. If the yield curve is upward sloping, then it must be the case that the risk premium is positive, which compensates the investor for holding the riskier long-term bond. The fact that risk premia on long-term bonds are typically positive explains why the yield curve is most often upward sloping.

A historical inspection of the average slope of the term structure over a long period can give us some idea of the size of the risk premium. Figure 7.14 shows that from 1985 to 2023, the difference between the interest rate on a 10-year Treasury bond (5.2%) and that on a three-month Treasury bill (3.4%) has averaged nearly 2 percentage points. The risk premium varies over time, but it has mostly been positive around 2%.

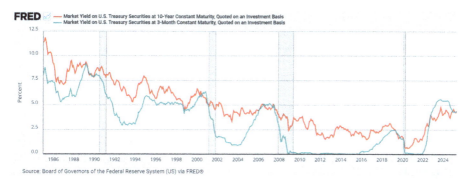

Figure 7.14: Infrequent yield curve inversions.
Note: Figure provided by the Federal Reserve Economic Database (FRED) of the Federal Reserve Bank of St. Louis.

We can also see that, quite infrequently, the three-month treasury bill has risen above the 10-year treasury. This would suggest an inversion of the yield curve, where the longer end of the yield curve sits lower than the short end. This indicates that the risk of holding long-term bonds is dominated by the risk of holding short-term bonds—which means the risk premium turns negative. The figure shows the negative risk premium is most evident during 2023. A negative risk premium suggests that long-term treasuries trade at a discount. Over the years, economists have identified that these periods of long-term treasuries trading at risk discounts occur when there is a lot of risk on the short-term of the yield curve, which seems to be followed by recessionary pressures roughly about one year after the yield curve initially inverts.

Risk spreads provide one type of information and the term structure another. For example, an economic slowdown or recession does not affect the risk of holding government bonds that are held to maturity. However, the immediate impact of a pending recession is to raise the risk premium on privately issued bonds. And—while the impact of a recession on companies with high bond ratings is usually quite small—the lower the initial grade of the bond, the more the default-risk premium rises as general economic conditions deteriorate.

Figure 7.15 shows the annual GDP growth over four decades, superimposed on shading that shows the dates of recessions. During these shaded periods, GDP growth is usu-

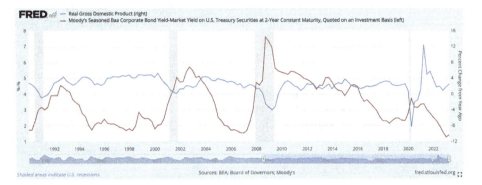

Figure 7.15: Bond risk (Baa bond yield minus two-year Treasury rate) and economic activity (real GDP growth).
Note: Figure provided by the Federal Reserve Economic Database (FRED) of the Federal Reserve Bank of St. Louis.

ally negative. On the right axis, the figure shows the spread between yields on Baa-rated bonds and U. S. Treasury bonds. We can clearly see that when risk spread rises, output growth falls.

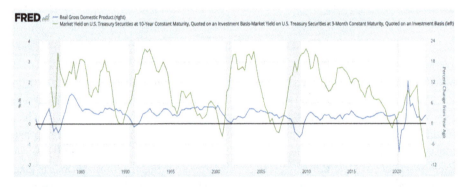

Figure 7.16: Bond risk (10- minus two-year Treasury rate spread) and economic activity (real GDP growth).
Note: Figure provided by the Federal Reserve Economic Database (FRED) of the Federal Reserve Bank of St. Louis.

Figure 7.16 shows annual GDP growth and the slope of the yield curve, measured as the difference between the 10-year and three-month yields. We can see that when the term spread falls, GDP growth tends to fall about one year later, more or less. When this term spread falls below zero, this is consistent with a yield curve inversion. The figure shows the term spread became flat roughly one year before the 1991 recession. And for the 2001 and 2008 recessions and the COVID downturn, the yield curve inverted roughly one year prior to the onset of those economic recessions.

Overall, the graph shows the yield curve is a solid leading indicator of recessions. It shows GDP growth in the current year is strongly correlated with the slope of the yield curve one year earlier: and if we shifted GDP growth one year earlier, then the troughs in the two lines clearly move together. This shows that the yield curve is a valuable forecasting tool for timing recession. However, the yield curve is less useful for predicting the severity of a recession and it did not predict the depth or duration of the Great Recession of 2007–2009.

Thinking About It...

Bond prices and quantities are determined by supply and demand forces. Higher prices encourage more bond issuance and discourage more bond purchases. Bond market reaches equilibrium where the supply and demand curves intersect. Various factors can shift these curves. Government deficits, business conditions, and inflation expectations may shift bond supply. Wealth changes, inflation expectations, and risk perceptions may shift bond demand.

Different bonds have different interest rates based on their risk levels. Rating agencies (Moody's, S&P, Fitch) evaluate bond creditworthiness. Ratings range from AAA (highest quality) to C/D (lowest/default), which characterize investment grade vs. speculative ("junk") bonds. U. S. Treasury bonds serve as a benchmark for other bonds. Interest rate spreads indicate relative risk between different bonds.

The term structure of interest rates shows the relationship between bonds of different maturities but similar risk. A yield curve plots various interest rates of bonds of different maturities in a snapshot of time (e. g., today), with the term of the maturity ranging from the short maturities on the left to longer maturities on the right. Yield curves are usually upward sloping, indicating that longer-term bonds typically trade at higher yields.

7.4 Glossary

Benchmark Bond Reference security (typically U. S. Treasury) used to price other bonds.

Bond Demand Curve The relationship between price and quantity of bonds investors demand, typically sloping downward.

Bond Rating Assessment of creditworthiness by rating agencies that estimates the likelihood a borrower will make promised payments.

Bond Supply Curve The relationship between price and quantity of bonds people are willing to sell, typically sloping upward.

Co-movement Tendency of different bond yields to move together when U. S. Treasury yields change.

Commercial Paper Short-term, unsecured debt instrument issued on a discount basis with maturity under 270 days.

Expectations Hypothesis Theory stating long-term interest rates equal the average of current and expected future short-term rates.

Fallen Angels Bonds that were once investment-grade but were downgraded to junk status.

Inflation Risk Uncertainty about how inflation will affect the purchasing power of bond returns.

Interest Rate Risk Potential for capital losses when selling bonds before maturity due to interest rate changes.

Interest Rate Spreads The percentage differences between various interest rates, often used as market signals.

Junk Bonds Bonds rated below investment grade, carrying higher default risk and yields.

Liquidity Premium Theory (LPT) Enhanced version of expectations hypothesis that includes risk premium compensation.

Market Clearing Process where prices adjust until quantity supplied equals quantity demanded.

Rating Downgrade Lowering of an issuer's bond rating due to deteriorating financial conditions.

Risk Premium Additional yield required by investors to compensate for increased risk of longer-term bonds.

Term Structure of Interest Rates Relationship among bonds with same risk characteristics but different maturities.

Yield Curve Graphical representation of interest rates across different maturities at a specific point in time.

Yield Curve Inversion When short-term interest rates exceed long-term rates, often predicting recession.

8 Equities and the Stock Market

Contents

In the previous chapters, we discussed how bonds are debt instruments. Stocks, which are also known as common stock or equity, are shares in a firm's ownership. Stocks first appeared in the 16th century as a way to finance the voyages of explorers. The idea was to spread the risk through joint-stock companies. These companies were organized to issue stock and used the proceeds to finance several expeditions at once. In exchange for investing, stockholders would receive a share of the company's profits. This chapter outlines the basics of stocks and the equity market.

8.1 Background on Common Stock

The idea of common stock is one of shared ownership and shared risk. Essentially, a group of investors would pool resources to collectively own the company and divide up the profits while spreading the risk of the venture. Historically, this facilitated an increase in international trade in the 16th and 17th centuries bringing about the age of mercantilism.

A powerful idea that solidified the viability of the stock market is the concept of 'apportionment' of ownership. Ownership of a profitable venture was often deemed valuable, and apportionment implies that an investor could sell her portion of ownership in the venture independently—not needing the permission of the other co-owners. The number of portions, or shares, of ownership that could be sold could be made arbitrarily large by selling them in ever smaller denominations.

Since shares were issued in small denominations, and were also made transferable, an owner could sell them to someone else and investors could buy as little or as much as they wanted. This increased participation, which thickened the market of stocks.

In the past, investors used to receive paper stock certificates—most stockholders no longer do. Information is all computerized, which is safer to store and makes it easier to transfer. Computerization reduced transaction costs of trading stocks, increasing participation again.

https://doi.org/10.1515/9783111193120-011

The ownership of common stock entitles the stockholder to participate in the profits of the enterprise. It also entitles the stockholder to have a say in the management of the firm, since stockholders are able to vote at the firm's annual meeting. Another advantage of stock ownership is that investors have *limited liability* in the firm. Even if the company goes bankrupt, the maximum amount a shareholder can lose is their initial investment. However, in the event of liquidation, as the firm experiences a financial strain, a stockholder is a residual claimant. This means the stockholder is paid last, only after all other creditors have been paid.

To sum up, the market for stocks is thick with wide participation because of the many advantages it offers: 1) an individual share is only a small fraction of the company's value and is highly transferable, 2) a large number of shares are outstanding, 3) prices of individual stocks are often low, 4) stockholders are residual claimants, 5) stockholders have limited liability, and 6) shareholders can have some influence in the management of the firm.

8.2 Measuring the Stock Market

Many thousands of stocks are being traded every day around the world. While investors typically concentrate their holdings on a smaller subset of all the stocks currently trading, it is useful to measure the overall market. Investors need to understand the dynamics of the stock market. They typically evaluate the connections between stock values and economic conditions. To do this, they need to be able to measure the level of fluctuation in all stock values (even if they do not hold them all). This concept is the value of the stock market. We refer to this overall measurement as a *stock market index*.

There are many stock indexes around the world. They tell us how much the value of an average stock has changed, and how much total wealth (or equity) has gone up or down. They also facilitate comparisons by providing benchmarks for investor performance. One can tell whether a money manager has done better or worse than "the market" as a whole.

The Dow Jones Industrial Average (DJIA) is the first and most widely known stock market index. It is based on the stock prices of 30 of the largest companies in the U.S. It tracks the value of purchasing a single share of each of the stocks in the index. The percentage change in the DJIA over time is the percentage change in the sum of the 30 prices. The DJIA is a price-weighted average, which gives greater weight to shares with higher prices. Therefore, the behavior of higher priced stocks dominates the movement of this price-weighted index.

Another popular index is the Standard & Poor's 500 Index. The S&P500 is constructed from the prices of the 500 largest firms in the U.S. economy. It tracks the total value of owning a single share of all 500 firms. It uses a value-weighted index where larger value firms carry more weight. For example, if a firm is priced at $100 and has 10 million shares outstanding, its total market value—or market capitalization—is worth

$1 billion. A price-weighted index like the DJIA gives more importance to stocks that have high prices. But a value-weighted index like the S&P 500 gives more importance to companies with a high market value—their price per share is not necessarily relevant.

Both types—price-weighted and value-weighted indexes—are useful because they answer different questions. Changes in price-weighted indexes give information on the performance of a typical stock, whereas changes in value-weighted indexes more closely resemble changes in the economy's overall wealth.

Other important indexes in the U. S. include the Nasdaq Composite Index and the Wilshire 5,000. The Nasdaq is a value-weighted index of over 3,000 companies traded on the over-the-counter (OTC) market. It is mainly composed of smaller, newer firms and has typically been dominated by technology and Internet companies. The Wilshire 5000 is the most broadly based index in use; it covers all publicly traded stocks in the U. S. with readily available prices. As a value-weighted index, the Wilshire is probably the most comprehensive measure of overall market wealth.

Stock market indexes can be pulled directly from the web into Python via the Pandas package with the Yahoo Finance overlay as follows:

```
#CAUTION We need to use yfinance library to override
#pandas_datareader to yahoo data

import pandas_datareader.data as pdr
import yfinance as yf
yf.pdr_override()
```

The following snippet of Python code produces a chart of daily values of the four major U. S. stock market indexes between January 2, 2020, and September 10, 2023. The code graphs four indexes each with a different scale in the vertical (y) axis—two for the main chart and one in a sub-graph or inset.

```
fig = plt.figure(figsize=(11, 8))
#fig = plt.subplots(figsize=(11, 5))

ax1 = fig.add_axes([0, 0, 1, 1])
ax1.set_title('Stock Market Indexes',fontsize=30)
color = 'tab:red'
ax1.plot(market['^DJI'],color='red', label='Dow Jones',ls='solid', lw=2.5)
ax1.set_ylabel('Dow Jones',color='red',fontsize=30)
ax1.tick_params(axis='y',colors='tab:red', labelsize=18)
ax1.tick_params(axis='x',colors='black', labelsize=20)
plt.grid(True)

ax2 = ax1.twinx() # Instantiate a 2nd axis that shares the same x-axis
color = 'tab:green'
ax2.set_ylabel('Nasdaq', color='green', fontsize=30)
```

```
ax2.tick_params(axis='y',colors='green', labelsize=18)
ax2.plot(market['^IXIC'], color='green',label='Nasdaq',ls='solid', lw=2.5)

#Inset
ax3 = fig.add_axes([0.085, 0.63, 0.6, 0.35 ])
ax3.plot(market['^DJI'],color='black', label='Dow Jones',ls='solid', lw=3.5)
ax3.legend(loc='lower right', shadow=True, fontsize='x-large')
plt.grid(True)
#plt.savefig('Stockmkts')
```

This code produces Figure 8.1, which clearly shows all three indexes are highly correlated. All three indexes experienced a substantial drop following March of 2020, because of COVID, and finally bottomed out by the end of 2022. While most of 2022 was a
rocky year for stock markets, coinciding with a major increase in headline inflation, 2023
marked a moderate recovery, with the DJIA mostly moving sideways and the S&P500 index and the Nasdaq seeming to grow faster, buttressed by bullish expected returns on
superconductors, hardware, and software connected with an expansion of artificial intelligence.

Figure 8.1: Three major stock market indexes.

While over the long run, all these indexes show strong co-movement, at shorter
windows, differences often arise. Many countries around the world have a stock market
and each has an index. Many of them are value-weighted indexes. Investors view global
stock markets as a means to diversify risk away from domestic markets. However, global
stock markets are typically strongly correlated.

8.3 Valuing Stocks

Investors in equities often differ on how stocks should be valued. Some believe they can predict changes by examining graphical patterns or past movements in particular stocks. These types of investors are known as *chartists.*

Others estimate the value of stocks based on their perceptions of investor psychology and behavior. They monitor other investors' trading patterns and follow suit—which is called free riding—or, conversely, bet against them. They also monitor trading chatter on social media and move to invest with the herd. These types of investors are collectively known as *behavioralists.*

Yet other types of investors estimate the value of stocks based on both their current assets and on estimates of future profitability. They pore over financial statements, they attend earnings meetings, and they forecast macroeconomic activity. These types of investors trade based on the fundamentals of a company. The *fundamental value* of a stock is based on the timing and uncertainty of the returns it brings.

Chartists and behavioralists question the usefulness of fundamentals in understanding the level and movement of stock prices. Instead, they are more concerned with internalizing correctly and responding quickly to financial news.

We can use the information we have already studied to compute the fundamental value of stocks. A stock represents a promise to make monetary payments on future dates, under uncertain circumstances. These payments are usually made in the form of dividends. These dividends are typically issued from the proceeds of a company when they have a good quarter. In other words, dividends are distributed to the owners of a company when the company makes a profit. When a company is sold, the stockholders receive a final distribution that represents their share of the purchase price.

8.4 The Dividend Discount Model

There are two potential returns from holding a stock. One is future dividends and the other is the potential for future capital gains, which can be earned any time the share value appreciates above the price that the share was originally bought at. Since both dividends and share prices are incurred in the future, they must be discounted to the present to evaluate the desirability of the underlying stock.

According to the *Classical Theory of Asset Prices,* the price of an asset equals the present-value discounted expected future incomes or returns. Following this definition, the price of a share of stock must equal the discounted future dividend payment and, if the stock is sold, the discounted future price. For example, the *dividend discount model* suggests that today's price (P_t) of a share of stock that issues a dividend one year from today (D_{t+1}) must be equal to:

$$P_t = \frac{D_{t+1}}{(1+i)} + \frac{P_{t+1}}{(1+i)},$$

which means that for a given interest rate (i_t), the higher we expect the dividend payment or the price of the stock to be next year, the more valuable it is to hold this stock today, and, therefore, the higher its price today (P_t). This equation can easily be extended to an arbitrary investment horizon of n years:

$$P_t = \frac{D_{t+1}}{(1+i)} + \frac{D_{t+2}}{(1+i)^2} + \cdots + \frac{D_{t+n}}{(1+i)^n} + \frac{P_{t+n}}{(1+i)^n}.$$

Dividend payments are not typically guaranteed. A firm might have a bad quarter and turn in no profits to distribute to the owners. At other times, the firm's management might decide to reinvest the profits in, for example, property, plant, or equipment for the firm, rather than issue out dividend payments to the owners. Alternatively, they might buy back some of the firm's own stock with quarterly proceeds. This makes it more difficult to apply the equations above to price a share of stock.

Case in point, if a company currently pays no dividends, investors must estimate when the company will begin paying dividends and use the present-value framework. This requires investors to have some extra information about annual dividend payments.

For example, an investor expects some dividend payment (P_t) at any given period t. Assume that the investor receives a dividend payment at a specific period t. She does not need to formulate a guess in this case; she sees this payment materialize to the realized value (D), so that $(D_t = D)$. If the investor assumes the dividend payments will grow at some constant rate g per year, then the dividend payment next year will be $D_t = D(1+g)$ and the dividend payment in n years will be $D_t = D(1 + g)^n$. With this information, we can rewrite the price equation as follows:

$$P_t = \frac{D(1+g)}{(1+i)} + \frac{D(1+g)^2}{(1+i)^2} + \cdots + \frac{D(1+g)^n}{(1+i)^n} + \frac{P_{t+n}}{(1+i)^n}.$$

As the planning horizon n gets arbitrarily large, it becomes more difficult to forecast what the price in n years will be. In this case, investors might not attempt to forecast that distant future price (P_{t+n}) at all and consider a *buy-and-hold strategy* instead. Presumably, holding the stock 'forever' would pay dividends forever, which would turn the stock into something like a consol (a bond with no maturity). This would modify the equation above into:

$$P_t = \frac{D(1+g)}{(1+i)} + \frac{D(1+g)^2}{(1+i)^2} + \cdots + \frac{D(1+g)^n}{(1+i)^n}.$$

By mathematical properties of geometric progressions, as n grows very large (toward infinity), it can be shown that the equation above reduces to the following equation:

$$P_t = \frac{D(1+g)}{(i-g)}.$$

This relationship is the dividend discount model. The model tells us that stock prices should be high when dividend payments are high (*D*), when dividend growth is rapid (*g* is large), or when the interest rate (*i*) is low.

8.5 Assessing Risk in Stocks

The dividend discount model of the previous section abstracted from risk. However, dividend payments are rarely guaranteed. Stockholders are residual claimants, which means they get part of the profits only after everyone else is paid, including bond holders. In addition, when investors buy stocks, they often finance their purchase. Essentially, they often put up some of their wealth to buy shares of the firm and borrow the rest. The borrowing creates leverage, and leverage creates risk. The higher the level of debt used to finance equity purchases, the higher the leverage, and the greater the owners' risk.

For example, let's say a firm needs $10,000 for computing equipment. The firm wants to calculate the return on its investment in the first year following the $10K capital expenditure. Once installed, the firm will have an equal probability of earning $900 from the equipment during a bad year of sales or $1,500 during a good one. The $10,000 investment can be financed in equity (with stocks) exclusively, or it can be part equity (stock) and part debt (bonds). Let's say that equity can be obtained at a 10% interest rate.

Table 8.1 shows the risk and expected returns from financing the $10,000 investment with different combinations of equity and debt. The first row shows the case when the investment is fully financed with 100% equity. In other words, the firm does not take on any level of debt to finance the expenditure. Column *b* in the first row shows zero percent financing through debt, which means that the cost of borrowing 10% of zero means a zero dollar payment (see column *c*), since no bonds are issued to finance the expenditure. Under this scenario, the payment to equity holders (column *d*) ranges from $900 in bad times to $1,500 in good times.

Table 8.1: Returns to debt and equity holders of a $10K investment under different financing schemes.

(a) Percent equity (%)	(b) Percent debt (%)	(c) Required payments on 10% bonds ($)	(d) Payment to equity holders ($)	(e) Equity returns (%)	(f) Expected equity returns (%)	(g) Standard deviation of equity returns (%)
100%	0	0	$900–$1,500	9–15%	12.0%	3%
50%	50%	$500	$400–$1,000	8–20%	14.0%	6%
30%	70%	$700	$200–$800	6.7–26.7%	16.7%	10%
20%	80%	$800	$100–$700	5–35%	20.0%	15%

Column *e*, in the first row, shows that in percentage terms, equity returns range from ($900/$10,000 = 9%) to ($1,500/$10,000 = 15%). Since there is an equal probability of having a bad year or a good year, the expected equity returns are:

$$(1/2) \times 9\% + (1/2) \times 15\% = 12\%.$$

The equity returns can deviate plus or minus 3% from this expected 12% equity return, since they range from 9% to 15%. Column *g*, in the first row, indicates that at 3%, the standard deviation of these expected returns is quite low when the investment is fully financed with equity.

The second row in the table shows what happens when half of the investment is financed with equity and the other half is financed by issuing bonds. In this scenario, since the firm issues $5,000 worth of bonds, at a 10% interest rate, the bond holders have to be paid ahead of equity holders to the tune of $500 (10% × $5,000). This $500 required payment to bond holders is shown in column *c*.

Looking at column *d* in the second row, since equity holders are residual claimants, in the bad times the equity holders would receive $900, but now that bond holders get paid $500 first, the leftover return for equity holders in bad times is $400. Similarly, the equity return in the good times would be ($1,500 – $500 = $1,000). This means that the payment to equity holders would range between $400 and $1,000. Column *e* in the second row shows that, as a share of the $5,000 equity financing, the equity returns range between 8% ($400/$5,000) and 20% ($1,000/$5,000).

The second row shows that when 50% of the investment is financed with debt, the expected equity returns increase from 12% (under zero percent debt shown in the first row) to the 14% that column *f* shows (under 50% debt in the second row). However, column *g* in the second row shows that, at 6%, the standard deviation is now much higher when some of the investment is financed with debt. Therefore, debt financing has increased the risk of the investment.

The third row shows what happens to the risk and expected returns of the investment when $3,000 is financed with equity and the firm issues $7,000 worth of bonds. The fourth row shows the case when the computing equipment is purchased with $9,000 of capital raised though bond issuance and a mere $1,000 of equity is used. We can see that the larger the position of the investment that is financed with bonds, the higher the bond payment obligation that has to be made ahead of issuing returns to the equity holders (the payment amount increases as we climb down column *c*). As the debt issuance gets larger, the dollar amount of equity returns (column *d*) gets smaller.

However, the equity returns are larger (column *e*) because the equity used is lower at higher debt levels. As we take on more debt to finance the $10K investment, expected returns increase from 12% to 20% (as we climb down the rows in column *f*). This may lead to the conclusion that financing investment with debt could be desirable, because expected equity returns increase at higher levels of debt. Importantly, these higher expected returns carry much higher degrees of risk—shown in column *g*, where standard deviations rise from 3% to 15%—because of what is known as *leverage*. In other words, a higher level of debt is used to chase higher returns, and this carries higher risk because debt claimants are paid ahead of equity holders.

8.6 Portfolio Risk

The dividend-discount model is useful when looking at the price and risk of holding a single stock. Many investors, however, collect a basket of various stocks into a portfolio. The returns from a portfolio can be simply calculated as the weighted sum of the stocks the portfolio contains.

```python
import pandas_datareader.data as pdr
import yfinance as yf
yf.pdr_override()

stocks = ['MSFT', 'AAPL', 'PG', 'GDX', 'SBUX', '^GSPC', '^IXIC' ]

begn = dt.datetime(2007, 1, 1)
endn = dt.datetime(2023, 9, 21)

# 'MSFT' , '^GSPC' ...
ticker = [stocks[0] , stocks[1]]
ticker

datos = pd.DataFrame()
datos[ticker] = pdr.get_data_yahoo(ticker, start=begn, end=endn)['Adj Close']
datos.head()
fech_range=len(datos.index)
fech_range

datos.head()
fech_range=len(datos.index)
fech_range
```

```
MSFT      AAPL
Date
2023-09-14      175.047684      336.782562
2023-09-15      174.320541      328.350555
2023-09-18      177.268906      327.197113
2023-09-19      178.364563      326.789459
2023-09-20      174.798676      318.954102
```

Financial analysts often normalize share price data so that it can be more easily compared across companies. Normalization involves converting both stock prices to an index so we can plot them as if they were both starting at the same $100 share price. Then, the period-by-period return of a stock can be calculated as the one-period change in the share price:

$$\text{return} = \frac{P_{t+1}}{P_t} - 1.$$

Or, alternatively, it can be calculated with a log transformation, which is known as log returns, as follows:

$$\text{return} = \log\left(\frac{P_{t+1}}{P_t}\right).$$

And then compute their returns with a log transformation, which can be easily done in a single line of Python code.

```
#Compute log returns
stock_returns = np.log(datos / datos.shift(1)).dropna()
stock_returns
```

We can calculate mean returns over an arbitrary period of time and annualize the returns by assuming 250 trading days in a year. (We also multiply by 100 to express in percentages.)

```
#Each individual stock return is:
100*stock_returns[['AAPL' , 'MSFT']].mean()*250
AAPL     16.065956
MSFT     25.168108
dtype: float64
```

This analysis shows that from 2007 to 2023, the annualized returns for Microsoft were considerable higher than those of Apple. If we are interested in calculating the portfolio return from holding these two stocks, we simply need to know how we distribute our portfolio among the various returns. In other words, we need a set of weights. For example, if 100% of our portfolio consisted of Apple stock exclusively, the portfolio return would be exactly equal to the 16% of Apple's return. On the other hand, if we only had Microsoft stock in our portfolio, our portfolio's return would be 25.1%.

The portfolio return is calculated by multiplying each stock times its associated weight and summing all the weighted returns. If the portfolio was equally weighted among the two stocks (50% Apple and 50% Microsoft), the portfolio's return would be 20.6%:

```
weight = np.array([0.5 , 0.5])

#Portfolio's Return
prtfol_ret = (np.dot(stock_returns[['AAPL' , 'MSFT']].mean()*250 , weight))
str(round(100*prtfol_ret,1) ) + '%'

'20.6%'
```

If the portfolio were more heavily weighted to Apple (say 80%), its return would be pulled down by the lower return on Apple:

```
weight = np.array([0.8 , 0.2])

#Portfolio's Return
prtfol_ret = (np.dot(stock_returns[['AAPL' , 'MSFT']].mean()*250 , weight))
str(round(100*prtfol_ret,1) ) + '%'

'17.9%'
```

And similarly, if most of the portfolio were heavily weighted on Microsoft (say 80%), the portfolio's return would be higher:

```
weight = np.array([0.2 , 0.8])

#Portfolio's Return
prtfol_ret = (np.dot(stock_returns[['AAPL' , 'MSFT']].mean()*250 , weight))
str(round(100*prtfol_ret,1) ) + '%'

'23.3%'
```

Each stock has a return, and each stock has its own risk. As we saw in previous chapters, the risk of a given stock can be measured by the standard deviation of its return (what we call "return volatility", or simply "volatility") over some period.

The previous code snippets show we can append **.mean()** to a Python object (in this case our numpy array containing the two stocks) to calculate the mean values. We can do the same for variances by simply appending **.var()**. Then taking the square root and multiplying by 100 obtains the standard deviation in percentages for each stock.

```
#Each individual stock's standard deviation is:
100*stock_returns[['AAPL' , 'MSFT']].var()*250**0.5

AAPL    0.507711
MSFT    0.643379
dtype: float64
```

We can see that Microsoft has a slightly higher standard deviation, suggesting that it is a somewhat riskier stock to hold than Apple. But how risky is a portfolio that holds both stocks?

Calculating portfolio risk is a more difficult proposition than simply combining the weighted returns of each stock to calculate the overall portfolio return. This is because, while both stocks carry their own level of risk, their risk may not be independent of each other. The risk of holding Microsoft may be somewhat related to the risk of holding Apple.

We need to account for that relationship. It is not enough to measure how each stock return varies over time. We also need to determine how both stocks co-vary with each other over time. This is accomplished with a covariance matrix. Figure 8.2 shows the general form of a covariance matrix between two stocks: **a** and **b**. The northwest quadrant shows the covariance of stock **a** with itself. This is the same as the variance of stock **a**.

Cov(stock a, stock a)	Cov(stock a , stock b)
Cov(stock b , stock a)	Var(stock b)

Figure 8.2: A covariance matrix.

We call the line that cuts through the northwest to the southeast quadrants, the main diagonal. The main diagonal of a covariance matrix holds the variances of each stock. Therefore, the off-diagonals show the covariance among the various stocks in our portfolio. The northeast quadrant shows the covariance of stock **a** and stock **b**, while the southwest quadrant shows how stock **b** co-varies with stock **a**. These two quadrants should show the same value, because the order in which we place the stocks does not affect their covariance. The covariance of x and z must be the same as the covariance of z and x.

From this we learn two properties of covariance matrices: One, their main diagonal contains variances, so the main diagonal must only contain positive values. Two, covariance matrices are symmetric, meaning their values are mirror images of each other across the main diagonal. The following snippet of Python code shows the covariance matrix of Microsoft and Apple's returns for a period that spans 2007 to 2023:

```
covmat = stock_returns.cov()*250
covmat
```

	MSFT	AAPL
MSFT	0.101727	0.051618
AAPL	0.051618	0.080276

We can see the positive values of the main diagonal of the covariance matrix and their symmetry across the main diagonal. The covariance matrix suggests that Microsoft returns show a larger variance over the period, indicating that they are somewhat riskier than Apple. The off-diagonal shows that Microsoft and Apple co-vary positively. However, the strength of that relationship in the risk of both stocks can be more easily interpreted with a correlation matrix.

A correlation matrix essentially divides the covariance matrix through by the standard deviations of the stock in each quadrant. Figure 8.3 shows a generic correlation matrix for two stock returns.

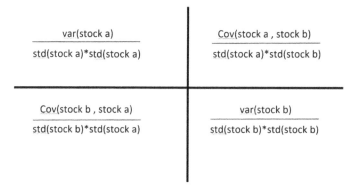

Figure 8.3: A correlation matrix.

Dividing the main diagonal elements of the covariance matrix by the square of the standard deviation of each stock is tantamount to dividing the variance of each stock by itself. This should make sense. Each stock should be perfectly correlated with itself.

The off-diagonal elements show the correlation coefficient between the stocks. The correlation values can range from –1 (or –100%) for a perfectly negative correlation to +1 (or 100%) for a perfectly positive correlation. The closer the value it is to zero, the weaker the strength of the relationship between the stocks and the more independent their risk is from each other.

The following Python snippet shows that Microsoft and Apple stock are positively correlated with a 57.1% correlation coefficient. (Note that we never need to annualize a correlation matrix since it does not contain average daily values, so no need to multiply times 250).

```
corrmat = stock_returns.corr()
corrmat

          MSFT      AAPL
MSFT    1.000000      0.571205
AAPL    0.571205      1.000000
```

Now that we have some measure of the volatility of each stock, as well as how both stocks co-vary, we can now determine the portfolio's risk. A simple equation for the portfolio's variance (Ω) that contains two stocks is given by:

$$\Omega = (\omega_1\sigma_1 + \omega_1\sigma_1)^2,$$

where the weights must add up to one ($\omega_1 + \omega_2 = 1$) and (σ_1) and (σ_2) are the standard deviations of each stock. Applying the quadratic formula, we have the following equation:

$$\Omega = \omega_1^2\sigma_1^2 + \omega_2^2\sigma_2^2 + 2\omega_1\sigma_1\omega_2\sigma_2\rho_{12},$$

where ρ_{12} is the correlation coefficient between the two stocks. The following snippet of Python code calculates our two-stock portfolio's variance:

```
weights = np.array([0.5 , 0.5])
```

```
#Portfolio variance
prtfol_var = np.dot(weights.T , np.dot(stock_returns.cov() *250 , weights))
prtfol_var
```

```
0.07131000992322262
```

Again, it is easier to interpret a standard deviation than a variance. The portfolio's volatility is simply given by the following equation:

$$\Omega^{\frac{1}{2}} = \sqrt{\omega_1^2\sigma_1^2 + \omega_2^2\sigma_2^2 + 2\omega_1\sigma_1\omega_2\sigma_2\rho_{12}},$$

which can be easily coded in Python:

```
#Portfolio volatility
prtfol_vol = np.dot(weights.T , np.dot(stock_returns.cov() *250 , weights)) ** 0.5
100*prtfol_vol
#print (round(prtfol_vol, 4) * 100) + ' %'
```

```
26.7%
```

Combining all this together, we find that if, since 2007, we have had an equally weighted portfolio with 50% stock in Apple and 50% stock in Microsoft, the portfolio return would have been 20.6% and the portfolio volatility would have been 26.7%.

If more weight in our portfolio had leaned toward Microsoft (say 20% Apple and 80% Microsoft), we have already shown the portfolio return would be higher (than 20.6%) at 23.3% (pulled up by the higher performing returns of Microsoft during the period). But the code below shows the portfolio volatility would also be somewhat higher (at 29.1% up from 26.7%) since a larger portion is held in the riskier Microsoft stock:

```
weights = np.array([0.8 , 0.2])
#Portfolio volatility
prtfol_vol = np.dot(weights.T , np.dot(stock_returns.cov() *250 , weights)) ** 0.5
prtfol_vol
str (round(100*prtfol_vol,2) ) + '%'
```

29.13%

As we discussed in previous chapters, risk can be characterized as either idiosyncratic or systemic. As we saw earlier, idiosyncratic risk can be mitigated by diversification or hedging strategies. On the other hand, systemic risk is, to some extent, "undiversifiable."

We now set out to disaggregate our calculated portfolio's risk into the diversifiable versus the systemic risk.

Systemic Risk = Portfolio Variance – Weighted (annualized) Stock Variances.

First, we need the annualized variances of each stock, recalling that Microsoft looks slightly riskier.

```
weights = np.array([0.5 , 0.5])
#Annualized stock returns for stock 1
stock1_var_ann = stock_returns['MSFT'].var()*250
stock1_var_ann
0.1017
```

```
#Annualized stock returns for stock 2
stock2_var_ann = stock_returns['AAPL'].var()*250
stock2_var_ann
0.0802
```

Then, applying our equation above shows the idiosyncratic risk is 0.026:

```
idyo_risk = prtfol_var - (weights[0]**2 * stock1_var_ann) -
↵   (weights[1]**2 * stock2_var_ann)
str (round(idyo_risk, 3) ) + '%'
0.026%
```

So subtracting this idiosyncratic risk from the portfolio's variance will give us a way to quantify systemic risk.

```
### The rest of the universe must be systemic risk
systm_risk_alt1 = prtfol_var - idyo_risk
```

```
systm_risk_alt1
0.04550083616621645
```

Showing that risk associated with the economy-wide factors is almost twice as large as the idiosyncratic risk. We can alternatively calculate systemic risk and check that both alternatives find the same number.

```
#Alternatively...
systm_risk_alt2 = (weights[0]**2 * stock1_var_ann) + (weights[1]**2 *
↪  stock2_var_ann)
systm_risk_alt2
0.04550083616621645
```

```
#check
systm_risk_alt1==systm_risk_alt2
True
```

8.7 Monte Carlo

Monte Carlo simulation (MCS) methods were invented by Ulam, Neumann, and Metropolis in the 1940s as a set of numerical techniques that use random sampling for computing approximate estimates or for simulating uncertain outcomes. MCS is useful for analyzing both deterministic and probabilistic systems with numerical approximations when an analytical solution may be difficult to reach.

MCS converts a complex, multi-dimensional, difficult problem in integral calculus into an easier problem of descriptive statistics. It can also be useful when best/worst/ base case scenarios may not be enough for decision-making and, instead, we need to quantify the probability and impact of all outcomes.

MCS may help when we need a better understanding of risk of complex financial models so long as we have some answers to the following questions:

- 1. What are the independent variables/risk factors/features that drive the model?
- 2. What are the correlations across time and among these probabilistic/stochastic variables?
- 3. What theoretical probability distribution best approximates their real-life behavior?

MCS methods are based on two of the most important theorems in probability and statistics: the law of large numbers and the central limit theorem (CLT). The law of large numbers shows that when we simulate/estimate data samples, convergence to the true mean is often guaranteed as the sample size gets larger. The CLT proves the sampling distribution of the mean approaches a normal/Gaussian distribution as the sample size gets large. See Figure 8.4.

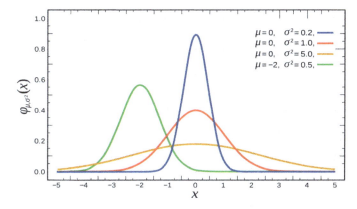

Figure 8.4: Normal distributions.

Sampling error is independent of the dimension of the variable and goes to zero asymptotically as the square root of the sample size increases. Therefore, sampling errors/fluctuations from the true estimate are normally distributed due to CLT. MCS requires a large number of iterations; in order to increase accuracy by a single digit, MCS iterations need to increase by a factor of 100.

Implementing a sound framework for building an MCS requires a few steps:

Step 1. We must formulate how dependent variables are affected by independent variables. Let's say that those independent variables denote risk factors for a given investment strategy.

Step 2. We must specify the probability distribution of each risk factor. This requires: (i) assuming some initial values for the risk factors and deciding the frequency of the measurement; (ii) specifying how each risk factor changes over time; and (iii) specifying how each risk factor is affected by other risk factors.

Step 3. We need to draw a random value from the probability distribution of each independent risk factor.

Step 4. We want to compute the value of each risk factor based on that random value.

Step 5. We need to compute target/dependent variables based on the computed value of all risk factors.

Step 6. Repeat Step 3 through Step 5 as many times as necessary in a process called iteration.

Step 7. Collect and analyze descriptive statistics of all iterations.

There are some challenges to conducting a MCS successfully. First, we often need to specify how each independent variable changes over time, but the degree with which it varies (its serial correlation) usually changes over time. We also need to specify how each variable is affected by other variables of the model, but the relationships among input variables/risk factors also usually change over time.

MCS typically requires fitting a theoretical probability distribution to the actual outcomes. However, probability distributions of variables usually change over time, which likely means nonlinear dynamics. Therefore, convergence to the best estimate is often nonlinear, making it slow and costly, so it may not occur quickly enough to be of any practical value to trading or investing.

8.8 Forecasting Stock Prices with MCS

Let's say we want a daily forecast of a given stock. We begin with the growth rate between a stock price today and its price yesterday. Let g denote the daily growth rate:

$$g = \frac{P_{today}}{P_{yesterday}} - 1.$$

This growth rate (g) describes the return from holding the asset between yesterday and today. This return can also be approximated by a log return (r). Therefore, the daily stock return can be calculated as follows:

$$r_t = \ln\left[\frac{P_{today}}{P_{yesterday}}\right].$$

Now, we can begin with an identity:

$$P_{today} = P_{today}.$$

Multiplying and dividing by $P_{yesterday}$ does not change the identity:

$$P_{today} = P_{yesterday} * \frac{P_{today}}{P_{yesterday}}.$$

We can now leverage the following condition: $e^{\ln(x)} = x$, which always holds, so that we have the following:

$$P_{today} = P_{yesterday} * e^{\ln\left[\frac{P_{today}}{P_{yesterday}}\right]}.$$

Substituting our definition for the daily return gives us the following equation of the price of a stock, which allows us to describe today's price as a function of yesterday's price as well as the daily return between yesterday and today, as follows:

$$P_{today} = P_{yesterday} * e^{[r_t]}.$$

We now make two main assumptions that allow us to make predictions about the stock price with MCS. First, we assume we know yesterday's price, but we do not know the daily return (r_t). Second, we assume the daily return is a random variable.

There are several ways to model a random variable. One way to model returns as a random variable is to focus on two typical behaviors of returns. Past returns often have a certain degree of persistence. This means that while they may tend to revert to their long-term averages at relatively high frequency, these averages themselves might move (often more slowly). This is typically referred to as *drift*. On the other hand, daily returns typically fluctuate at high frequencies. The spreads of those daily fluctuations are typically referred to as *volatility*. This means that past returns often exhibit both drifts and volatilities at various degrees.

Therefore, we decompose daily returns into their drift plus their volatility. The drift of the daily return of a stock is a rough approximation of the future's return of the stock given by:

$$\text{drift} = \mu - \frac{1}{2}\sigma^2,$$

where μ is the historical mean and the σ^2 is the variance of the returns. As we discussed in previous chapters, the volatility is given by the standard deviation (σ) of the data. However, given our assumption of randomness in daily returns, we randomize the volatility with a Z-value from a standard normal distribution so that our volatility becomes $\sigma * Z$. So, we decompose daily returns in the following way:

$$r_t = \mu - \frac{1}{2}\sigma^2 + \sigma * Z.$$

Explaining Z-values

Z-values correspond to the distance between the mean return and each realization of the return, expressed as the number of standard deviations. The following snippet of Python code shows how to generate Z-values.

```
#Example for randomization
# ex_rnd generates pseudo-random probabilities between 0 and 1
ex_rnd = np.random.rand(3,2)
ex_rnd
```

```
array([[0.33038299, 0.74209251],
       [0.2674843 , 0.43495548],
       [0.10300313, 0.53848152]])
```

```
# norm.ppf(ex_rnd) coverts those probabilities to standard
# deviation distances from mean zero
norm.ppf(ex_rnd)
```

```
array([[-0.43885587,  0.64980997],
       [-0.6204393 , -0.1637716 ],
       [-1.25961893,  0.09660893]])
```

```
# We can combine both in a single step to generate Z
Z = norm.ppf(np.random.rand(4,2))
Z
```

```
array([[ 1.96149132,  0.29616807],
       [ 1.55218724, -0.33373723],
       [ 2.12196049,  0.68014503],
       [ 0.10329107, -1.26732179]])
```

These Z-values can be leveraged to simulate randomness in predicted values of the price of a share of stock, which we will accomplish via MCS.

We can combine our stock price equation with the decomposition of the daily return from earlier to arrive an equation for the share price at a given period, (say, today):

$$P_{\text{today}} = P_{\text{yesterday}} * e^{[[\mu - \frac{1}{2}\sigma^2] + \sigma * Z]}.$$

This equation gives us a single value for the price forecast today. But there is randomness involved. To deal with that randomness, we will want to repeat the calculation many 1,000s of times with an MCS.

Moreover, we can predict future prices by projecting this equation into the future in a recursive manner. This means that if we start from the previous price (recall that we assume we know this initial price), and we calculate the daily return between yesterday and today, we can calculate the price for today. Subsequently, we can repeat the analysis. Now that we know today's price, we can calculate the return between today and tomorrow and predict tomorrow's price. We can then repeat this process on an on. For example, if we wanted to predict the daily price of a share of stock for the next 364 days, we could begin with an arbitrary initial price at period 0 say (P_0) and proceed as follows:

$$P_t = P_0 * r_t,$$
$$P_{t+1} = P_t * r_{t+1},$$
$$P_{t+2} = P_{t+1} * r_{t+2},$$

$$\vdots$$

$$P_{t+364} = P_{t+363} * r_{t+364}.$$

The following snippet of Python code enters various stock prices into Jupyter lab:

```
Establish the time frame of interest
empz = dt.datetime(2020, 1, 1)
acab = dt.datetime(2023, 3, 20)
```

Designate the specific equities of interest

```
tickers = "MSFT AAPL GOOG AMZN NFLX".split()   #.split converts string to list
ticker_m  = "^GSPC ^DJI ^IXIC ^RUI".split()

import pandas_datareader.data as pdr
import yfinance as yf
yf.pdr_override()
```

Read the Data

```
stocks_ = pdr.get_data_yahoo(tickers, start=empz, end=acab)
```

We then select the share price of Netflix (NFLX) to predict and calculate the mean and the variance of its log returns, which allows us to calculate the drift:

```
#<<<<<<<<<<<<<<<<<<<<<<<<<<<<
# SELECT WHICH STOCK TO FORECAST
stock = stocks.NFLX
#>>>>>>>>>>>>>>>>>>>>>>>>>>>>
pctDelta=stock.pct_change().dropna()
log_returns = np.log(1 + pctDelta)
type(log_returns)
pandas.core.series.Series

u = log_returns.mean();
u
-0.0010496

var = log_returns.var();var
0.0015083
```

We now calculate the drift and the standard deviation. The drift of the log returns is a rough approximation of the future returns of the stock. Recalling the equation, we can code it into Python as follows:

$$\text{drift} = \mu - \frac{1}{2}\sigma^2.$$

```
drift = u - (0.5 * var)
drift
-0.0018038

stdev = log_returns.std()
stdev
0.0388375
```

Now that we have values for the drift and the variance for the stock, we can simulate as many paths for as many periods as we want. Each path corresponds to an independent simulated history of the price we are modeling with MCS. That path can be as long or short as we want:

```
# Set up the number of periods (days) to predict
t_periods = 252

# Simulate paths of daily log returns
# for the stock we want
simulations = 6

daily_returns = np.exp(drift + stdev *
 ↵   norm.ppf(np.random.rand(t_periods, simulations)))

# 6 sets of 252 future stock prices
daily_returns.shape
(252, 6)
```

This Python snippet sets up a simulation for six different paths of a share price of Netflix for 252 trading days; so our simulation will look like the following:

$$P_t = P_0 * r_t,$$
$$P_{t+1} = P_t * r_{t+1},$$
$$P_{t+2} = P_{t+1} * r_{t+2},$$
$$\vdots$$
$$P_{t+252} = P_{t+251} * r_{t+252}.$$

The question now is which price (P_0) to begin from? Since we want to forecast the price, we can begin with the most recent price available.

```
S0 = stock.iloc[-1] #The last price available in the list 'stocks'
S0
377.6000

#We now create a placeholder (matrix of zeros) of the same size as daily
 ↵   returns
price_list = np.zeros_like(daily_returns)
price_list.size
price_list.shape
(252, 6)
```

```
#And fill the first row of price_list with S0
price_list[0] = S0

#Now we can build a loop to simulate
#the 6 simulated paths of the chosen
#stock price for the next 252 days:
for t in range(1, t_periods):
    price_list[t] = price_list[t-1] * daily_returns[t]

plt.figure(figsize=(6,3))
plt.plot(price_list)
```

The last two lines of the Python snippet chart the six simulated paths. See Figure 8.5.

Figure 8.5: Six simulated paths for the price of NFLX.

We can append these six simulated paths to the historical price of Netflix splicing where the price ends and our simulations begin (connecting where the last value of the price is available with the first value of the simulated paths). The following snippet of Python code accomplishes this. See Figure 8.6.

```
fig, ax1 = plt.subplots(figsize=(11, 5))

color = 'blue'
plt.grid(True)
plt.xticks(fontsize=12)
plt.yticks(fontsize=12)
```

```
ax1.plot(fechas0, stock, color="k", label=tickers[4])
ax1.legend(loc='lower right', shadow=True, fontsize='x-large')
plt.xlim([allfechas[0]], [allfechas[-1]])
plt.ylim((0, 800))    # set the ylim to bottom, top

ax2 = ax1.twinx()
ax2.plot(fechas1, price_list, label='Forecasts')
ax2.set_yticks(np.linspace(0, ax2.get_yticks()[-1], len(ax1.get_yticks())))
ax2.legend(loc='upper left', shadow=True, fontsize='small')
plt.yticks(color='white')
plt.grid(False)
plt.ylim((0, 800))    # set the ylim to bottom, top

plt.show
```

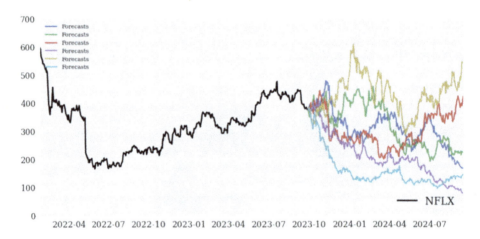

Figure 8.6: Six forecasts for the price of NFLX.

As we covered before, there is a substantial amount of randomness introduced in MCS; therefore, we need to run a very large number of simulated paths. We can simulate a much larger set of paths, then we can compute the mean (μ) and standard deviation (σ) across all paths for each period. The following snippet of Python code simulates 500 paths of the price of Netflix. See Figure 8.7.

```
# Simulate paths of daily log returns of the stock we want
simulations = 500

daily_returns = np.exp(drift + stdev *
↪    norm.ppf(np.random.rand(t_periods, simulations)))
```

```
#We now create a placeholder (matrix of zeros) of the same size as daily
 ↪  returns
price_list_large = np.zeros_like(daily_returns)
price_list_large.size
price_list_large.shape
#price_list
(252, 500)


#And fill the first row of price_list with S0
price_list_large[0] = S0


#Now we can build a loop to simulate the 500 simulated paths of the
 ↪  chose stock price for the next 252 days:
for t in range(1, t_periods):
    price_list_large[t] = price_list_large[t-1] * daily_returns[t]


#price_list is now 500 paths

plt.figure(figsize=(6,3))
plt.plot(price_list_large);


plt.figure(figsize=(6,3))
plt.plot(price_list);
```

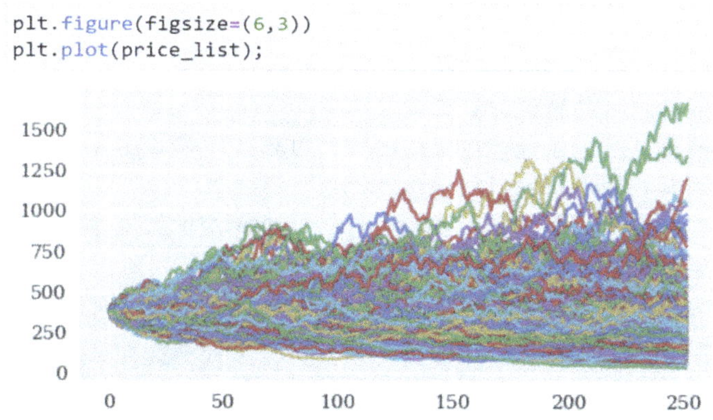

Figure 8.7: 500 forecasts for the price of NFLX.

We can use the following formula to construct a 90% confidence interval (with a Z-value of 1.64) such that $\mu \pm 1.64 * \sigma$ creates an upper and lower bound where 90% of the simulated paths fall within, as follows:

```
price_list_large_m = price_list.mean(1)
price_list_large_sd = price_list.std(1)
```

```
price_list_large_hi = price_list_large_m + 1.96*price_list_large_sd
price_list_large_lo = price_list_large_m - 1.96*price_list_large_sd
```

We can then graph the price of Netflix and append it to the forecast (from the mean across all paths) and the 90% confidence interval. The following snippet of code accomplishes this. See Figure 8.8.

```
fig, ax1 = plt.subplots(figsize=(11, 5))

color = 'blue'
plt.grid(True)
plt.xticks(fontsize=12)
plt.yticks(fontsize=12)


ax1.plot(fechas0, stock, color="k", label=tickers[4])
ax1.legend(loc='upper right', shadow=True, fontsize='x-large')
plt.xlim([allfechas[0]], [allfechas[-1]])
plt.ylim((0, 900))    # set the ylim to bottom, top


ax2 = ax1.twinx()
#ax2 = ax1.twiny()
ax2.plot(fechas1, price_list_large_m, color="b", label='Mean Forecast',
    ↪   linewidth=1, linestyle='dashdot')
ax2.plot(fechas1, price_list_large_hi, color="r", label='90% Confidence
    ↪   Interval', linewidth=2, linestyle='dotted')
ax2.plot(fechas1, price_list_large_lo, color="r", linewidth=2,
    ↪   linestyle='dotted')

ax2.legend(loc='lower left', shadow=True, fontsize='x-large')
plt.grid(False)
plt.ylim((0, 900))    # set the ylim to bottom, top
plt.xticks(color='white')
#plt.yticks(color='white')

plt.show()
```

We interpret this (dotted red) interval as follows: If we were to repeat this simulation, say 100 times, the forecast would lie within this interval 90 of those 100 times. The width of this interval suggests the accuracy of our forecast. The narrower this band, the more confident we can be about our forecast in the dashed red line.

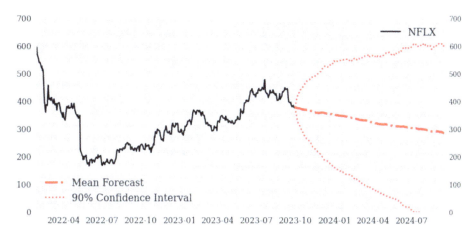

Figure 8.8: Out-of-sample forecast for the price of NFLX.

Thinking About It...

Stocks emerged in the 16th century as a way to finance trading voyages through joint-stock companies. The key innovation was "apportionment"—the ability to divide ownership into transferable shares. Modern stocks offer several advantages, including limited liability, transferability, and voting rights in company management. The most common way to measure overall stock market performance is through market indices; for example, the *Dow Jones Industrial Average* (DJIA) and the *Standard & Poor's* (S&P 500).

Individual stock measurements are typically shown with some common metrics such as returns from price changes (in logs or in levels). Based on returns, measurements of risk may be obtained, including standard deviation of returns (volatility), variance of returns, correlation with other stocks, and covariance with other stocks.

We can also measure groups of stocks collected into a portfolio. When measuring a portfolio of stocks, we need to consider: the *portfolio's return*—calculated as the weighted sum of individual stock returns based on their proportion in the portfolio—and the *portfolio's risk*—which is more complex and must account for: individual stock variances, correlations between stocks, and covariances between stocks. The portfolio's risk can be further decomposed into systemic risk and idiosyncratic risk.

There are many ways to predict stock prices. One way to conduct forecasting primarily is through Monte Carlo simulation (MCS) methods. Beginning from historical price data to calculate the initial parameters, MCS can generate multiple price paths by repeatedly applying a forecast equation. Each path represents a possible future trajectory of the stock price. However, MCS faces several challenges in implementation: first, relationships between variables often change over time; second, probability distributions may not remain stable; third, convergence to accurate estimates can be slow; and finally, the approach requires significant computational resources for meaningful results.

8.9 Glossary

Apportionment The foundational concept that allows ownership in a company to be divided into independently transferable portions (shares), enabling partial ownership to be sold without requiring permission from other owners.

Behavioralists Investors who base their trading decisions on perceptions of market psychology and investor behavioral patterns, often monitoring social media sentiment and trading patterns to inform their decisions.

Buy-and-Hold Strategy An investment approach where stocks are purchased with the intention of keeping them for an extended period, treating them similarly to perpetual bonds that pay regular dividends.

Chartists Investment analysts who attempt to predict stock price changes by examining graphical patterns and historical price movements, focusing on technical analysis rather than company fundamentals.

Common Stock Shares in a firm's ownership that entitle stockholders to participate in profits and vote at company meetings, while maintaining limited liability for losses.

Dividend Discount Model A valuation method that determines a stock's fundamental value based on the present value of its expected future dividend payments.

Drift In stock price modeling, the general directional trend of returns, calculated as the historical mean return minus half the variance.

Free Riding A trading behavior where investors monitor and copy other investors' trading patterns, essentially following the market rather than conducting independent analysis.

Fundamental Value The estimated worth of a stock based on both current assets and projected future profitability, determined through analysis of financial statements and macroeconomic conditions.

Historical Mean The average return of a stock over a specified past period, used as a key component in calculating drift for price forecasting models. This represents the central tendency of returns over time.

Joint-Stock Company An early form of business organization that issued stock to finance ventures, spreading risk among multiple investors who shared in potential profits.

Leverage The use of borrowed money to finance stock purchases, which can amplify both potential returns and risks in investment positions. The text notes this as a significant factor in determining overall investment risk.

Limited Liability A key feature of stock ownership where the maximum amount an investor can lose is their initial investment, even if the company goes bankrupt.

Market Capitalization The total value of a company calculated by multiplying the current stock price by the number of outstanding shares.

Monte Carlo Simulation A numerical technique using random sampling to simulate multiple possible future paths of stock prices and estimate probable outcomes.

Over-the-Counter (OTC) Market A decentralized market where stocks, particularly of smaller and newer companies, are traded directly between parties rather than on a centralized exchange.

Portfolio Risk The combined risk of multiple stocks held together, which accounts for both individual stock volatility and the correlations between stocks.

Residual Claimant The position of stockholders in receiving payment last, after all other creditors (including bond holders), during company liquidation.

Return Volatility The degree of variation in a stock's returns over time, typically measured by the standard deviation of returns.

Stock Market Index A measurement tool that tracks the overall performance of a group of stocks, providing a benchmark for market performance.

Value-Weighted Index A stock market index, like the S&P 500, where companies with a larger market capitalization have a greater influence on the movement of the index.

Part IV: **Machine Learning**

9 The Basics of Machine Learning

Contents

In Webster's Dictionary, artificial intelligence (AI) is defined as:

> "A branch of computer science dealing with the simulation of intelligent behavior in computers."

A subset of AI is known as machine learning (ML), which Webster's defines as:

> "The process by which a computer is able to improve its own performance (as in analyzing image files) by continuously incorporating new data into an existing statistical model."

Machine learning was originally inspired by how the brain works. This was a branch that became known as neural networks. Analysis is structured around a simple framework of input and output signals within a large network of interconnected neurons, which resembles the human brain. This chapter presents a basic overview of machine learning algorithms that begin by replicating the input-output mechanism of a neuron.

9.1 Neural Networks

In a network of neurons, each neuron receives inputs from other neurons. These inputs have varying degrees of strength (called weights). A network is defined by the number of neurons and their weights. For example, the human brain has approximately 10^{11} neurons, each with 10^4 weights.

When an input leads to an output, its weight leaves an in-print. Therefore, the strength of the signal can adapt from input to output. If a neuron fires along the same path, the signal can be reinforced, increasing the weight, which fixates the path in a process called learning. Weights adapt during the learning process. There are two main aspects of this type of network: *reinforcement* and *modularity*.

Reinforcement: "Neurons that fire together wire together" (known as Hebb reinforcement).

https://doi.org/10.1515/9783111193120-013

Modularity: Different areas perform different functions even if using the same input-output structure.

A neural network is composed of inputs and outputs connected through a "machine" like the brain. The machine facilitates learning though reinforcement and modularity. Examples of inputs are features, attributes, predictions, and predictive variables. Examples of outputs include classes, targets, dependent variables, and responses. Examples of machines include sets of algorithms, techniques, models. See Figure 9.1.

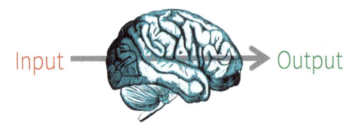

Figure 9.1: A biological neural picture.

A human brain—or a machine learning algorithm—is a vast complex network of inputs and outputs too difficult to fully understand. One way to model it, even absent full understanding, is to reduce the network to a primordial unit as a *first principle*. First-principle: an irreducible unit of understanding that begins as an assumption but cannot be decomposed into smaller units. This is a starting point of analysis. A first-principle concept of machine learning is the perceptron, a concept invented by the psychologist Frank Rosenblatt in 1957.

A perceptron is a collection of inputs and weights that are fed into a machine, which combines (as a simple dot product) the inputs and the weights to yield an output. See Figure 9.2.

The perceptron has a collection of inputs, $x_1, x_2, \ldots, x_n$, which is chosen by the modeler. Typically, an extra term (called the bias) is added to the inputs, which could shift the x's directionally (up and down). This is the analog concept to an intercept in linear regression.

The perceptron has a vector of weights $w_{0j}, w_{1j}, \ldots, w_{nj}$, which assign the importance to the inputs. The dot product of the inputs and the weights $W^T X$ produce the outputs Z_j.

The outputs of the perceptron are determined by a simple method: First, choose/obtain the inputs and, second, multiply the inputs by the respective weights. See Figure 9.3.

This can be done in a few lines of code in Python:

```python
def forward(Theta, X, active):
    N = X.shape[0]
```

```
# Add the bias column
X_ = np.concatenate((np.ones((N, 1)), X), 1)

# Multiply by the weights
z = np.dot(X_, Theta.T)

# Apply the activation function
a = active(z)

return a
```

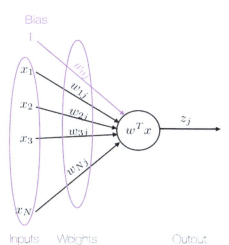

Figure 9.2: A picture of a perceptron.

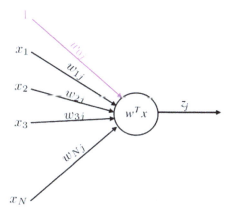

Figure 9.3: A perceptron.

The inputs are often chosen by the analyst/modeler. But how are the weights obtained? Through a process called *training*. We assume the output is a binary outcome giving a value of zero or one.

Binary outcome. *It can only take two mutually exclusive values: True/False, On/Off, which can be represented with a value of one or zero.*

The training procedure is as follows: (1) If the output is correct, do nothing; (2) if perceptron incorrectly outputs zero, add the input to the weight vector; (3) if perceptron incorrectly outputs one, subtract the input from the weight vector. If a correct set of weights exists, the process converges.

Perceptrons are simple yet powerful machines. Given enough inputs, perceptrons can learn many things. Learning is only constrained by the inputs/features included in the system.

9.2 Machine Learning Tasks

One common task of ML algorithms is *classification*, which is the process of separating inputs into classes of inputs. For example, we can use a perceptron to classify between zero class and one class in two dimensions.

Take points laying in a two-dimensional x-y axis. See Figure 9.4.

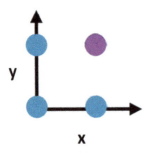

Figure 9.4: A classification example.

Each point has a corresponding value in the (x, y) axis where the darker color represents the value of one, or "true", and the lighter color represents the value of zero, or "false" in Figure 9.5.

Now we can classify between two conditions: True = 1 and False = 0. Perceptrons work well in finding linear boundaries between classes by relying on a single hyperline in two dimensions (2D) (or a single hyperplane in 3D) to separate the data points.

For example: It is possible to separate points that have a $(x = 1)$ AND $(y = 1)$ placement from other points. See Figure 9.6.

It is also possible to separate points that have a $(x = 1)$ OR $(y = 1)$ placement from other points. See Figure 9.7.

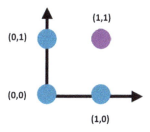

Figure 9.5: A classification example with ordinal binary values.

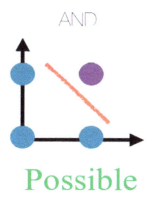

Figure 9.6: Separating between true and false for "AND."

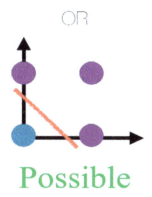

Figure 9.7: Separating between true and false for "OR."

Finally, it is also possible to separate points that have a $(x = 1)$ NOR $(y = 1)$ placement from other points. See Figure 9.8.

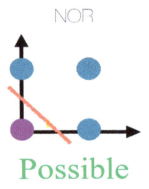

Figure 9.8: Separating between true and false for "NOR."

But classification is not always possible when no single line can separate the inputs. For example, it is not possible to separate points that have a $(x = 1)$ XOR $(y = 1)$ placement from other points (XOR is short for "excluding-or," which means an "OR" condition excluding the "AND" condition). This means finding points where $(x = 1)$ XOR $(y = 1)$, but not $(x = 1)$ AND $(y = 1)$. This cannot be accomplished with a single line in our example. See Figure 9.9.

Figure 9.9: Separating between true and false for "XOR."

9.3 Linear Regression

Another common task of ML algorithms is linear regression. Recall the perceptron was just a graphical representation of the dot product of the inputs and the weights $W^T X$, which gives the outputs Z_j. This can also be thought of simply as a linear regression, where the output of the perceptron is simply the line that best fits a collection of inputs.

Let's say that we have data organized in the $x - y$ plane. The y data is what we want to understand, and we assume it depends on the x data. Therefore, the output (y) is a function of inputs $\vec{x_i}$, where each point is represented by a vector. So in the simplest case $y \approx f(\vec{x_i})$, let's say we have a single input x_1, we add a bias term x_0 to account for the intercept. A perceptron algorithm can estimate the weights for each input that best fits the line $y = w_0 x_0 + w_1 x_1$.

Regression analysis in machine learning requires finding the weights (w_0, and w_1) that provide a line that best fits our data. So, whether we are doing classification analysis or regression analysis, everything hinges on finding the weights. Machine learning treats the issue of finding weights as an optimization problem.

Optimization problem. *A mathematical analysis that is conducted to find an optimal condition or an optimal value, which often involves an objective to maximize or minimize some function, which sometimes is subject to a constraint, and it often involves iteration (repeating the process).*

Optimization problems often require three pieces: 1) the objective function to optimize, 2) a set of constraints, and 3) an algorithm necessary for optimization. The goal of perceptrons in machine learning often involves prediction. Therefore, the function to optimize is some measure of prediction error. The constraints involve representing the problem. This is where the analyst or the modeler brings to bear her institutional knowledge of the particular task to accomplish. The algorithm required for optimization is often a general-purpose tool applied to the task. Often the same algorithm can be chosen for different tasks. A popular algorithm used in optimization is what is called *gradient descent*.

Concept box: *Gradient descent*:

Picture a person who is blindfolded and dropped from a helicopter somewhere in a mountain range. She cannot take off her blindfold and her goal is to find the valley where it is safe. She is looking to descend from wherever she is down to the lowest point in the area. She cannot see, but she is armed with a walking stick. One way to find the valley is to use her walking stick to palpate in every direction touching the walking stick in every direction around herself and wherever she detects the biggest drop (largest gradient descent) step in that direction.

Then repeat the process (iteration), using her walking stick in every direction and step in the direction where the biggest drop is. She keeps descending down the mountain through the biggest directional drops. Wherever she might be in the mountain, she always palpates in a circle and she always moves toward the direction with the biggest drop. She keeps repeating the process.

When she gets to a position where upon palpating around, she does not find a drop in any direction, she has reached the valley. In other words, using her walking stick she cannot find another direction in which to move farther down, so she has reached her goal. However, she may just found a lowest point in an immediate area (a local valley). Has she found the lowest point in the whole mountain range (the global valley)?

With her current walking stick, she has no way to conclude whether she has found a local or a global valley. One thing to do is to exchange her walking stick for a longer one to facilitate a larger step. Imagine she gets a much larger stick that allows her to palpate and leap over longer distances. An advantage of a larger step size is that she could presumably reach the valley faster (since she is traveling faster) and she lowers the likelihood of getting stuck in a local valley. The disadvantage of a bigger step size is that she could skip right over a given valley. She could end up traveling faster, but also spending more time traveling without finding the global valley because she is more likely to repeatedly skip over it, multiple times and, potentially, forever.

The task of machine learning is centered around formulating a hypothesis that we have some functional form that allows us to combine inputs with weights to produce some output. This hypothesis $h_w(X)$ is a function of inputs X and weights w.

The learning procedure can be described as follows:

1. We begin with a vector of inputs or features X^T.
2. We have a hypothesis that involves the dot product of inputs and weights (w). We apply the constraint and the learning algorithm to the hypothesis $h_w(X)$ and we get a predicted output.
3. We compare the predicted output to the observed output and we get an error function.
4. We use the error to rescale the weight and loop into another step for the hypothesis. See Figure 9.10.

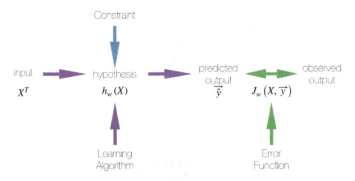

Figure 9.10: Machine learning path.

This is an iterative process repeating i times, which means the algorithm first makes a prediction. Then, from its prediction, the algorithm registers an error function—quantifying the difference between the predicted value from the weight-contingent hypothesis $h_w(X)$ and the actual value y—and feeds the error function J_w back into the learning algorithm before repeating the process again.

It is common to assume a functional form for the error to be quadratic. Quadratic errors have two nice properties:

1. The signs of the errors do not offset each other because the square of a number is always positive, whether the number is positive or negative. This means that if one

iteration has an error of –3 and the next iteration yields an error of +3, without assuming a quadratic we run the risk that the two errors offset each other, and we could conclude incorrectly that the algorithm performs without error across the two iterations.

2. A quadratic error penalizes larger errors more than smaller errors. A quadratic error of two is four, while a quadratic error of three is nine.

So, the error term J_W can be written as minimizing the sum of squares across i iterations.

$$J_W = \frac{1}{2m} \Sigma_i [h_W(X^{(i)}) - y^{(i)}]^2.$$

Gradient descent involves finding the minimum error by updating the weights W while following the slope of the error function (keeping track of how the error responds to the vector of weights $\vec{W}$) and iterating (repeating) until we converge to the lowest possible value of the error.

The algorithm requires taking a stand on two conditions:

1. How large should the step size α be?
2. What values should the weights start from $\vec{W}^{(0)}$ (called initialization).

The following formula shows how the error function varies with respect to the weights on a given iteration i:

$$\frac{\delta}{\delta W_i} J_W = \frac{1}{m} X^T (h_W(X) - \vec{y}).$$

The function that updates the weights each iteration is given by:

$$W_i = W_i - \alpha \frac{\delta}{\delta W_i} J_W.$$

These can be easily coded into Python as follows:

```
oldJ = 0
err = 1

Js = []

#alpha=0.9 #step too large for convergence

while err > 1e-8:
    Hs = np.dot(X, weights)              #null hypot
    deltas = alpha/M*np.dot(X.T, (Hs-y))   #
```

```
count += 1
weights -= deltas

J = np.sum(np.power(Hs-y, 2.))/(2*M)
Js.append(J)
err = np.abs(oldJ-J) #Error updating (compares old and new error)
oldJ = J

if count % 1000 == 0:
    print(count, J, err, weights.flatten())

print(count, J, err, weights.flatten())
```

The full training/learning procedure is given below:

The process will iterate (repeat) while the error is larger than some arbitrary value (1e-6), typically called *"tolerance"*. Once the error climbs down to a value equal or lower than this, the learning algorithm has converged to a low error given an optimal set of weights $\vec{W}$ and outputs $\vec{y}$.

Application. Let us apply this to the following question.

Can daily movements in the 1-year U. S. Treasury rate be explained by movements in the 10-year Treasury rate?

In essence, we want to conduct a linear regression between the 1-year and the 10-year treasuries and find whether they are related. Let our output y denote the 1-year treasury and our input x_1 denote the 10-year treasury rate. The form of the regression is given by $y = w_0 + w_1 x_1$, where w_0 represents the intercept of the line we want to fit and w_1 represents the slope of the line. Essentially, we are using a single feature (the 10-year treasury) to explain or predict a single output (the 1-year treasury) given two weights for intercept and slope of a best fit line.

Let's say that we collected 11 points of data for both treasury rates and graph them. See Figure 9.11.

The first thing to do will be to add an arbitrary vector of 11 values to initialize the bias (11 zeros, 11 ones,... the values do not matter because the algorithm will update them through the learning procedure) and append them to the vector of features; in this case, X just has the one feature (11 values of the 10-year treasury).

```
M, N = X.shape
#Add w0 for the bias / intercept
X = np.concatenate((np.ones((M, 1)), X), axis=1)
```

We then decide on a step size and initialize the weights.

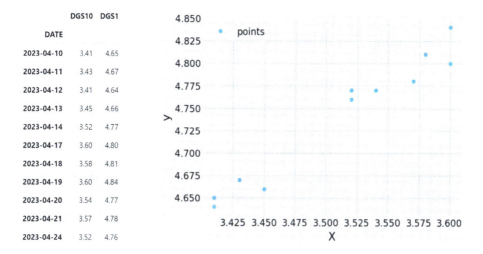

DATE	DGS10	DGS1
2023-04-10	3.41	4.65
2023-04-11	3.43	4.67
2023-04-12	3.41	4.64
2023-04-13	3.45	4.66
2023-04-14	3.52	4.77
2023-04-17	3.60	4.80
2023-04-18	3.58	4.81
2023-04-19	3.60	4.84
2023-04-20	3.54	4.77
2023-04-21	3.57	4.78
2023-04-24	3.52	4.76

Figure 9.11: Scatter diagram: 10-year and 1-year U. S. Treasury rates.

```
#step size
alpha = 0.01

#for weight initialization
epsilon = 0.2

weights = 2*np.random.rand(N+1, 1)*epsilon - epsilon
count = 0
```

The full learning/training procedure is given below:

```
oldJ = 0
err = 1

Js = []

#alpha=0.9 #step too large for convergence

while err > 1e-8:
    Hs = np.dot(X, weights)                    #null hypot
    deltas = alpha/M*np.dot(X.T, (Hs-y))    #

    count += 1
    weights -= deltas

    J = np.sum(np.power(Hs-y, 2.))/(2*M)
```

```
Js.append(J)
err = np.abs(oldJ-J) #Error updating (compares old and new error)
oldJ = J

if count % 1000 == 0:
    print(count, J, err, weights.flatten())

print(count, J, err, weights.flatten())
```

The last few lines instruct that every third iteration the algorithm should print the value for the hypothesis, the error, and the weights in brackets $[w_0, w_1]$ representing the predicted value of the intercept and slope.

This sample output shows that it took 54 iterations for the downhill technique to reach the lowest value (the value to reach the tolerance specified) with final values for the intercept and slope of 0.3125 and 1.2602. See Figure 9.12.

```
3 6.481033880569607 2.1482819178276387 [0.07862968 0.43920033]
6 2.7457628900446993 0.9100743216255114 [0.16029944 0.72607008]
9 1.1633941200725042 0.385533791172888 [0.21346013 0.9127831 ]
12 0.49305696438305646 0.16332325965017458 [0.24806518 1.03430732]
15 0.20908276447974944 0.06918845508701255 [0.27059296 1.11340225]
18 0.08878308118981629 0.029310230731826356 [0.28526005 1.16488132]
21 0.03782065445474645 0.01241666214044565 [0.29481085 1.19838612]
24 0.016231493919196247 0.005260058144982944 [0.30103163 1.22019204]
27 0.0070856980349172346 0.0022283138174846043 [0.30508501 1.23438354]
30 0.003211271115672111 0.0009439792821027532 [0.30772769 1.24361905]
33 0.0015699484688508037 0.0003998980468023787 [0.3094522  1.24962888]
36 0.0008746333439523497 0.0001694095078197856 [0.3105791  1.25353921]
39 0.0005800743515310304 7.176789997947553e-05 [0.31131703 1.25608305]
42 0.0004552872415086216 3.0404092359550064e-05 [0.3118018  1.25773748]
45 0.0004024204085211524 1.288118772779605e-05 [0.31212179 1.25881302]
48 0.0003800210839531873 5.457978767642508e-06 [0.31233453 1.25951178]
51 0.00037052867674959746 2.313292844517722e-06 [0.31247747 1.25996531]
54 0.0003665040129177521 9.811129585719086e-07 [0.31257498 1.26025923]
54 0.0003665040129177521 9.811129585719086e-07 [0.31257498 1.26025923]
```

Figure 9.12: Learning output.

Charting the error function reveals that by the 40th iteration, the downhill climb largely reached the bottom and by 54th the process has converged. See Figure 9.13.

Plotting the line with our estimated values of the slope and intercept reveals that the two treasury rates are positively correlated. For every 1% increase in the 10-year rate, we would, on average, expect a 1.26% increase in the 1-year treasury. See Figure 9.14.

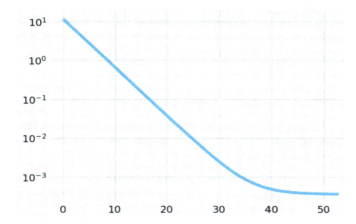

Figure 9.13: Learning output curve.

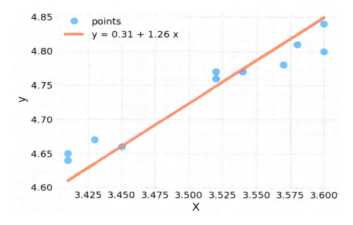

Figure 9.14: A line fit.

9.4 Classification

Classification is another typical ML task. When doing classification, probability is a critical tool. Linear regressions extend lines in a straight direction from positive infinity to negative infinity, well outside a range of acceptable values for probabilities that take on values between zero and one.

Therefore, linear regressions that we built based on our hypothesis of a dot product of weights and features, may be less useful for classification tasks. The good news is that we can build on the learning algorithm we used for linear regression by incorporating new hypotheses into otherwise the same procedure.

In the case of linear regression, the hypothesis was itself the dot product of inputs and weights (w). We now rewrite it ahead of the hypothesis step so the hypothesis can take other forms. This will allow us to apply other learning algorithms. The rest—prediction, error collection and weight updating—remains the same.

More generally, most ML hypotheses will require what is called an *activation function* ϕ. In the case of linear regression, the activation function was the identity matrix, meaning no activation was required beyond collecting the weights and inputs and deriving the dot product, denoted by $Z \equiv X^T w$. Therefore, if the activation function was the identity matrix $\phi = I$, the hypothesis was itself the dot product $\phi(z) \equiv X^T w$. For classification objectives, we will consider other activation functions ϕ.

Logistic Regression. Logistic regression predicts the probability of a value belonging to a given class. Imagine you have 11 clients with a savings account at a bank you manage who applied for a loan in the first trimester of last year. Your clients' savings accounts ranged from $10K to almost $80K and you can find which clients qualified for the loan (1) or failed to qualify for the loan (0). See Figure 9.15.

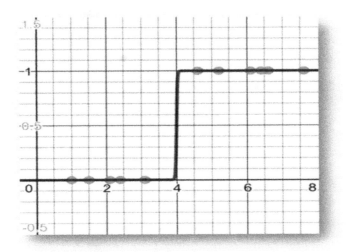

Figure 9.15: Logistic regression with a short sample of loan clients.

Simple inspection reveals a clear-cut threshold of $40K. It seems like all clients with savings exceeding that number qualified for the loan and those below the $40K did not. So there is a clear transition from not being able to take out a loan to qualifying for one at an amount of $40K of savings.

This indicates any client with less than $40K in savings will have a 0% chance of qualifying for the loan, and any client with savings greater than $40K will have a 100% chance of getting it. Because there is a distinct separation at $40K, a logistic regression is going to "jump" from 0% to 100% at that boundary.

Of course, real life rarely works out this way. Let's say you gathered more client data since then and got a more realistic picture, where the middle of the range has a mix of clients qualifying and not qualifying for the loan. The way to interpret this is the probability of clients qualifying for a loan gradually increases with more savings, which can be used as collateral against repayment failures.

Because of this overlap of points in the middle, there is no distinct cutoff when clients qualify, but instead a gradual transition from 0% probability to 100% probability ("0" and "1") of getting a loan. See Figure 9.16.

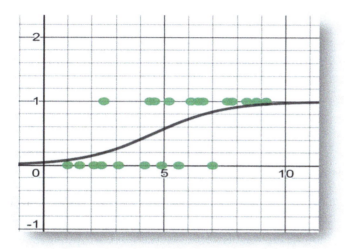

Figure 9.16: Another logistic regression with an augmented sample of loan clients.

More generally, this logistic regression results in a curve indicating a probability of belonging to the *true* (1) category, which in this case means *a client gets a loan*. As savings increase, the number of qualifying clients also increases and, thus, the probability of getting a loan increases.

A *Logistic Regression* is a classification tool that predicts a true or false value for one or more variables. Training data must have outcomes of 0 (false) or 1 (true), but the regression outputs a probability value between 0 and 1.
–   An S-shaped curve (a logistic or sigmoid function) is fit to the points and then used to predict probability.
–   If a predicted value (the y-axis) is less than 0.5 it is typically categorized as false (0), and if the predicted value is greater than/equal to 0.5, it is typically categorized as true (1).

For linear regression, the activation function was an identity. For logistic regression, the activation function will be a sigmoid function to predict the probability of a value belonging to a given class. Using the sigmoid/logistic function, we can map weighted inputs to a range between zero and one $[0, 1]$. See Figure 9.17.

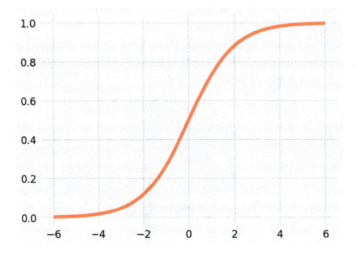

Figure 9.17: A sigmoid function.

And at a certain threshold (say 0.5), the value is classified as True = 1 above it and a False = 0 below it. See Figure 9.18.

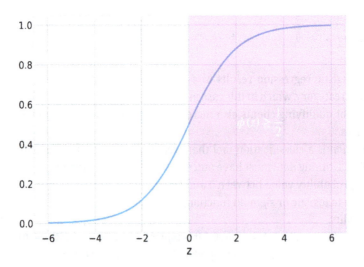

Figure 9.18: A sigmoid function with a binary outcome.

Since we now have a binary outcome, we are going to need a different error term. For linear regression, the error function was the square difference. For logistic regression, the error function is called cross entropy, which is given as follows:

$$J_W = -\frac{1}{m}[y^T \log(h_W(X)) + (1-y)^T \log(1 - h_W(X))],$$

which measures the distance between two probability distributions, where

$$h_W(X) = -\frac{1}{1 + e^{-X\overrightarrow{W}}},$$

which converts the labels to probabilities; for example, an instance with a label = 1 has a probability 1 of belonging to that class. The gradient descent formulas are the same as those used in linear regression.

Linear and logistic regressions share the same learning procedure, except for the activation function and the corresponding error function.

Different activation functions $\phi(z)$ are essentially different algorithms (just change the error... the rest is the same). Activation functions should typically be: nonlinear, differentiable, nondecreasing. They should also have the ability to compute new features, where each layer builds a more complex representation of the data. See Figures 9.19 and 9.20.

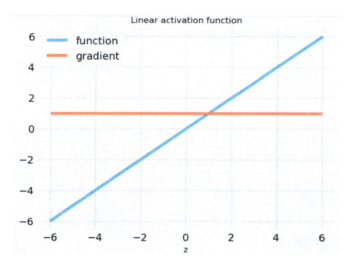

Figure 9.19: A linear activation function.

Rectified linear (RELU) functions have become popular because they are easier (faster) to train than sigmoids, resulting in faster learning because it is a stepwise linear regression (lower degree of nonlinearity than sigmoid). See Figure 9.21.

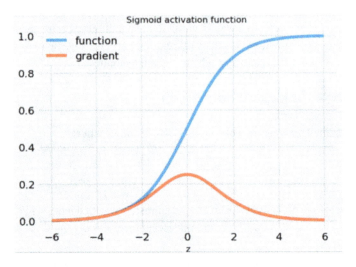

Figure 9.20: A sigmoid activation function.

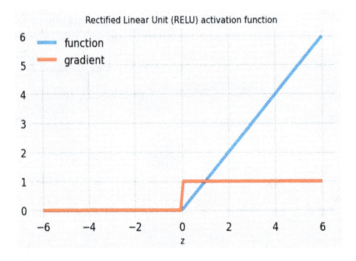

Figure 9.21: A RELU activation function.

9.5 Forward Propagation

Having multiple activation functions allows us to generalize the concept of the perceptron. Forward propagation uses the perceptron for any activation function.

Forward propagation is a multilayer perceptron system involving four steps: 1. Obtain the inputs. 2. Multiply the inputs by their respective weights. 3. Calculate the output using a selected activation function. 4. Use the output of this perceptron as an input for the next. See Figure 9.22.

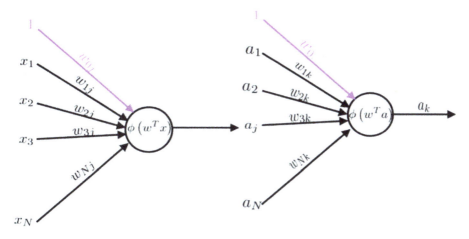

Figure 9.22: Forward propagation.

This means we construct multiple layers of perceptrons, where the output of each perceptron can feed as an input into the next layer. However, as we saw earlier in a single perceptron setting, updating the weights required calculating an error term and feeding it back to the algorithm so the weight could be updated.

One way to propagate the errors backward and update the weights is to have a RELU activation function for each input on the first layer and then have a linear activation function on the second layer, which builds up the linear regression from the values computed by the RELUs in the previous step. See Figure 9.23.

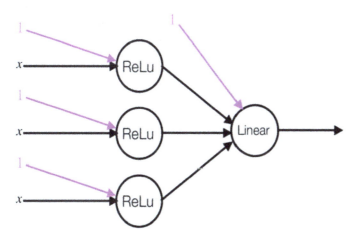

Figure 9.23: RELU propagation.

We need to quantify our errors to determine how correct our predictions are. As discussed before, this is achieved with loss (J_W) functions: Two common ones are the quadratic loss function and cross entropy.

In a process called *regularization*, extra penalty terms are typically added to the error functions. This minimizes the value of each weight, which allows the algorithm to converge faster by constraining the parameter space within which we look for the true values.

Two common penalty terms involve adding the absolute value of the weights, called the Least Absolute Shrinkage and Selection Operator, or LASSO:

$$\widehat{J_W} = J_W + \lambda \Sigma_{ij} |\omega_{ij}|$$

or adding a quadratic term for the weights:

$$\widehat{J_W} = J_W + \lambda \Sigma_{ij} \omega_{ij}^2,$$

which is called an "L2" Ridge regression.

LASSO drives less important weights to zero, while Ridge makes the weights roughly equal across all features. These are two different methods to speed up convergence and feature selection.

9.6 Backward Propagation

Once forward propagation is accomplished, and a measure of error is quantified in each layer, we must move backward and update the weights. The error at the output layer is a weighted average difference between the predicted output and the observed one.

Let δ^L be the error for the final layer, written as the difference between the predicted value (h_ω) and the data (y). We then move backward to the previous layer by multiplying δ^L times the derivative of the activation function as a way to propagate backward through the layers until the first layer is reached, where the inputs have no errors $\delta^L \equiv 0$ by definition.

Application: The MNIST Database. In 1994, the National Institute of Standards and Technology (NIST), which is part of the U. S. Commerce Department, developed a large database of handwritten digits to facilitate image processing and optical recognition systems to speed up mail sorting for the U. S. Post Office. This modified NIST dataset, or MNIST, consists of 70,000 28 × 28 black-and-white images of handwritten digits extracted from two NIST databases—one written by American Census Bureau employees (60K images) and one by American high school students (10K images). The MNIST dataset became the original canonical dataset for deep learning with 70,000 grayscale images of handwritten digits between zero and nine. Since there are 10 categories of numbers (one category per digit), 7,000 images can be used for training and 1,000 images for testing (algorithm validation) for each number.

We can write a deep learning algorithm that will recognize these numbers. To do this, we build a neural network with three layers: One input layer (X), one hidden layer (σ), and one output layer (Y)—with two perceptrons (θ) that connect the layers.

The inputs are each of the 28 × 28 pixels for each of the digits. Each pixel takes on a value from zero to one, ranging from white to black, with any value in between corresponding to any shade of gray. See an example of these looked like in Figure 9.24.

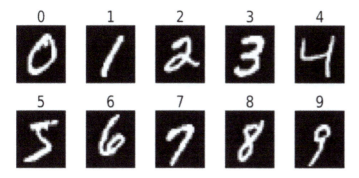

Figure 9.24: National Institute of Standards and Technology modified numbers (MNIST).

We first stack the value of 28 × 28 into a 784 × 1 column vector containing all these values. We specify a single hidden layer composed of 50 neurons, which we can parcel out as a 50 vectors, and the output layer should have 10 vectors, one for each of the digits 0–9. The forward propagation stage moves sequentially from the input to the output layer. At the end, the value of the guess with the highest probability is quantified. Then we propagate backward along the lines described previously.

We add a bias term on the input and hidden layers for forward propagation. The bias is not needed for backward propagation. Figure 9.25 shows the process.

The forward propagation algorithm can be written in a few lines of code.

```
def forward(Theta, X, active):
    N = X.shape[0]

    # Add the bias column
    X_ = np.concatenate((np.ones((N, 1)), X), 1)

    # Multiply by the weights
    z = np.dot(X_, Theta.T)

    # Apply the activation function
    a = active(z)

    return a
```

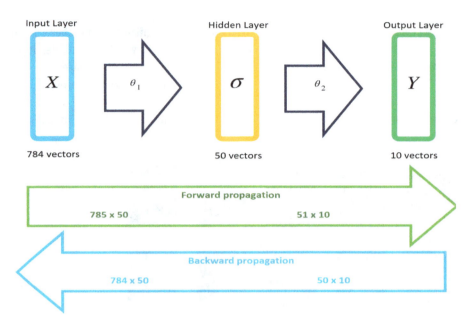

Figure 9.25: The propagation process in machine learning.

Then, the *predict* function effectively implements the actual model. It forward propagates the inputs through all the layers with the correct activation functions at each step and returns the final output.

```
def predict(Theta1, Theta2, X):

#Layer 1 (recursive output of layer 1
# becomes input to layer 2)
    h1 = forward(Theta1, X, sigmoid)

#Layer 2
    h2 = forward(Theta2, h1, sigmoid)


# classify according to
# which class has highest prob.
    return np.argmax(h2, 1)
```

Then, the backward propagation algorithm returns the information from the output layer back to the input layer. This algorithm is built on top of the single-gradient descent, which is extended to incorporate multiple layers, where the weights for each layer need to be adjusted separately.

```python
#This algorithm will go through the entire #sample (all inputs)
#exactly once (1 EPOCH)


def backprop(Theta1, Theta2, X, y):
    N = X.shape[0]    # num of inputs
    K = Theta2.shape[0] #nu of layers

    J = 0

    Delta2 = np.zeros(Theta2.shape)
    #same shape as two input matrices
    #theta1 and theta2

    Delta1 = np.zeros(Theta1.shape)

    for i in range(N): #Running for all N inputs together so this is an
    ↳   epoch
        # Forward propagation, saving intermediate results
        a1 = np.concatenate(([1], X[i]))   # Input layer

        z2 = np.dot(Theta1, a1) #weight * input value
        h2 = sigmoid(z2)        # HYPT IS SIGMOID FUNCTION
        a2 = np.concatenate(([1], h2))   # Hidden Layer

        z3 = np.dot(Theta2, a2)
        h3 = sigmoid(z3)   # Output layer
        a3 = h3

        y0 = one_hot(K, y[i]) #Converts our output to a vector of zeros
        ↳   and ones

        # Cross entropy
        J -= np.dot(y0.T, np.log(a3))+np.dot((1-y0).T, np.log(1-a3))

        #-------------------------------------------------------------
        # Calculate the weight deltas (propagating the error backwards)
        delta_3 = a3-y0 #predicted minus actual

        #Propagate the error of the output layer delta_3 to the hidden
        ↳   layer (delta_2)
        delta_2 = np.dot(Theta2.T, delta_3)[1:]*sigmoidGradient(z2)
```

```
#Update each of the weight matrices
Delta2 += np.outer(delta_3, a2)
Delta1 += np.outer(delta_2, a1)


J /= N  #Calculate the avg error across all samples

#Calculate the gradient for each weight matrices
Theta1_grad = Delta1/N
Theta2_grad = Delta2/N

#Return the average error for the epoch and
#the gradients for each weight matrix
return [J, Theta1_grad, Theta2_grad]
```

The training procedure essentially remains the same as what was discussed for linear regression. This facilitates graphing cost functions and accuracy curves for the algorithm. The ancillary files include the Python code for identifying a single digit with 92% prediction accuracy from the MNIST dataset (also provided). See Figures 9.26 and 9.27.

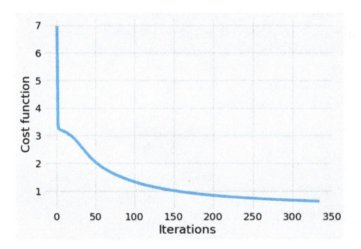

Figure 9.26: Cost function.

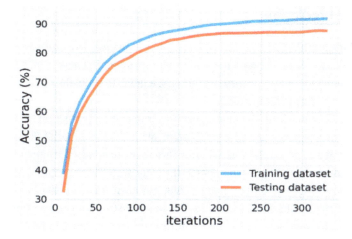

Figure 9.27: Training and testing accuracy.

9.7 Data Considerations

In the typical practice of machine learning, many details must be considered. For example, many algorithms are linear—or use Euclidean distances—that are heavily influenced by the numerical values/units used (cm vs. km, for example). Therefore, using features with very different range of values in the same analysis can cause numerical problems. To avoid scaling difficulties, it is common to rescale the range of all features so that each feature follows within similar ranges of values.

One simple method is to convert the raw data to fall within a range of values falling between zero and one, $x \in [0, 1]$, in what is called *unity-based normalization.*

$$\hat{x} = \frac{x - x_{min}}{x_{max} - x_{min}}.$$

In the context of machine learning, this pre-processing of data is also called *feature scaling.* For some purposes, the modeler might want to extend the scale from zero to one to arbitrary values, say $x \in [a, b]$. This can be done with a simple adjustment to the formula:

$$\hat{x} = a + \frac{(x - x_{min})(b - a)}{x_{max} - x_{min}}.$$

Other methods to pre-process raw data before feeding it to machine learning algorithms include normalization ($\hat{x} = \frac{x}{\|x\|}$) and standardization ($\hat{x} = \frac{x - \mu_x}{\sigma_x}$). There are myriad other methods to pre-process and filter the data prior to beginning the learning algorithm.

9.8 Inference and Prediction

The objective of machine learning is *statistical inference*, which involves learning something from the data—not to repeat the data back, but to infer something new from the data. So we want to find a hypothesis, a story, a summary, a label, that fits the data. An important concern is what is called *overfitting*.

The typical outcome of a machine learning algorithms is to make a prediction from the data. Imagine that the pre-processed data we fit an algorithm is the material that it uses to "learn." Think of it as a practice exam. When we are ready to obtain a prediction from our machine learning algorithm, we implement the algorithm. Think of this as an exam with high stakes. Overfitting relates to "memorizing" the answers to practice questions instead of generalizing to questions we have not seen before (inference). Machine learning algorithms can be very susceptible to overfitting—meaning they can have a tendency to "regurgitate back" the answers to the practice exam instead of correctly answering the new "exam questions."

A common approach to address the major concern of overfitting is to withhold some portion of the data the algorithm is to learn from, thereby splitting the data into two subsets: *Training* and *Testing*. So a machine learning algorithm proceeds in two stages. First, the algorithm is trained using only the training dataset. Second, we evaluate results in the previously unseen testing dataset.

Broadly speaking, learning in machine learning algorithms can be supervised by a human or it can be left unsupervised. In the category of machine learning algorithms that involves *supervised learning*, the human analyst supervises the connection between the training and the testing. The analyst may decide how much the algorithm needs to train and how much it needs to be tested. In a simple example of *unsupervised learning*, all the human analyst needs to do is to provide the data and prompt the algorithm for an outcome, and the algorithm trains a random portion of the data and tests over another portion. The algorithm splits the sample between training and testing at a random point.

Generally, there may be different rules on how to split the sample. One way to do this is with a multiple split, effectively splitting the dataset in an arbitrary number of (k) parts. Then, train the algorithm separately in k parts and evaluate in one. To mitigate the randomness of that choice, training can be repeated k times in order to average the results. This is called *k-fold cross validation*.

Since we now have two facets of learning—training and testing—there opens an opportunity for error in both. So, now we have to track error in training and error in testing. The overall error in the model is called the *bias*. And the difference between the training error and the testing error is called the *variance*. The model's complexity is driven by the number of features, the number of hyper-parameters to estimate, the number of layers in the forward and backward propagation, and other aspects of the model.

It is generally difficult for a machine learning algorithm to learn from an overly simplistic model. In principle, as the model increases in complexity, the error in both testing and training will typically decline. Therefore, as the model increases in complexity, the bias will decline as the errors in training and testing begin to decrease (often in tandem). Thus, the more complex the model, the less error in training. Think of this as getting the practice questions in advance. The more attention (complexity) you dedicate to the practice, the better your performance will be in the practice questions. So, the error in testing decreases monotonically with the model complexity—the more complexity, the less error in training.

On the other hand, while some complexity will decrease the error in testing, too much complexity may begin to increase the testing error again. So, there may be an inflection point in testing error where an optimal level of complexity reduces testing error, but more complexity than that optimal level will begin to increase the testing error again—even if the training error continues to decline. This means that an overly complex model will see further reductions in training error along with increases in testing error. In other words, the difference between the training and testing errors (the variance of the model) widens as the complexity of the model increases.

An overly complex model reduces the bias (as the error in training declines) but increases the variance (as the error in testing increases). This means there is a trade-off between bias and variance in machine learning algorithms. The hope is to minimize the bias *and* the variance, so the objective is to find a "sweet spot" level of complexity. Too little complexity and the algorithm is more prone to biased predictions. Too much complexity and the algorithm will have a tendency to yield more variance in its predictions (with differing results every time we run it).

Why is it the case that too much complexity will generally increase the error in testing? Think about adding complexity as paying more attention (studying more). If we pay little attention (i. e., the model is overly simplistic) we may be prone to large errors in practice questions (training) and in the exam (testing). As we begin to pay more attention and study more, we may learn a lot from our practice questions, which should help prepare us for the exam. So paying more attention (increasing complexity) should help reduce error in both training and testing. However, more and more complexity relies more and more on proper training. So adding more and more complexity would be like *memorizing the practice questions*, which would further reduce the error in training, but it may not help—indeed it may increase—the error in the exam (testing). In other words, unless the exam is an identical copy of the practice questions—in which case the objective would be *recall*, rather than *learning*—too much complexity (memorizing the practice questions) will yield excellent performance in training and comparatively poorer performance in testing. This is related to the issue of overfitting, which we discussed earlier, where in-sample predictions can be made to look artificially great but out-of-sample forecasts can be widely inaccurate.

Imagine we computer-simulate a mountain range with randomly placed peaks, slopes, plains, and valleys. We also simulate a virtual hiker represented by a machine learning algorithm. And we now task the simulated hiker (our algorithm) with finding the deepest valley—the point with the lowest altitude—in our simulated mountain range. The algorithm is nearly blind. It cannot see the whole mountain range. It can only see one (simulated) step in every direction. In other words, the hiker does not get a global view of the valley; it gets a local view. We endow the virtual hiker with the ability to look one step into every direction, learn where the lowest point is within that confined circle step, and step into that lowest local point. Once it has moved, repeats the process, looks around, learns where the lowest point is and moves there.

In this story, *walking is learning*. So, the size of the simulated step is the learning rate. Imagine that we, humans, supervise the algorithm by modulating (or fine tuning) the learning rate of the algorithm. If the learning rate is very high, the step size is too large, so the virtual hiker jumps across many peaks and valleys in every bound, making it highly unlikely it will ever find the lowest valley. If the learning rate is high, the step size is moderately large, so the hiker may find the general region of the valley, but it jumps across multiple spots within the valley never finding the lowest point. In both of these cases we would say *the algorithm never converges*. Conversely, if the learning rate is slow (think baby steps), the algorithm may find both the general region of the valley and the lowest point in that valley, but it may take a long time to find it. In this case, we would say *the algorithm converges (too) slowly*. Therefore, the objective is to find the optimal step size (the optimal learning rate) that does not endlessly jump over the lowest point, and it does not take too long to find it.

9.9 A General Scaffolding for Machine Learning Algorithms

We do not want to build a machine learning algorithm from scratch every time. The good news is that neural networks are extremely modular in their design. Modular code allows easy expansion to an arbitrary number of layers. The structure of a neural network can be described as a list of weight matrices and activation functions.

Activation functions are important. They are essentially similar algorithms with different specifications for the quantification of their error terms. Activation functions generally need to be nonlinear and nondecreasing. The AI engineer also needs to keep track of the gradients of the activation functions. This means that activation functions must also be differentiable. Differentiability is important for the gradient descent feature of learning optimization (remember the hiker who is blindfolded in our earlier example descending into the lowest point of the valley).

Activation functions can be used to compute new sets of features because they can be appended to each additional layer in the neural network scaffolding of a machine learning algorithm. Each layer builds up a more abstract representation of the data.

Again, a machine learning algorithm is modular in design, which means the AI engineer can use most (similar blocks) of the same code and only tweak what she needs

for her particular application. For example, the next few lines of Python code instanti-
ate an *activation function base class*, which provide an interface to both the activation
function and its derivative.

```python
class Activation(object):
    def f(z):
        pass

    def df(z):
        pass
```

This code snippet will help calculate an activation function and its derivative. Then,
this base class can be applied to functional forms of various activation functions. Below,
we can extend the base class with multiple activation functions.

```python
class Linear(Activation):
    def f(z):
        return z

    def df(z):
        return np.ones(z.shape)

class ReLu(Activation):
    def f(z):
        return np.where(z > 0, z, 0)

    def df(z):
        return np.where(z > 0, 1, 0)

class Sigmoid(Activation):
    def f(z):
        return 1./(1+np.exp(-z))

    def df(z):
        h = Sigmoid.f(z)
        return h*(1-h)

class TanH(Activation):
    def f(z):
        return np.tanh(z)
```

```
def df(z):
    return 1-np.power(np.tanh(z), 2.0)
```

Then we describe the model with a set of weights. First, we initialize the weights. Then, we specify how many layers we want in the algorithm. Then we can modularize so that we can easily add or subtract layers from the algorithm as needed. All of this is shown below:

```
#Define an initialization function to be called several times
def init_weights(L_in, L_out, epsilon = 0.12):
    return 2*np.random.rand(L_out, L_in+1)*epsilon - epsilon

#Specify how many layers are needed
hidden_layer_size = 50
num_labels = 10

#Initialize the weights
# so that we can easily add/remove layers
Thetas = []
Thetas.append(init_weights(input_layer_size, hidden_layer_size))
Thetas.append(init_weights(hidden_layer_size, num_labels))
```

Next, we specify a model, where *sigmoid* is an object that contains both the sigmoid function and its gradient as defined in the previous snippets.

```
model = [] #the model will be a python list with even elements=weights
 ↪   and odd elements=activations)

#Layer 1
model.append(Thetas[0])
model.append(Sigmoid)

#layer 2
model.append(Thetas[1])
model.append(Sigmoid)
```

Prediction involves *for-looping* to the forward propagation function for each layer and its corresponding activation function. The following snippet defines a *forward propagation function* as well as a *predict* function. The *predict* function now takes the entire model as input and it must loop over the various layers.

```python
def forward(Theta, X, active):
    N = X.shape[0]

    # Add the bias column
    X_ = np.concatenate((np.ones((N, 1)), X), 1)

    # Multiply by the weights
    z = np.dot(X_, Theta.T)

    # Apply the activation function
    a = active.f(z)

    return a


def predict(model, X):
    h = X.copy()

    for i in range(0, len(model), 2):
        theta = model[i]
        activation = model[i+1]

        h = forward(theta, h, activation)

    return np.argmax(h, 1)
```

Finally, once the algorithm has been initialized with weights and beginning from the input layer, it has propagated forward through the various layers and activation functions and has arrived at a prediction in the output layer, a predicted value is reached. Then, the algorithm will comb backward from output back to input to update the weights and proceed propagating forward again. *Backward propagation* is similar to forward propagation, but starts at the end and goes backward through each layer and its corresponding activation function, taking account of the prediction errors along the way and updating the weights accordingly. At the end, it returns the list of the changes of all the deltas and the overall error is updated before beginning the forward propagation again. Machine learning is an iterative process.

As we have discussed, a machine learning algorithm includes: input layers, hidden layers, and output layers. These can be organized in different ways in what is called *neural network architectures*. In the figure below, the yellow nodes are the input layers, the green nodes are the hidden layers, and the red nodes are the output layers. See Figure 9.28.

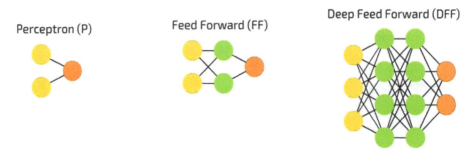

Figure 9.28: Neural network architectures.

In this chapter, we have discussed the perceptron (P), and the feed forward (FF) architectures. A deep neural network (DFF) is essentially a neural network with more layers (and possibly more neurons in each layer). It is not just scale that makes the FF algorithm 'deep.' Importantly, DFF allows for more connections between nodes across layers. Propagation in DFF takes longer, it generally requires more time to converge, and it requires more computing power.

Another type of architecture is known as an *Auto-Encoder* (AE), which has two distinct features. One, there are fewer neurons in the hidden layer than there are inputs. Two, the outputs to be computed are the same as the inputs. See Figure 9.29.

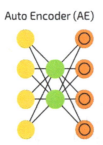

Auto Encoder (AE)

Figure 9.29: An auto encoder.

So why bother? Because the AI engineer may not be interested in learning about the outputs. AE is useful if the objective is to find the value of the nodes in the hidden layer that facilitates an accurate and reliable recovery of the inputs. An AE grabs the input data and finds an internal representation of the data (finds features from the data). Then, from those features, can the model guess what the input was? In other words, the objective may not be to learn about new outcomes from the features, but to learn about the features so that the neural network can recover the inputs. AE is useful for file (e. g., zip) compression, noise reduction, and dimension reduction, among other applications.

FF neural networks proceed from input to output through hidden layers. Deep learning just adds more layers and more connections between nodes, but information still flows from the inputs to the outputs. Another type or neural network is a *recurring neural network (RNN)*. Information is circular (it recurs) in an RNN so it goes back from the output to the input. RNNs accomplish this circularity by adding an extra input that corresponds to the previous output. So, the objective is to recall what the last output was and use it to try to guess what the next answer should be. Each output depends implicitly on all previous outputs. In RNNs, input sequences generate output sequences. Instead of stacking layers next to each other, RNNs stack layered networks next to each other. Many large language models (LLMs) are built as RNNs.

Thinking About It...

Machine learning was inspired by biological neural networks. Neural networks consist of interconnected neurons that receive weighted inputs. A perceptron is the basic unit, combining inputs and weights to produce outputs. Learning occurs through weight adjustment based on input-output patterns. Machine learning tasks include *classification*: separating inputs into classes (e. g., AND, OR, NOR operations), and *linear regression*: fitting lines to data points.

Key technical concepts include: *gradient descent*: an optimization algorithm for finding minimal error; *activation functions*: including linear, sigmoid, and RELU functions; *forward propagation*, which involves moving data through network layers; and *backward propagation*, which requires updating weights based on error calculations.

Machine learning can be used for a large number of applications. In this chapter, we discussed an application to predict binary outcomes in a loan approval example and recognizing handwritten digits using neural networks.

9.10 Glossary

Activation Function A mathematical function that determines the output of a neural network node. Common types include linear, sigmoid, and RELU (Rectified Linear Unit) functions. It transforms the input signals into output signals.

Artificial Intelligence (AI) A branch of computer science dealing with the simulation of intelligent behavior in computers.

Backward Propagation (Backprop) The process of calculating gradients and updating weights from the output layer back to the input layer to minimize prediction errors.

Bias Term An extra input added to neural network layers that allows the model to learn patterns that do not pass through the origin, analogous to the intercept in linear regression.

Binary Outcome A result that can only take two mutually exclusive values (e. g., True/False, 0/1), commonly used in classification problems.

Classification The process of categorizing inputs into distinct classes or categories. A common machine learning task where the goal is to predict which category new data belongs to.

Cross Entropy An error function used in classification tasks that measures the difference between predicted probability distributions and actual values.

Epoch One complete pass through the entire training dataset during the learning process.

Forward Propagation The process of moving data through a neural network from input layer to output layer, where each layer's outputs become inputs for the subsequent layer.

Gradient Descent An optimization algorithm that iteratively adjusts weights to minimize error by moving in the direction of the steepest descent of the error function. It is analogous to a person who is blindfolded using a walking stick to find the lowest point in a valley.

LASSO (Least Absolute Shrinkage and Selection Operator) A regularization technique that adds the absolute value of weights to the error function, helping drive less important weights to zero.

Linear Regression A machine learning task that finds the best-fitting straight line through a set of points, used for predicting continuous values.

Logistic Regression A classification algorithm that predicts the probability of a binary outcome using a sigmoid function to map inputs to values between 0 and 1.

Machine Learning (ML) The process by which a computer improves its own performance by continuously incorporating new data into an existing statistical model.

Neural Network A network of interconnected nodes (neurons) that processes information through weighted connections, inspired by the human brain's structure. Each neuron can receive inputs from other neurons and produce outputs based on those inputs.

Overfitting An unwanted result of overusing the available data or parameters in a model, which may lead to "too-good-to-be-true" replication of the in-sample data we have, but very poor learning about the data/question we are investigating and we want to know more about. It regurgitates back what we know but it does not provide much insight on what we do not know. Overfitting is a major concern in machine learning algorithms.

Perceptron A fundamental unit of neural networks invented by Frank Rosenblatt in 1957, consisting of inputs and weights that are combined to produce an output. It serves as the basic building block for more complex neural network architectures.

Regularization A technique to prevent overfitting by adding penalty terms to the error function, constraining the model's parameters. Common types include LASSO and Ridge regression.

RELU (Rectified Linear Unit) An activation function that outputs the input directly if positive, and zero otherwise. Popular in modern neural networks due to its computational efficiency.

Ridge Regression A regularization technique that adds squared weights to the error
function, helping make weights roughly equal across all features.

Weights Numerical values that determine the strength of connections between neurons in a neural network. These values are adjusted during the learning process to
improve the network's performance.

Index

https://doi.org/10.1515/9783111193120-014